D0549453

Music and Youth Culture

Music and Youth Culture

Dan Laughey

Edinburgh University Press

© Dan Laughey, 2006

Edinburgh University Press Ltd
22 George Square, Edinburgh

Typeset in 11/13 Ehrhardt
by Servis Filmsetting Ltd, Manchester, and
printed and bound in Great Britain by
MPG Books Ltd, Bodmin, Cornwall

A CIP record for this book is available from the British Library

ISBN 0 7486 2380 9 (hardback)
ISBN 0 7486 2381 7 (paperback)

The right of Dan Laughey
to be identified as author of this work
has been asserted in accordance with
the Copyright, Designs and Patents Act 1988.

Contents

List of Figures and Tables

Figures

Tables

Preface

The relationship between music and youth culture is fraught with clichés. All the theorising imaginable, therefore, could not have provided me with a better understanding of this subject area than the thoughts and feelings of those young people that I have talked to over the past few years. It is difficult, in fact, to be sure of a particular moment when I started to write this book. The research began the day before 9/11 but many of the ideas emerged a long time before that. My Masters dissertation in 1999 covered similar ground, but perhaps the inspiration came a few years earlier during secondary school teacher training. As part of my training I devised a short – and very primitive – questionnaire for a Year 11 class. One question asked, 'Which item of popular culture would you choose to donate to your school library: A. a novel, B. a film, C. a computer or video game, D. a television show, or E. a music album?' Every one of the thirty respondents chose E. Subsequently I organised a lunchtime music club which met each week to exchange tastes and news about the latest 'thing'. At the same time I read several fascinating studies into children and television but wondered why, when music seemed to be far more important to young people, there was little comparable research into youth and popular music. The spark was lit and here is the end result. The discerning reader will note, however, that the term 'popular music' is conspicuous by its absence. Young people tend not to describe their music – consumed or produced – as 'popular' and in any case the range of different descriptors that they do use suggest the inadequacy of a singular category. 'Popular music' says just as little about music experienced in everyday life as 'youth' says about the different characteristics of young people's everyday lives.

Many individuals and several institutions have helped to bring about this publication, and I certainly do not have the will or inclination to name them one by one. Perhaps most importantly of all, I would like to acknowledge a three-year University of Salford Research Studentship that helped to fund the research contained herein. The supervision of Professor Brian Longhurst has provided an invaluable source of ideas and guidance that leaves its influence both within and beyond the confines of this book. Thanks are also due to Professor Tia DeNora, Professor Derek Scott, Dr Greg Smith and Professor Sheila Whiteley for providing useful comments on the work in progress. I would like to thank colleagues at the School of Cultural Studies, Leeds Metropolitan University, for their encouragement and support. Further thanks are due to Sarah Edwards at Edinburgh University Press for her invaluable editorial advice.

I am grateful to all those members of staff at schools and colleges who participated in this research by assisting me in the arrangement of interviews with their students. Of course, I am also indebted to all those young people who volunteered to be respondents. The interest in and response to the fieldwork surpassed all expectations.

The archival research for this book has benefited from the help of staff at several public libraries in north-west England, the Mass-Observation Archive at the University of Sussex and the Blackpool Leisure Parcs Archive – thanks to Ted and Ann Lightbown for their assistance. The warm hospitality of several cheap guest houses in Brighton and Blackpool deserves a mention too.

Last but by no means least, I would like to thank my family – and especially my mum and dad, Win and Bill Laughey – for fully supporting (i.e. paying for) my studies and being my fiercest critics. During the course of researching and writing the book I have started a family of my own, and so I would like to dedicate *Music and Youth Culture* to Nicky, Harry and another who is yet to take breath.

CHAPTER 1

Introduction

Music is considered by many to be the highest form of art and culture. Music is also considered by many to epitomise their values and tastes, as well as those of other people. Music is very often a product of its time – both a reflection of the 'here and now' and a 'recaller' of memories. Meantime, music and youth are usually deemed to hold a special relationship with each other. Music is delivered and sold to youth audiences, and young people on the whole are fans of one music genre or another. Any attempt to study young people's relationship to music, therefore, is immediately faced with a list of commonly held assumptions – and the above name but few – that need critical evaluation. I could wax lyrical about how my love of music has evolved since a very tender age. I will resist this temptation, however, because this book is partly motivated by a desire to appreciate the role of everyday music beyond those texts, artists and genres that are consumed for personal pleasure. Youth and music may represent a special relationship but young people – like everyone else – exhibit all kinds of different preferences that can frequently lead to pressure, conflict and division. Having said this, the research contained herein shows that different kinds of music and different kinds of young people retain a remarkable bond that has withstood the test of time since at least the early twentieth century (and probably earlier). And whilst not every young person is a music follower, I will argue that music retains a social and cultural force of identification and presentation in nearly all young people's lives, whether they like it or not.

What follows is an attempt to understand how music interacts with young people's everyday lives. In relation to a considerable and expanding body of previous research in this subject area, I will adopt an interactionist perspective to shed light on orthodox structuralist frameworks for conceptualising youth music cultures. Structuralist approaches to studying youth music cultures as macro social units or 'collective wholes' have dominated sociological and cultural analysis for at least the past fifty years. Structuralism and subsequent post-structuralist modifications have wielded their influence in particular through the theories of Roland Barthes (1993, first published in 1957) who showed how cultural texts and objects acquire meanings in what they are not as well as what they are. Barthes set out to understand signs (in the sense of units of meaning, such as a word or image) and developed a structuralist approach which is now known as 'semiotics' – a method of textual analysis which reads language as a signifying system that is capable of generating cultural myths. In *Subculture* (1979), Dick Hebdige perceptively draws similarity between semiotics and a literary critical approach to the study of lived culture. He then suggests that semiotics is able to reject the literary canon in favour of reading

> the normally hidden set of rules, codes and conventions through which meanings particular to specific social groups (i.e. those in power) are rendered universal and 'given' for the whole society. (1979: 9)

These 'rules, codes and conventions' form the dominant ideology that serves to maintain the status quo over subordinate groups through a process called 'hegemony' (Gramsci 1985) as applied to music and youth subcultures by Hebdige.

To whatever extent semiotics can read hegemonic struggles by youth cultures in the subversive meanings that they attach to everyday texts and objects such as music, the method cannot probe beyond the textual 'end product' to examine the contextual 'means' by which these ends are formulated. Rather than seek out 'hidden meanings' through textual analyses such as semiotics, as have so many structuralist perspectives on subcultures, club cultures and post-subcultures, the empirical methods deployed in this book – interviewing, simple observation and a questionnaire-based survey – are designed to contextualise young people's music consumer and producer practices through their own everyday actions and narratives. The interactionist approach deployed here argues that the macro-structures of cultural industries and texts – such as music – are subject to constant change in response to actions and meanings that are generated on the micro-social level.[1] Youth music practitioners in this study are therefore contextualised as diffused audiences and performers for both mediated and co-present music phenomena; not as homogeneous members of subcultural worlds whose music is radically appropriated to exist in harmony with autonomous beliefs or styles. By the same token, this study avoids a narrow focus on specific music cultures (e.g. rock fans) and instead assesses how various types of music made accessible across multimedia as well as public contexts might be used to cut heterogeneous socio-cultural identities within quite tightly defined demographic and geographic characteristics. To this end, the field where I have located my youth sample has been further and higher education institutions (mostly schools and colleges) around the close-knit Bolton, Manchester and Salford segment of the Greater Manchester conurbation in north-west England. My fieldwork and the theoretical insights that emerged are informed by archival research into early accounts of young people's music cultures and media in the same geographical area.

Informed by wider theoretical developments in the sociology of consumption and everyday life as well as cultural and media studies, the research presented here is less interested in how young people are located within music structures than in how music interacts with the structures of their everyday lives. Classic structuralist accounts of youth subcultures (e.g. Clarke and Jefferson 1973; Willis 1978) have tended to locate music alongside other artefacts within an all-embracing style as homology. In the case of punks, for example, a preference for heavy rock music was not understood in relation to everyday education, work and leisure contexts, but solely in relation to syntagmatic leisure contexts in which the punk style – heavy rock, outlandish hairstyles, leather boots and jackets, safety pins and homemade clothes – was collectively lived out. This study, in stark contrast, intends to situate music in relation to the various leisure and non-leisure contexts recurrent in young people's lives. Music is not presumed to fit into spectacular systems of signification that are opposed to dominant social and cultural forces but is instead situated in the localised interactions that typify the ordinary, routine and mundane circumstances of young people's everyday experiences. Theories of everyday life that work outside the orthodox neo-Marxist paradigm of effects and resistance (exemplified by Hall 1992) towards a paradigm of performance and enactment (Finnegan 1997a; Abercrombie and Longhurst 1998) keep more in sympathy with this research agenda.

With regard to specific theories of consumption in everyday life, I am particularly interested to explore the merits of perspectives that relate music consumer to producer practices rather than those that clearly distinguish one from the other. As such, this book is aligned to the ethnographic turn in media studies of audiences although it disassociates itself from many ethnographic studies that have continued to use the vocabulary of incorporation and resistance. Those studies that maintain a structuralist paradigm have focused on the ways in which youth cultures resist incorporation into dominant national and global structures, but have largely been reluctant to detail ethnographically those localised everyday interactions where resistance is presumably located (Bennett 2000). In particular, a focus on symbolic as opposed to actual resistance (e.g. P. Cohen 1992) has meant that artefacts such as music have been bestowed with meanings exclusively applicable to youth *against* rather than *within* parental cultures. The interactionist approach endorsed here, on the other hand, situates young people's music practices in relation to local and inter-generational contexts of uses and influences. In contrast to structuralist formulations that effectively define youth as an intra-generational, extra-local unit, my fieldwork and archival findings will reveal the significance of familial as well as peer group networks to young people's music practices, and the significance to these practices of concrete local places containing conventions and traditions more than 'symbolic defences of communal space' (Hebdige 1979: 39).

Notions of tastes and performances as applied to youth music cultures will be intended to accommodate the characteristics of respondents' mediated as well as their co-present practices. Whilst the majority of music media were accessible to all in the sample, particular media such as the Internet afforded variable levels of user involvement. In the case of public music practices, there were also variable levels of involvement in – added to variable degrees of accessibility to – such practices. Unlike structuralist models of youth music cultures that have discussed the inequalities experienced by collective groups or even a whole generation of young people so defined by a single demographic characteristic, the research agenda here attempts to detail the variations in access to and involvement in music practices *within* these collective units. Conceptualisations of distinction (Bourdieu 1984) deployed in studies of club cultures (Thornton 1995), for instance, have tended to operate on a simplistic level that has distinguished between clubbers and non-clubbers. Much finer distinctions as well as belongings perceived by respondents in terms of their own and others' music practices, however, will be conceptualised in this study to evince the complexities of practitioner involvement and accessibility. Whereas the literature on youth subcultures has generally avoided any prolonged examination of media consumption because of its concerns to analyse subversive practices that are opposed to the ideological functions of media productions, I will explore the complementary relationship between mediated and co-present music practices, each of which accorded similar significance to young people on the basis of empirical analyses.

Furthermore, a focus on the enactment of tastes, narratives and performances through processes of presentation and identification will inform a fluid, dynamic model of the role that music plays in respondents' everyday life narratives. Previous research (e.g. Frith and McRobbie 1990) has overstated the emotional relationship between young people and their musical affiliations where emphasis has been placed on fanatical or enthusiastic consumption at a given moment in time. A key consideration in my deployment of an ethnographic interviewing method – in which I made return visits to several respondents over a sixteen-month fieldwork period – was to account for temporal changes in respondents' presentations of and identifications with specific music cultures. Accounts of permanent changes in music tastes over the fieldwork period proved to be few and far between, but the conservatism suggested by this finding could be explained by the mostly broad, omnivorous music tastes articulated by these young people. Respondents' broad music tastes also explained why changes in these tastes were rarely permanent but frequently temporary in aiding the articulation of everyday life narratives about particular moods or actions. Two types of narratives about music tastes and performances that accorded to different timeframes will thus be substantiated: narratives that are embedded – frequently in family contexts – through memories facilitated by (domestic) music experiences; and narratives that are radically contextualised (Ang 1996) – frequently in peer group contexts – in immediate relation to the whims of music fashions.

Youth as a concept

Taken at face value, the concept of 'youth' appears to be reasonably straightforward. Youth refers to people within a particular age band who are neither immature children nor fully fledged adults. This definition of youth offers a starting point but not much else. Wyn and White (1997) problematise this common sense of youth as it derives from an orthodox approach to thinking about age as an essentially biological process:

> Although each person's life span can be measured 'objectively' by the passing of time, cultural understandings about life stages give the process of growing up, and of ageing, its social meaning. (1997: 10)

Understanding youth as a social and cultural rather than a biological concept is further reinforced by changing historical values, beliefs and attitudes to young members of society. The concept of 'youth' is actually a relatively recent one and is difficult to trace much further back than the early seventeenth century. In the Middle Ages the associated concept of childhood was only loosely acknowledged, given that children were expected to be independent from the age of seven (Aries 1962). Youth followed well behind childhood as a widely recognised phase in the life course and only became widely used in the 1950s when it was initially applied to a particular type of gendered (male) and class-specific (working-class) young people (Frith 1986). Despite the relatively late arrival of 'youth' as a social and cultural phenomenon, classic studies of young people in terms of adolescence (e.g. G. S. Hall 1904) and delinquency (e.g. Robison 1936) had already inspired a large body of theory and research about young people during the first half of the twentieth century. It is not the intention of this book to review the early psychological and sociological literature on youth. However, the legacy of this literature should not be underestimated and it clearly influenced much of the early work on subcultures that will be discussed in Chapter 2.

Ideas about adolescence and delinquency (now sometimes referred to as anti-social behaviour) continue to occupy much research time and money but have been countered by other ways of thinking about youth from contemporary perspectives in sociology, social policy and cultural studies. Some of these perspectives have been influenced by the subcultures literature but others have cast doubt on an understanding of youth as a set of fixed, homologous and non-hierarchical experiences. As such, ideas about the fluidity of youth lifestyles and consumption (Miles 2000; Roberts and Parsell 1994), youth governance in relation to criminalisation (Muncie and Hughes 2002) and youth transitions through employment, education and leisure activities (Wallace and Cross 1990; Furlong and Cartmel 1997) have all offered fresh approaches to the concept of youth. The opening lines of Steven Miles's *Youth Lifestyles in a Changing World* speak volumes about the tired emphasis on delinquency and subcultures that has dogged so-called 'classic' sociologies of youth: 'For too long social scientists have portrayed young people as excluded risk-taking troublemakers motivated by nothing more than their own rebellious self-interest' (Miles 2000: 1). I would extend this comment to numerous cultural studies scholars and a significant generation of academics and journalists who have written about youth culture as though they were still living in 1968 among their fellow hippies. More recent authors have better understood the complexities and flexibilities of youth transitions from one context to another; from one set of identities to a different set. Rather than conceive of youth during a static moment of rebellious leisure, new perspectives have tried to grasp the 'plethora of transitional transitions' (2000: 11) experienced by young people in everyday life contexts. Miles's discussion of 'lifestyle' is particularly apt at approaching the dynamics of youth experiences by embracing the interplay between structure and agency, and expressing young people's social mobility both upwards and

– where the emphasis has usually been placed by youth sociologists – downwards.

As well as offering a dynamic examination of lifestyles, new perspectives on youth transitions have helped to inform how youth might be situated in relation to music and other cultural practices. A major limitation of much youth cultural and particularly subcultural research has been to only fleetingly examine the activities of routine, workaday young people outside their more creative and visible – indeed, 'spectacular' – leisure-based activities. This book is therefore less interested in how young people interact with music and wider social structures than in how music is situated in the fast-moving and changing structures of their everyday lives – and how this ultimately impacts upon the transient nature of successive youth generations:

> During the last two decades, changes in patterns of educational participation, delayed labour market transitions and an extension in the period of dependency have all had implications for the lifestyles which young people adopt and for the ways in which they spend their free time. (Furlong and Cartmel 1997: 53)

The 'transitions' approach to understanding youth has been particularly helpful in showing how the concept is not determined by objective structural categories such as age and class but is subject to social and cultural changes in the experiences and practices of being young. Perhaps the most notable change that has occurred during the last twenty to thirty years – particularly in Western societies – has seen the protraction of youth as a life stage. Wallace and Kovatcheva (1998: 181–4) argue that the endless revivals of youth cultural styles in Eastern and Western Europe, such as 1970s disco, point to a present-day concept of youth that no longer applies merely to young people and their supposedly distinctive, original, possibly subcultural activities. The very idea that 'youth subcultures' might exist today is therefore problematised not so much by the notion of 'subculture' as by that of 'youth'.

Situating music in youth culture

Much early work around youth and music (e.g. Adorno various; Hall and Whannel 1990, first published in 1964) started with the music and applied it – often without sound empirical evidence – to a given youth culture or generation. However, there are important exceptions to this rule. A strand of thinking about youth culture and music from the perspective of those characterised by the former concept can be traced back to a pioneering analysis of 'youth culture' as a social entity (Parsons 1942). Following in this tradition, Mungham (1976), Murdock and McCron (1976) and Frith (1978; 1983; 1986) were among the first youth sociologists who both worked alongside exponents of a youth cultural studies tradition but at the same time redressed the lack of empirical insights that had thus far informed an understanding of youth (music) cultures. My own account of young people's music uses and practices, and the ways in which they are narrated and performed so diversely and vividly, owes much to these broader perspectives on youth and social change. The value of this body of work as a rejoinder to the seminal textual analyses of youth culture (e.g. Hall and Jefferson 1993) will be made explicit in the following chapter but for now a short example will suffice. Whilst semiotic or historical readings of youth subcultures have suggested quite uncritically the working-class position of youth subcultures, more rigorous sociological research (Stewart 1992; Hollands 1990) has demonstrated the complexity of social class, given that a typical lengthening of the transitional phase among more affluent young people has led to greater parity in levels of disposable income experienced by youth of all social classes.

Consistent with the concept of youth 'in transition' between varying degrees of leisure, education and employment, this book approaches an analysis of music only in relation to all the other everyday activities of young people. Ian K. Birksted's (1976) research into how a group of teenage boys viewed their school performance to be inextricably affected by work, leisure and holiday activities points towards a wider concern to contextualise routine, recurrent, temporal phenomena. Like school performance for these teenage boys, music for many young people that I researched could feature across leisure, work and education times but would hold different levels of attention in accordance with the various contexts in which it was consumed and produced. Moreover, experiences of music and other activities across leisure, work and education contexts were not easily distinguishable. Indeed certain work activities were often motivated by a desire to accumulate the necessary financial capital for leisure and even education activities. Likewise, certain education contexts such as school breaks were also important contexts for leisure activities. The way in which these different types of activities closely juxtaposed with each other to banish the segregated notion of hedonistic weekends at leisure or long holidays without work, and to instead shift certain leisure times towards weekday nights, would problematise any suggestion that these young people could find the time and commitment required for spectacular subcultural or indeed club cultural pursuits.

Situating music in juxtaposition with the everyday transitions of youth cultures is also helpful in order to understand how the process of growing up can correspond to changing contexts of leisure. Theories of subculture have tended to assume that public contexts free from parental controls accommodate the spaces for youth musical expression. For many interviewees of different ages in this research, though, the parental home (but very rarely the street corner) provided a central context for what they perceived to be leisure time.[2] As well as facilitating rest and recuperation from education and work time, a young person's home and those of others often accommodated multimedia entertainment technologies, cheaper or even free food and drink, warmth, hygienic amenities, security and familiarity. Moreover, someone's parents were always likely to be eating out or away from home to allow temporary escape from the everyday regulations of these domestic leisure contexts. As might be expected, public music practices would be easier to access and more likely accessed as young people grew older. Indeed private/mediated music practices offered an alternative to the drawbacks associated with access to public/co-present ones, whilst co-present music practitioners tended to explain their activities without reference to mediated choices. This latter point perhaps indicates why studies that overstate co-present music practices within subcultural (e.g. Hall and Jefferson 1993) or localised art worlds (Finnegan 1989) rarely encounter mediated music influences. As these initial findings show, though, it is unhelpful to focus on the public/co-present to the ignorance of the private/mediated music practices given that the activities associated with each set of practices provided definite choices in response to my respondents' other everyday leisure, work and education activities.

Book structure

The aims of this book are fivefold and generally correspond to the intentions of particular chapters. First, I aim to analyse classic theories of youth music cultures as subcultures – together with contemporary revisions of these classic theories in terms of club cultures and post-subcultures – from an interactionist methodological standpoint. A second aim of the research is to apply sociological and cultural theories of everyday life to young people's music consumption and production in general, and their enactment of tastes, narratives and performances in particular. Third, the aim is to situate contemporary young people's music cultures within a historical context by exploring an early period of mass music activity among British youth prior to the post-war phenomena of subcultures. Fourth, and informed by extensive empirical information, I aim to contextualise the local sites of everyday interaction wherein young people's music cultures and media are enacted and influenced, detailing the similarities as well as the differences between their involvement in mediated and accessibility to co-present music experiences. The fifth and final aim of this book is to evince the relationship between young people's music media and public music practices, which by necessity will demand a model for indicating the relationship between private and public consumer as well as local and global producer practices. These five aims underpin how the book is structured, chapter-by-chapter details of which now follow.

Following this introduction, Chapter 2 reviews the literature on subcultures, club cultures and post-subcultures from an interactionist perspective. My argument here is that the prevalent deployment of semiotics, structuralism and postmodernism in understanding post-Second World War youth cultures has resulted in a dearth of empirically informed, sociologically detailed accounts of young people's localised interactions with familiar others. Instead of focusing on young people's relations to the people and places that provide meaningful everyday sources of reference and influence, youth cultural studies – particularly those derivative of the European tradition of critical and cultural theory – have tended to locate respondents in collective, intra-generational units that share homologous commitments to spectacular deviances or symbolic resistances. In turn, much previous research into the role of music in youth cultures has worked within a structural Marxist framework centred on the effects of and resistances to the commercial function inherent in mass music texts that young people have consumed throughout the twentieth century to the present day. Such a framework persists in theories of fandom, club and taste cultures that are also guilty of a narrow focus on intensely committed, emotional consumer practices. Theories of post-subcultures, on the other hand, go some way to rejecting structuralist perspectives but continue to deploy subcultural discourses, besides sometimes showing a postmodernist aversion to rigorous social research.

Rather than presuppose a static youth cultural world characterised by certain musical ideologies and political affiliations, then, I will suggest an interactionist approach to the study of young people that attempts to understand their everyday cultural values *within* rather than *against* those cultural values of other social groups. This approach is therefore able to evince heterogeneous youth (music) cultures through understanding dynamic intergenerational and local relations that are complemented rather than contrasted to relations with globally mediated phenomena. A dynamic interactionism used to problematise structuralism as a framework for understanding music cultures and media is then further outlined with reference to archival research in Chapter 3. The archive in question is the

Mass-Observation Archive, named after the social research organisation that generated its ethnographic material. This chapter will interpret the findings of Mass-Observers located in north-west England who observed youth music and dance practices during the pre-war and intra-war years (1936–49). These practices and the various contexts in which they were enacted (ballrooms, dance schools, living rooms) are seen to resonate in particular with ideas about the 'carnivalesque' (Bakhtin 1984) and every-day consumer tactics which escape the influence of producers (de Certeau 1984). I will argue that the notion of what might be termed 'promenade performances' of demonstration and display afforded by varying levels of involvement and competence in dancing practices illustrates the significance of interactive processes of cultural exchange – or cultural transmission (Fine and Kleinman 1979) – scarcely evident in many con-temporary youth cultural accounts.

Theoretical frameworks other than those reliant upon a dichotomy between dominant parental and resistant youth cultures are assessed in Chapter 4. This chapter applies various concepts associated with the soci-ology of consumption together with theoretical accounts of everyday life to young people's music consumer and producer practices. Propelled by a relatively recent tradition of media audience ethnographies, research that can be defined as owning an interactionist dimension has attempted to detail the complex relationships between music texts and young people's everyday, local contexts. I will therefore discuss the merits of approaches to young people's music practices that are situated in everyday narratives, self-identities and self-presentations as well as specific localities. These approaches possess the potential to contextualise the differences encoun-tered by young people in their everyday experiences of music consumption and production. In particular, the notion of self-presentation (Goffman 1969a) combined with those previously discussed ideas about the 'carniva-lesque' and tactics will inform contextual analysis of differential display and demonstration by youth music practitioners through promenade per-formances. Instead of focusing entirely on how music structures youth cul-tural values, the theoretical concerns endorsed throughout this chapter will anticipate later fieldwork intentions to situate music in relation to all the other cultural practices that characterise young people's daily social interactions. It will be argued that the starting point for situating music in young people's lives should be the individual, peer group or familial con-texts through which consumer and producer practices are learnt.

Chapters 5 and 6 present research findings from fieldwork that provide empirical support for the main arguments presented earlier in the book. During the fieldwork period (July 2001–June 2003), in order of significance,

I conducted fifty-two interviews either with groups or individuals, a questionnaire-based survey with 232 respondents, and simple observation at fifty-four diverse research locations where public music functioned to some degree. Mediated music uses and influences are the concern of Chapter 5 only in so far as they relate to the 'other' type of music experience (i.e. the co-present type). Although mostly private/domestic contexts provide the situations for music media consumption, I will show how mediated music consumption is a pervasive feature of these young people's public leisure as well as educational and work contexts. Differences in music media uses among the sample will be understood along an involvement continuum from intensive to casual media consumption. Implicit to this focus on young people's heterogeneous consumer involvement in specific music cultures will be a rejection of subcultural and club cultural – as well as many post-subcultural – accounts of youth music consumption framed within homologous structures of style. This chapter will also focus on mediated music influences and argue that such influences need to be understood through contexts of reception as much as the music texts themselves. Family and peer group influences in domestic and educational contexts will be shown to stamp very localised meanings on global music media products. Media uses and influences will then be conceptualised in reference to the earlier theoretical discussion of literacies and narratives. The productive outcomes of young music consumers' media literacies as well as their everyday life narratives will be radically situated in relation to those contexts through which these literacies are learnt and these narratives are articulated.

Chapter 6 will build upon analyses in the previous chapter by initially presenting those distinct facets of young people's public music practices before combining such facets with those identified as distinctive to mediated music practices. Differences in public music practices among respondents will be partly understood along an accessibility continuum from exclusiveness to inclusiveness. However, for such differences in young people's co-present music experiences to be fully understood it will be deemed fit to combine scales of accessibility with those of involvement as devised in analysis of mediated music experiences. As a result, a dual configuration of analyses of mediated music involvement and co-present music accessibility will result in four groupings of youth music practitioners regardless of their preference for either music media or public music practices: *clubbers*, who access exclusive co-present contexts and intensively consume mediated music; *surfers*, who also access exclusive co-present contexts but tend to casually consume music media; *exchangers*, who tend to enact inclusive public music practices but are intensively involved in media uses; and *drifters*, who also enact inclusive public music practices and are casually involved in media uses. The rest of Chapter 6 will propose various applications of these four groupings. Developing theoretical discussion about performances, I will conceptualise respondents' presentations of and identifications with their public music practices through interactionist perspectives on impression management and judgement as well as age playing techniques. After discussing perceptions of space/place in respect of localised meanings and media influences in respect of globalised meanings that are exerted upon co-present music contexts, this chapter finishes by outlining a notion of promenade performances as first proffered in Chapter 3. These performances of display and demonstration will return to interactionist concerns about how young people's everyday music cultures are situated in intergenerational and local contexts.

Chapter 7 ties together the theories and research on music and youth cultures. Here I will advocate a situational interactionist model for the study of everyday youth music cultures and media which conceptualises contexts, practices, involvement and accessibility in terms that support previous theoretical propositions and fieldwork/archival analyses. This model will then be applied to a more thorough examination of two central themes to have emerged in the course of this study: those of intergenerational narratives and localised performances. The overall conclusions (Chapter 8) will evaluate the extent to which the five aims of this book have been successfully addressed and will present their theoretical outcomes. Where this study of music in young people's everyday lives attempts to contribute to the knowledge and understanding of its subject area is in the rejection of dominant structuralist and postmodernist theoretical frameworks in favour of the adoption of a less frequently undertaken interactionist approach. This approach will conceptualise youth music consumers as diffused audiences and performers rather than homogeneous participants of an exclusive, collective subcultural or club cultural world.

Notes

1. This is a brief and necessarily generalised distinction between structuralist and interactionist perspectives. I would recommend Cuff et al. (1990) for a more detailed exposition of these perspectives and their theoretical agendas.
2. Roberts et al.'s (1990) longitudinal survey of approximately four thousand young men and women aged 16–19 years – similar to the ages of most of the respondents in my sample – in mid-1980s Scotland also revealed the importance of domestic settings for listening to recorded music on a regular basis, partly due to economic constraints.

CHAPTER 2

Subculture, Club Cultures and Post-Subcultures: Music/Social Interactions?

What is a subculture? There is no simple, catch-all definition and this chapter will show how an understanding of subculture is inextricably dependent on competing methodological approaches. To understand the theories and research into youth and music subcultures that represented a substantial area of scholarly activity in the USA and Britain during the latter half of the twentieth century, it is first necessary to trace the process by which subcultural ideas arose from wider perspectives on culture and society. Early developments in cultural studies from different critical traditions in North American social research, and European literary and cultural theory, had a fragmentary impact on subsequent studies of subcultures. A consequence of such an impact was the tendency for British cultural studies of youth groups and their musical affiliations – the most influential of which derived from the Centre for Contemporary Cultural Studies (CCCS) at the University of Birmingham – to adopt an almost entirely structuralist perspective on subcultures as exclusive signifying systems.[1] In the USA, by contrast, and particularly through the work of the Chicago School (of sociology and criminology), subculture was conceived to be a phenomenon to which every individual in any everyday context potentially could belong. Of interest to US researchers were the ways in which subcultural groups interacted with and overlapped each other. Although this distinction between traditional North American and European cultural studies is not clear-cut in all cases, it is significant to later formations of subculture.

If it follows that studies of youth subcultures were influenced by earlier ethnographies from Chicago School sociologists in the 1920s and 1930s (Hebdige 1979: 75), it is puzzling to discover how little they seem to have been influenced by interactionist perspectives that subsequently aided interpretation of these early studies and informed their predecessors. Due to the weighty influence of the CCCS literature on more recent accounts of club cultures and post-subcultures, and despite the numerous critiques of subculture included in these and other accounts,[2] interactionist analyses of subcultures are conspicuous by their absence (early exceptions here are Fine and Kleinman 1979; Mungham 1976). The club cultures and post-subcultures literature furthermore shares many of the flaws found in the study of subculture which it has intended to supersede. I will argue that the most fundamental criticism of subcultural theory in general and British subcultural studies in particular has been the construction of closed semiotic spaces that define youth groups homogeneously *against* other groups and ignore the everyday interactions between young people (and others) *within* these different groups. The concept of club cultures, whilst a useful rejoinder to the semiotic bias of subcultural accounts, should be criticised similarly for lacking detailed sociological examination of young people's everyday lives. The postmodernist slant to the post-subcultures argument deserves credit for occasionally moving beyond the dominance-resistance model of structuralism but, perhaps reflecting contemporary cynicism about empiricism, also tends to lack applied social research. Incorporated into this analysis are studies that more promisingly depart from structuralist and constructionist tendencies towards an analysis of young people that does not presuppose collective cultural identities channelled through music, fashion and other ostensibly omnipresent forms of intensive consumption. Instead, these contributions together with my own are more likely to reject the sociology of youth subcultures by diverting attention to the dynamic interactions experienced by young people in everyday contexts of cultural consumption.

Culture to subculture

It is from the North American tradition of social and cultural research that the concept of 'subculture' first emerged and from which interactionist studies of subculture developed – in stark contrast to the structuralist traditions of early European cultural studies. Two pioneering studies from the Chicago School, although not alluding to the precise term 'subculture', paved the way for such a concept by ethnographically detailing the activities of a particular cross-section of the wider US population. First, Paul G. Cressey (1932) and a team of observers began a project in 1925 to investigate what were perceived in criminal terms as 'taxi-dancers'. Taxi-dancers were usually young females who offered themselves for hire to male dance partners in return for half of the patrons' charges, the other half of which would be retained by the proprietors of the Chicago dance halls who employed the taxi-dancers. Interpreting multiple observers' accounts of their experiences, Cressey states that the taxi dance hall

> is a distinct social world, with its own ways of acting, talking, and thinking. It has its own vocabulary, its own activities and interests, its own conception of what is significant in life, and – to a certain extent – its own scheme of life. (1932: 31)

This depiction smacks of concepts like argot and homology familiar to the subcultures literature that flourished in US academic circles from about 1960 (D. R. Cressey 1970) and Britain about a decade after.[3] The taxi dance hall was approached as a mysterious institution shunned by the wider population as the least socially acceptable form of dance entertainment on a scale of acceptability in which government-funded municipal ballrooms and dance schools were differentiated as of the highest status. P. G. Cressey could then locate the 'distinct social world' of the taxi dance hall in relation to competing social worlds to account for the everyday structural forces that shaped the micro-industry of dance entertainment.

The legacy of Cressey's study, therefore, was ethnographic observations of interactions among taxi-dancers and their customers that suggested ways in which the wider structure of an urban community situated these social interactions but also ways in which actors perceived themselves within the wider social structure. For example, fierce competition both among taxi dance halls, and between them and other dance institutions, fostered amalgamation of different ethnic groups in Chicago after dance-hall managers lifted exclusion policies for certain groups so as to attract a larger clientele. The consequence of the processes by which these structural market forces increased interactions between 'Italians', 'Poles', 'Filipinos' and 'Orientals' was increased racist violence between these groups, often caused by accusations of mixed ethnic sexual relations for which taxi dance halls were considered to be 'breeding grounds'. In order to deter these violent interactions, it was deemed necessary by structuring influences such as the police for these dance halls to revive exclusion policies whereby each manager would agree to serve clientele of a particular ethnic group. This historically informed location of structuring and inter-acting yet 'distinct' social worlds reveals much about each social world itself but has so rarely been of concern to analyses of magically vacuumed subcultural spaces. Although, for instance, Hebdige's (1979: 45) 'phantom history of race relations since the War' refers to the significance of racial relations in the formation of British youth subcultural identities, I agree with Simon Jones's criticism of this 'phantom history' of stylistic, ahistorical spaces for ignoring 'concrete experience and interaction' (1988: xxv).[4]

Second, William F. Whyte's participant observation of young people on the streets of Chicago undoubtedly influenced ethnographic research on youth subcultures. Whyte relied on informants from the youth groups that he participated in so as to retrieve 'insider accounts' of what later was referred to as delinquent subcultural behaviour (see Downes 1966: 1–11). Despite the influence of Whyte's *Street Corner Society* (1993, originally published in 1943) on social research methods, Andy Bennett (2000) has recently suggested that later research on subcultures

> began to shift away from the 'local' as a frame of reference for the acquired deviant sensibilities of youth and towards a new approach which suggested youth itself was capable of generating a series of norms and values, that youth was, in effect, a 'culture' or *subculture* in its own right. (2000: 15)

Whilst I agree with Bennett's statement, I would rather cite Cressey's (1932) study as a model of how a youth subculture is not created in an autonomous space but is negotiated through localised interactions shaped by structuring influences. The main drawback of Whyte's participant observation was that it focused on the leaders of these groups, not the followers; the extraordinary, not the mundane; the strikingly visible, not the private and concealed. As will be discussed in Chapter 4, my empirical aims to understand everyday youth cultural consumption and production avoided the production of 'exotic data' (Naroll and Naroll 1963) as associated with the participant observer in practice.

Following these pioneering studies into subcultural worlds or societies, Milton M. Gordon's article entitled 'The Concept of the Sub-culture and its Application' (1970, originally published in 1947) proffered perhaps the first sustained consideration of 'subculture' using that precise term. This concept would enable sociologists

> to discern relatively closed and cohesive systems of social organisation which currently we tend to analyse separately with our more conventional tools of 'class' and 'ethnic group'. (1970: 33)

The emphasis on 'organisation' here points to this early formulation of 'sub-culture' as essentially a subsection of the whole culture, whether this meant a regional or national culture. Subcultures were inclusive in that they had 'an integrated impact on the participating individual' who could in turn adopt a subcultural personality that might change with their varying degrees of social mobility (1970: 32). Although this early formulation of subculture alongside other North American studies suffered from ecological fallacies whereby everyday environments were perceived to generate – often hostile – effects on individuals, they were nevertheless informed by an empirical research tradition that was far less important to the European tradition of critical and cultural theory at this time.

These early models of subculture laid the foundations for later accounts of deviance from within this ethnographic social research tradition. Howard Becker's (1953) account of marijuana use by jazz musicians more usefully showed how the pleasures of drug use stem from a 'learning process' acquired through experiences that parallel becoming accepted deviant group members. The use of marijuana by musicians could be understand as a device to aid perception of their 'hip-ness' in contrast to the 'square-ness' of their audience, whose musical tastes were distinctly other than their own (Becker 1951: 139). These unavoidable if discouraged interactions with their audience in intimate performance contexts such as weddings impressed on these musicians the feeling that their musical tastes and, by extension, their lifestyles deviated from normal laypeople. As one jazz player said, 'outside of show people and professional people, every-body's a f– square. They don't know anything' (1951: 140). Drug use by these musicians was thus defined against 'square' drug use. As Becker noted, synonyms for marijuana 'change as [soon as] musicians feel that they have gained currency among outsiders' (1951: 144). Unlike accounts of a commonly structured deviant counter-culture that somehow escaped inter-action with other groups outside their 'new leisured class', Becker's study more convincingly suggested that it is these very interactions between deviant groups and outsiders which fostered perceptions of how certain subcultures could structure their everyday lives in contrast to other group cultures. Chris Jenks (2005: 56) offers a structuralist critique of Becker in which he argues that little is considered about how problems caused by the social structure mean that interactions between, say, the police and deviant individuals are always underpinned by 'power differentials'. To some extent this is a valid critique and yet Jenks neglects to understand Becker's point that social structures are both producers and the products of power rela-tions in everyday interactive contexts, and therefore need to be examined through precisely the kind of micro-ethnographic studies conducted by Becker and other interactionist researchers.

Ned Polsky's (1971) ethnography of the beat scene in New York in 1960 similarly highlighted the interactionist dimension of youth subcultural deviance. Drawing on interviews with a commendably large sample of 300 'beats', he noticed that 'the large majority of beats do not flaunt their phys-ical presence before the public gaze' (1971: 149) and instead structure their communal activities within timeframes that operate outside normal tourist hours. Inconspicuous 'badges' such as beards of certain lengths enabled one beat to identify another in everyday interactions motivated by a desire not 'to call the attention of outsiders to themselves' (1971: 150 and 151). Essentially, the beats considered their deviance to be slight, and through a means of negotiating and interacting with dominant social groups by taking temporary paid work, they believed that what was presently cate-gorised by outsiders as their deviance would be socially acceptable in the future. So when certain US states relaxed restrictions on marijuana use in large schools,

> Proselytizers for marihuana – beats, hippies and college users alike – interpret all this to mean that marihuana will be adopted by ever-widening segments of the population and one day replace liquor in the affections of most Americans. (1971: 173)

The important point made here by Polsky, then, is that youth subcultures can have conformist as well as deviant goals, mainstream as well as subter-ranean social ends. Therefore, what outsiders perceive to be deviance might amount to a misinterpreted definition of young people's mainstream political intentions. Polsky's views would appear to have owed much to the influence of Becker's earlier labelling theory (1963).

Before considering the theoretical turn towards youth subcultural resis-tance that emerged from the European tradition of cultural studies, a further study that critiqued commonsense assumptions about subculture from a labelling theory perspective – rather than proposing a radically alternative subcultural theory – was Stanley Cohen's (1980a) study of the mods and rockers in mid-1960s Britain. The behaviour and actions of youth subcultures were not the overriding factors by which they were defined as deviant. Polsky (1971) noted the reaction of beats to definitions of them by others:

> The individuals in question resent any label whatever, and regard a concern with labelling as basically square. (1971: 149)

The label 'beats' was therefore refused from within the 'beats' subculture and presumably created by outsiders. According to Cohen (1980a), mass media were the creators of the mods and rockers following societal reac-tion to their sensational reporting of disturbances between the two groups at English seaside resorts. Contrary to the lay view of news media as objec-tive carriers of information, in institutional contexts

> the information has been subject to alternative definitions of what consti-tutes 'news' and how it should be gathered and presented. The information

is further structured by the various commercial and political constraints in which newspapers, radio and television operate. (1980a: 16)

So *Folk Devils and Moral Panics* (1980a) – along with Jock Young's (1971) study of drug-taking – usefully focused on the transactional relationship between deviant groups and the moral panics which they evoked in the wider society. These panics were thus structured and constructed by dominant ideological apparatus such as mass media and the police. This metaphorical battleground between the dominant and the dominated was much more literally read by exponents of a resistance framework wherein mass media were charged with partaking in a dominant hegemonic agenda.

A striking instance of the differences between the traditions of North American and European cultural studies is the story of Theodor W. Adorno's aversion to US mass communications research after emigrating from his native Germany following the hostilities instigated by its Nazi government during the Second World War. Adorno's argument that popular music exerted a 'soporific effect upon social consciousness' (1945, quoted in Morrison 1978: 346) to distract the masses from realising the futility of capitalism has continued to pervade the study of music consumption to the present day. Despite his famous polemical attack on the stultifying popular 'culture industry' that rendered 'the masses redundant as producers' (with Horkheimer 1944: 150), Adorno nevertheless suggested in a footnote to 'On Popular Music' that 'The attitude of distraction is not a completely universal one. Particularly youngsters who invest popular music with their own feelings are not yet completely blunted to all its effects' (1992: 223). He further noted that a demographic focus on age differences had no room in his study. Tracing Adorno's thoughts to the period following his move to the US, David E. Morrison has shown that while Adorno recognised that

> young people were still capable of investing popular music with meaning, the radio industry itself, with its monotonous and repetitive 'plugging' fitted well the rhythms of the industrial process and undermined the possibility of such 'meaning'. (Morrison 1978: 344)

The US radio industry as such typified all that was aesthetically impoverished about contemporary culture in its broadcasting of standardised Tin Pan Alley songs and its elevation of Hollywood stars like Ginger Rogers to a level of idolatry that 'the girl behind the counter' emotionally relates to her predicament of 'missed fulfillment' (Adorno 1992: 222).

It is unfortunate but perhaps unsurprising given Adorno's distrust of the quantitative sociology advocated by Paul F. Lazarsfeld (Morrison 1978) that he failed to allow himself the necessary room to pursue his earlier hypothesis about meaningful youth music consumption. Perhaps the derogatory German meaning of *Kultur* with its racist and authoritarian undertones coupled with his own lambast of the capitalist-driven entertainment industry contradicted the value-free judgements of mass cultural and communications studies to such an extent that Adorno would have distanced himself from foreign research practices peculiar to democratic societies such as accessing government documents. Aversion to the empiricism of North American social research, however, was by no means a limitation of Adorno's and the Frankfurt School's critical theory alone. F. R. Leavis and Denys Thompson (1933) as well as T. S. Eliot (1948) were influential British contributors to a European tradition of literary studies in which a close scrutiny of texts was considered to provide the richest interpretations of their cultural value regardless of how these texts were used – presumably with far less scrutiny – by the majority of their readers.[5] Moreover, this tradition remained antagonistic to pragmatic analyses of popular culture and media in its concern to uphold a canon of authentic or organic literature (R. Williams 1966). So whilst the emergence of cultural studies in Europe sprang from more established traditions of literary and critical theory, the North American roots of cultural studies by contrast emerged from the social research ethos of sociology and mass communications studies. Perhaps this difference explains the fact that studies of subculture began within a North American tradition which was more likely to investigate such a grounded phenomenon. After all, youth subcultures were hardly represented in the kinds of texts that the European tradition considered worthy of scrutiny.

Youth subcultures

The syntagmatic shift from culture to subculture more or less independently construed by North American and European theorists has impacted on much of the literature on youth subcultures. I will show here that the tangible transition from understanding subcultures as deviant subsections of a wider culture to a European theoretical tradition that understood youth subcultures as vacuums of resistance was borne out of perceptions that the ideological function of mass media needed to be assessed by exploring signifying systems in texts. This new theoretical framework, epitomised by Stuart Hall's 'Encoding/Decoding' (1992, originally published in 1980), was a reaction in particular to empirical aspects of North American social and communications sciences that afforded little scrutiny to textual analyses.

The resistance thesis maintained by British CCCS theorists superseded that of deviance by developing a distinct methodology that Cohen (1980b: xxv) later called 'new subcultural theory'. Armed with the semantic weapons of semiotics, both CCCS staff and students produced a significant body of work throughout the 1970s that substituted deviance as a negotiation between differently adjusted social groups for resistance as a more politicised opposition between youth and dominant or parental culture. As such, CCCS work was removed further from examining interactions between subcultures and outsiders, towards a single-minded structuralist objective more in keeping with the 'great tradition' or 'ideal order' of artistic authenticity in European cultural and literary criticism. Two outcomes of this objective that contradict my aims in this book to formulate an understanding of everyday youth cultural practices will be discussed here: first, a limiting trend to analyse a singular social variable such as – in particular – social class rather than to accommodate multivariate analysis; and second, a preoccupation with decoding homologous styles.

First, class-specific youth subcultural resistance was based on the assumption that variations in age, gender and ethnicity had no bearing on a collective response to socio-cultural circumstances. John Clarke et al. were concerned with 'how "class" and "generational" elements interact together in the production of distinctive group-styles' (1993: 52). However, both these 'elements' were presupposed: for 'class', read working class; for 'generational', read youth. As Gary Alan Fine and Sheryl Kleinman (1979) have rightly pointed out,

> In the case of youth [. . .] it seems inadequate to deal with the wide range of belief systems (and subcultures) within that age group by means of the concept of a single demographically based subculture. (1979: 3)

Furthermore, 'While a small group can be studied as a closed system, it is erroneous to conceive of group members as interacting exclusively with each other' (1979: 8). Such criticism can be similarly levelled at John B. Mays's study of juvenile delinquency in inner-city Liverpool in which he concluded that each child within distinctly different youth groups 'exhibits the same symptoms' (1954: 147) of uncreative leisure pursuits which account for their impoverished social situation. Mays clearly believed that 'a love of good music or drama or literature' would somehow alleviate the material poverty in which his respondents lived, and he revealed a Leavisite sympathy characteristic of highbrow European cultural theory by claiming that 'cultivated' young people 'are so rarely met that their aesthetic deviation seems phenomenal' (1954: 73).

Whilst Mays painted a dim picture of British working-class youth, CCCS researchers tended to paint a very different picture of youth groups as heroic and subversive. Nonetheless, British cultural studies had maintained the 'great tradition' of tainting every subcultural group with the same brush. Presuppositions of social class and generational unity were fundamental to Clarke et al.'s dialectic analysis of youth subcultural resistance to the means of production governed by the dominant, ruling class of party politicians and media professionals among others. As David Muggleton (2000) has rightly argued, this *a priori* neo-Marxist framework rendered an assertion of the authentic origins of subcultural resistance very hard to falsify. The homogeneous working-class character of youth subcultures was thus romanticised as a lone oppositional voice against the hegemonic bloc successfully secured by the dominant with the consent of the subordinate parental culture. Subcultural youth was in this sense a class of its own, united in resistance and isolated from what were surely their differing socio-economic backgrounds as determined by their parents' occupations. This isolation from the parental culture, however, was demanded because incongruous class positions problematised the assumed unity of youth subcultural resistance. Such a narrow structuralist conception of subcultural resistance, then, effectively misrepresented the complexities of a 'generational element'. Moreover, a class-specific resistance in substitution for the more contested characteristics of deviance would mean that the new concept could only be applied empirically to the most marginal and atypical groups. Little prolonged consideration is afforded to non-resistant members of a youth generation who are thus structurally excluded from a presupposed, intensely political arena.

The archetypal study of the correspondence between social class and youth subcultures is Phil Cohen's (1992) participant observation of working-class communities in London's East End. Using not dissimilar language to previous deviant counter cultural studies, he observed 'generational conflict', a breakdown of family continuity and 'interpersonal tension' that was managed by young people via collective 'symbolic systems' (1992: 82). These symbolic systems were generated by working-class youth 'to retrieve some of the socially cohesive elements destroyed in their parent culture' (1992: 83) through social structuring such as the demolition of terraced housing and its replacement with alienating high-rise blocks. Again, this exclusive conception of youth as somehow a closed system in conflict with elders who experienced the same class structure begs the question about where any details of intercommunity relations between the generations were included in this hegemonic struggle. P. Cohen's notion of territoriality, for instance, only operates within a symbolic dimension of warfare or 'a magical way of expressing ownership' (1992: 85). Actual territorial resistance in interactive struggles between the generations would be an unthinkable event whilst the youth generation is assumed to operate within a symbolic system and the parental generation within a dominant hegemony. Another unlikely event would be youth subcultural resistance outside a narrow, politically circumscribed working class:

> I do not think the middle class produces subcultures, for subcultures are produced by a dominated culture, not by a dominant culture. (1992: 85)

The possibility that youth groups from different social classes could disseminate 'cultural information' to each other 'through individuals who perform particular structural roles in intergroup relations' (Fine and Kleinman 1979: 11) is too readily dismissed. Gary Clarke critiqued this study with the perceptive suggestion that 'Any empirical analysis would reveal that subcultures are diffuse, diluted, and mongrelised in form' (1990: 83).

This notion of *symbolic* territoriality has since been conceived semiotically in a somewhat different context as a *social* phenomenon with gender-specific outcomes:

> The teenage girl fan of Madonna who fantasises her own empowerment can translate this fantasy into behaviour, and can act in an empowered way socially, thus winning more social territory for herself. When she meets others who share her fantasies and freedom there is the beginning of a sense of solidarity, of a shared resistance, that can support and encourage progressive action on the microsocial level. (Fiske 1989a: 172)

This shared resistance, John Fiske suggests, might take the form of girl fans identifying with Madonna's feminist pop star persona while empowering their status in relations with boys in actual social contexts. However, this analysis is based on reading the texts which were entered for a music television channel's (MTV) competition in which viewers were asked to produce a video for a Madonna song. These texts, then, were produced by intensely motivated girl fans of Madonna, so that the experiences of boy fans or less avid followers of the pop star were excluded from such a preconceived sample. Furthermore, Fiske's theory that audiences radically reinterpret media texts lacked detailed sociological evidence to define more clearly how the micro-social and macro-social levels interact during the construction of fandom, at the phase of consumption.

Gender-orientated cases of subcultural resistance have been cited few and far between to the extent that no distinctively female youth subculture has yet to be uncovered. Hebdige (1979) has pointed to the subversive practices deployed by David Bowie lookalikes in imitating his extravagant, sexually ambiguous style of dress and performance but this expression of an 'alternative identity' (1979: 88) was interpreted in youth subcultural appearances rather than actions. Angela McRobbie and Jenny Garber (1993, originally published in 1975) prompted feminist critiques on the masculine-centred celebratory accounts of gender resistance by Hebdige and other – mostly male – CCCS theorists. They argued that prevalent connotations of the term 'youth' as 'young male' were not sufficiently demythologised by accounts of subcultures which ignored male and female interactions to such an extent that young females were uncritically deemed to be objects of sexual attractiveness. McRobbie later argued that

> If we look for the structured absences in this youth literature, it is the sphere of family and domestic life that is missing [. . .] It is this link between the lads' hard outer image and their private experiences – relations with parents, siblings, and girlfriends – that still needs to be explored. (1990: 71)

By extension, Hebdige's (1979) analysis of how certain masculine youth subcultures such as skinheads negotiated with as well as opposed the parental culture lacked reflexive social research tools to engage sufficiently in the private experiences of these subcultures outside their spectacular public appearances.

Hebdige's resistance thesis, nonetheless, deserved credit for at least stressing the role of subcultural identities other than those that were merely (working) class-based. However, none of the youth subcultures that he presents are convincingly decoded as displaying multiple social variables without threatening the resistance thesis itself. Rather, ethnicity in particular is a resource for resistant identities where the meaning of style has been understood by successive post-war British working-class subcultures. These urban, white youth populations appropriated reggae music, and the clothes and hairstyles of the Rastafarian figure, from immigrant Afro-Caribbean communities living in close proximity so as to create 'symbolic defences of communal space' (1979: 39). Like P. Cohen's (1992) class-based concept of territoriality, ethnic forms of resistant youth identities work in a magical, symbolic world rather than the social worlds inhabited by the cultures of parents and families, thus necessarily excluding consideration of interactions between these worlds. White middle-class youth subcultures – which Hebdige at least acknowledges in cases such as bohemian punks – are therefore less clearly associated with black cultural styles because such complexities cannot be easily positioned within the neo-Marxist resistance frame.

Second, the overstated importance placed by CCCS theorists on style as homology partly explains a tendency to only conceptualise resistance in terms of singular social variables. John Clarke and Tony Jefferson described homologous style as 'the selection of certain objects (clothes, hairstyles, music and so forth) which are relevant to the focal concerns of the group in question' (1973:17). Paul Willis had earlier formulated the concept of homology in his Ph.D. thesis on the social meaning of pop music:

> Homological analysis of a cultural relation [between a lifestyle and an artefact] is synchronic, that is the analysis takes a cross section of the nature of the relationship at one period of time. The homologous notion itself is not equipped to account for changes over time, or to account for the creation, or disintegration of homologies. (1972: 11–12)

Not only is this formulation effectively an admission that homology cannot account for the temporal flux of actions that determine a spectacular sub-cultural style, but it is also an entirely ahistorical formulation. Part of the practical appeal of homology which also indicated its flaw is hinted at by Fine and Kleinman (1979) in their more general criticism of subcultural research: 'Problems of collecting and reporting information are so exten-sive that many researchers settle for a synchronic analysis of subculture' (1979: 6). In the light of the above formulation of homology, Willis could certainly be regarded as such a researcher who mistakenly implies that 'the content of a subculture during the research is the content of the subcul-ture across time' (1979: 6). By pursuing the peculiarly timeless authentic-ity of contemporaneous youth subcultures, any intergenerational sense in which their homologous style might be thought to have evolved from pre-vious youth cultural relations is denied. G. Clarke (1990: 90), for example, cited a revival in swing music among British working-class youth in the early 1970s and hippy affection for pre-modern jazz in the mid-1960s. The 1990s indie youth music culture that borrowed heavily from the sounds of The Beatles, The Kinks and other British bands of the 'Swinging Sixties' without reviving *all* things mod – the scooters and hairstyles for example – was by no means the first to typify a retrospective relation to music arte-facts that cannot be explained by Willis's concept of homology.

As already discussed, social class was considered by early CCCS theo-ries to be the overriding factor that cut youth subcultural identities. The concept of homology clearly grew out of this consensus as Willis claims that 'the vast majority of young people involved with pop music are working class' and 'separated off into something like a class which is excluded from the privileges and modes of expression of the dominant class, simply by age' (1972: 8). So when Hebdige employed the concept in his semiotic analysis of punks, he maintained its original formulation and instead blamed 'traditional semiotics' for its inability to 'provide us with a "way in" to the difficult and contradictory text of punk style' (1979: 117). The homologous punk style was frankly more difficult to decode. For example, Hebdige argued that punks' use of the swastika sign was not consistent with a fascist homology but rather that it had no meaning other than its 'shock value'; 'its potential for deceit. It was exploited as an empty effect' (1979: 117). A new mode of post-structuralist semiotics, then, read the polysemic signifying practices through which subcultural meanings were produced rather than simply what meanings were produced. In one of many paradoxical conclusions drawn by the author, this new semiotics showed 'how the punk style fitted together homologically precisely through its lack of fit' (1979: 120). Hebdige's application of homology to punk subcultural resistance is unconvincing on two accounts. First, what should surely be semiotically interpreted as a contradiction to style as homology is considered to be a homologous style 'in denial'. And second, what are conceived as punks' signifying practices continue to exclude semiotic readings of the voices and actions of the practitioners themselves – punks. The resistance paradigm therefore 'precludes any kind of agency, choice or diversity' (Hodkinson 2002: 11–12) as presumably experienced by subcultural practitioners. The signifying practices detailed by Hebdige were ultimately read from spectacular appearances rather than actions. The notion of practices deployed in the research presented later in this book (see Chapter 4) will equate to everyday actions carried out by potentially every young person rather than magical appearances only sported by extraordinarily homologous youth.

The problem with decoding homologous youth subcultural styles, though, is caused not just by the one-dimensional structuralist assumptions of the concept of homology but by how it is decoded. I have argued earlier in this chapter that semiotics as a method was closely aligned to the European cultural studies tradition of literary and critical theory. It is a method of textual analysis which reads language as a signifying system that is capable of generating cultural myths. Barthes (1993) applied semiotics to a variety of everyday phenomena so as to decode particular myths inherent to French culture in the 1950s. Semiotics is best applied to such a generalisable subject matter. However, when semiotics was applied to the very specific, localised phenomena of youth subcultures, the resistance which was decoded also needed to be specified and any potential anomalies dismissed from analysis. As Stanley Cohen points out, 'This means that instances are sometimes missed when the style is conservative or support-ive: in other words, not reworked or reassembled but taken over intact from dominant commercial culture' (1980b: xii). As will be shown in the fol-lowing section, semiotic readings of the relationship between youth cul-tures and music artefacts have mistakenly celebrated 'every aspect or gesture that could be interpreted as a form of resistance' (Widdicombe and Wooffitt 1995: 20) following this neo–Marxist subcultural resistance frame-work. A rare instance in which the resistance thesis has not merely been critiqued but threatened by interpretations of empirical data is Michael Brake's study of a Canadian youth culture which 'is largely derivative, and uses elements of borrowed culture, and any oppositional force is highly muted' (1985: 145). Such interpretations are based on a wider considera-tion of how Canadian youth have fragmented national identities due to the linguistic, ethnic, geographical and climatic differences which characterise the second largest country in the world. British youth subcultures, by con-trast, were uncritically assumed to share collective identities in homolo-gous relations to their nation, class, ethnicity and so on, despite the cultural diversity of the wider British population. Semiotic analyses that have only decoded resistance using the oversimplified notion of homologous subcul-tural style have also mostly decoded resistance in the contexts of youth music cultures.

Rock, pop and fan cultures

If histories of youth subcultures invariably begin with the Teddy Boys, his-tories of rock and pop music often cast their anchor similarly in the mid-1950s. As such, there is an important issue to be untangled about the close relationship between music and youth cultures/subcultures in this post-war period.[6] I will argue here that the previously discussed resistance thesis as applied to youth subcultures – particularly by CCCS theorists – was extended to much of the literature on young people's rock and pop music consumption, whether they were identified as members of subcultures or not.[7] Moreover, semiotic readings of music media texts continued to out-weigh social research analyses which, where used, introduced an important interactionist perspective to the resistance debate. In this section I will first consider those studies on rock and pop youth cultures that remain firmly within what has been since referred to as the 'Incorporation/Resistance Paradigm' (hereafter IRP) (Abercrombie and Longhurst 1998). It will be shown that these studies insufficiently accounted for how rock and pop music interacted with the everyday lives of young people who were not easily labelled as subcultural members or specific types of emotional consumers such as teenyboppers. The second part of this section will then discuss youth cultural studies that outline more sophisticated analyses of rock and pop consumption in concrete contexts of social interaction, including some of the literature on fan cultures. These studies pave the way for this book's analysis of music as a general category (not bound to a particular genre) in young people's everyday lives.

First, early murmurings of later CCCS subcultural theory were evident in Stuart Hall and Paddy Whannel's (1990, originally published in 1964) analysis of pop song lyrics on themes of love and romance (this theoretical connection is also made by Laing 1994):

> They reflect adolescent difficulties in dealing with a tangle of emotional and sexual problems. They invoke the need to experience life directly and intensely [. . .] There is a strong impulse at this age to identify with these collective representations and to use them as guiding fictions. (Hall and Whannel 1990: 31–2)

Pop music was seen as one of the popular, mass arts embraced by the young generations of the post-war period whilst at the same time the classic arts – classical music included – were in demise. Pop stars *reflected* 'a youthful religion of the celebrity' (1990: 34). Teenagers used these popular arts to search for styles that not only afforded surface but also substantial meanings for their subordinate lives. Pop music expressed 'a strong current of social nonconformity and rebelliousness [. . .] the rejection of authority in all its forms, and a hostility towards adult institutions and conventional moral and social customs' (1990: 33). Similar vocabulary was used to conceptualise subcultural resistance. In this case, however, Hall and Whannel refer to teenage audiences in general. Their account of pop youth culture was importantly one of the first attempts to understand the relationship between young people and mass music media. Its main limitation was to be shared by many that followed it – an assumption that because mass media 'mirrors attitudes and sentiments which are already there' (1990: 28), it is justifiable to read youth cultural practices from messages contained in music texts.

This flawed assumption was also made by Simon Frith and Angela McRobbie (1990), who argued that the terms 'teenybopper' and 'cock rocker' were used by music media to construct and reflect a binary model of fandom in which most boys are targeted to acquire tastes for a heavier sound performed by male rock bands, while most girls are targeted to acquire tastes for an easy listening sound performed by young solo acts. As such, 'Pop songs aimed at the female audience deny or repress sexuality [. . .] few alternative readings are available' (Frith and McRobbie 1990: 380). Their argument was that subversive consumption of pop music is hindered by production and marketing strategies which 'situate both performers and audiences along clear gender lines' (Frith 1990: 420). A brief consideration by Frith of extraordinarily intense music magazine and video consumption led him to conclude that relations between audiences and performers were sexually charged because 'In fantasy terms possession is, by its very nature, erotic' (1990: 423). Despite this binary model of fandom presented by mass music media, teenage girls were still considered able to use music as a collective expression of resistance and detachment from parents and teachers (Frith and McRobbie 1990: 381). As Sue Wise recalled, 'Elvis's rise to fame was inextricably linked with the moral panic surrounding the behaviour of women and girls at his live performances' (Wise 1990: 396). The inadequacy of Wise's autobiographical account, and Frith's and McRobbie's media textual analyses, are that they neglect to contextualise this youth cultural resistance to the moral panics and constructed models of fandom that young people's interactions as music consumers ultimately generate. Where are the voices of fans – other than authorial voices – during contexts of fandom? Accounts of fandom that improve upon this lack of contextualisation are considered shortly.

David Robins and Phil Cohen (1978) evaluated the effects of Osmond-mania – caused by the male pop idol, Donny Osmond – on teenage girl fans in a youth club where they carried out participant observation during the mid-1970s. They too noticed that these girls used pop music as a collective means of resistance, this time against ridicule of their tastes from boys, who the male authors sympathetically felt 'aspired to more sophisticated tastes – progressive, reggae, and rhythm and blues' (1978: 56). These girls' group identification with the songs of Donny Osmond, though, amounted to 'imaginary emancipation' from the consciousness of motherhood and restricted career choices channelled through 'the hysteria of the live concerts, the fan mags and the rest, where suddenly, "as if by magic", this sub-generation was present to itself for the first time' (1978: 52). This is a very gloomy portrait of the empowering function of pop in the context of working-class teenagers' lives. Whilst the resistance thesis is maintained, collective youth cultural expression through music is merely experienced as a magical, imaginary escape from the 'real', everyday world of economic survival. As I argued in relation to the notion of territoriality (P. Cohen 1992), this dichotomy between symbolic and actual social systems denies any consideration of the dynamic interactions between youth groups and those groups *within* which they differentiate themselves – boys, girls, parents, teachers, the police and so on.

Paul Willis's formulation of a homologous youth cultural style pandered to semiotic readings which only accounted for gestures of resistance, but in *Profane Culture* (1978) he deployed ethnographic techniques such as participant observation and interviewing to analyse the social meanings of music for youth groups. His analysis of hippy and motorbike boy cultures reveals in both groups 'an inability to break from cultural forms into the kind of political activity or power struggle to change or challenge the main institutions of society' (Willis 1978: 6). Nevertheless, the motorbike boys used music in actively collective ways, opposing its commercial function by searching for original recordings of rock 'n' roll songs that were 'at least ten years out of date' which possessed 'the ultimate in musical value in their ontological genuineness' (1978: 62 and 64). Rock 'n' roll songs as authentic cultural artefacts were part of the homology of the motorbike boys, part of their collective identity:

> The music did have a distinctiveness, a unity of construction, a special and consistent use of techniques, a freshness and conviction of personal delivery, a sense of the 'golden', 'once and for all' age, which could parallel, hold, and develop the security, authenticity, and masculinity of the bike culture [. . .] Their preferred music, therefore, was clearly answerable to the restless movement of the bike boys' lives. (1978: 63 and 68)

Whilst I do not intend to question Willis's analysis of homologous music use other than to reiterate concerns about the concept of 'homology', I would argue that both the motorbike and hippy cultures which he observed were extraordinarily spectacular, profane and committed to a way of leisure rather than life. These youth music cultures are neither indicative of a wider youth population or of youth in particular if it is considered that – certainly in the case of motorbike boys – many participants are middle-aged men. What defined the motorbike boys' collective identity was its suppressed working-class rather than age-based character. Willis usefully related their leisure time to the financial problems that the motorbike boys endured in their mainly manual work occupations and domestic roles, but music would appear to be unused in these contexts, or at least it is not deemed significant enough to be investigated. On the contrary, for most youth groups with less intensively collective identities who do not distinguish so clearly between work and leisure lifestyles, an understanding of their music use in different everyday contexts is paramount, and fundamental to investigations in this book.

Before I assess accounts that offer a rejoinder to assumptions about music as an expression of subcultural resistance, Dick Bradley's (1992) understanding of youth and rock 'n' roll in the period 1955–64 provides a conventional history of disaffection with the dominant culture that excludes the voices of the many conformist young people who also liked rock 'n' roll:

> I believe that youth culture involves a resistance to atomisation and massification, and to the boredom, the loneliness, the fear and the experiential vicariousness they produce [. . .] this [rock 'n' roll] music-use, far from being congenial or 'homological' to the youth culture, actually acted as the most central and important 'styling' practice of all. (1992: 107)

In going a step further than CCCS theorists' conception of youth subcultural homologies, Bradley considered rock 'n' roll to be the driving force for productive youth cultural practices, of which music-making and music-listening were central. 'Resistant communality' among *the youth culture* (regularly referred to in the singular as if meaning a monolithic movement) was caused by a mass culture that atomised young people's creative experiences. The 'seriality' of mass entertainment technologies such as the cinema meant an 'invocation of (often illusory) togetherness' (1992: 95), so mass music was used to express a genuine togetherness among youth groups. As such, Bradley commits himself to the idea that youth cultural consumption of rock 'n' roll produced autonomous meanings, although he can only demonstrate this by his own decoding of hidden messages in lyrical and phonic content rather than by sociological data on young people's uses of these lyrics and sounds. What Tia DeNora rightly interprets as 'an epistemologically naïve move' in 'a tacit shift in many semiotic "readings" of music [. . .] from description of musical material and its social allocation to the theorisation of that material's "wider" significance and cultural impact' (2000: 28) is a move naively made by Bradley.

Second, more sophisticated studies of youth cultural consumption have placed less emphasis on the binary conflict between cultural dominance and resistance, and more on grounded uses and influences of cultural artefacts. If the 'massification' response by mid-1950s youth cultures was sympathetic with Adorno's (1991) fears about the culture industry, Frith's (1978; 1983) interpretation of youth in relation to mass culture is closer to that of Walter Benjamin's in his classic essay on mechanically reproduced art. Benjamin had a more positive view of mass culture in his belief that 'With the emancipation of the various art practices from ritual go increasing opportunities for the exhibition of their products' (1973: 218–19). The ritual function of a classic work of art was 'the location of its original use value' (1973: 217) – for example, in an art gallery or country house estate – but the mass reproduction of mechanical works of art enabled greater democracy of consumption through their increased availability (i.e. exhibition function) and new exchange value. Frith (1983) argued that

Benjamin's ideological perspective on mass culture improved on Adorno's pessimism by showing that 'the grasping of particular works by particular audiences was a political rather than a psychological event' (1983: 57).

Frith's interviews with secondary school students in 1972 were probably the first and still one of the few attempts to account empirically for young people's music use without resorting to rose-tinted participant observation of a presupposed youth cultural or subcultural world. These interviews informed Frith that 'kids pass through groups, change identities and play their leisure roles for fun' (1978: 53). Whilst identifying different music cultures such as a 'sixth form culture' (aged 16–18 years) that was mostly middle-class, progressive rock fans, and a fourth and fifth form culture (aged 14–16 years) of mostly working-class students with tastes for commercial pop, Frith suggested that

> The different youth groups' use of music were different not because some groups were more resistant to commercial pressures than others, not even because some groups were more organised in subcultural terms than others, but because the groups each had their own leisure needs and interests. (1983: 212)

These needs and interests were shaped by the social structure and relations of production of their town of residence, which was Keighley, a small town in northern England which contains both urban and rural communities. For instance, Frith problematised the assumption of much CCCS literature by noting that 'class relations in leisure are not straightforward' (1983: 253) and moreover, youth are not always at leisure but often have jobs that provide differing levels of personal, disposable income. So a young person from a middle-class family without a job might well have less money to spend on leisure and fashion than a young working-class person with a part-time job. On this basis, I tend to agree that 'Age remains a much better indicator of music use than class' (Frith 1978: 50) with the qualification that any given indicator of music use only presents a partial explanation. The one drawback of what is otherwise Frith's hugely insightful early work on youth music consumption is the contradictory manner in which he nevertheless deploys social class as well as age indicators to distinguish between different musical taste groups. What he might have explored in his initial suggestion that 'The ideological essence of [the sixth form] culture was its individualism' was the dynamics *within* this culture, and how, despite individualist tastes, sixth formers could still 'assert themselves as a group' (1978: 40 and 42). My fieldwork analysis in Chapters 5 and 6 will explore such dynamic interactions between different musical taste groups within this sixth form age range and slightly older.

Although Geoff Mungham's (1976) study assumed a sample of working-class youth, the Mecca dance hall that he used for participant observation and to interview the management served as a 'mass-dance' (1976: 82), a territorial space shared by youth of a particularly locality more than a particular social class. Contrary to the notion that music functions as a homologous relation to youth groups, Mungham observed that these dance-hall goers 'do not really go to soak up a particular kind of music – other than that which goes under the generic label "popular" – or because their friends go there, but in order to "meet people"' and, more specifically, strike up prospective sexual relations (1976: 82). There was 'an intolerance of deviations in dress, appearance, personal mannerisms or musical experimentation' at the dance hall and various management strategies aimed to foster a clientele who agreed to certain codes of 'propriety and "respectability"' (1976: 86). For example, all male dancers at Mecca halls were required to wear suits. Mungham found that these demands from management for a certain standard of self-presentation in the mass dance 'are eagerly endorsed by youth itself' (1976: 92). The author concluded that these working–class youth dancers were deeply 'conservative and quiescent' in their pursuit of financial security within a 'largely non-mobile' (1976: 102 and 90) predicament that they shared with other generations in their community. Whilst this study suffers from the same single variable analysis (i.e. class) of subcultural resistance – as was identified earlier in this chapter – it is an unusually realist youth cultural account that considers spheres of work as well as leisure, and of conventional as well as spectacular leisure activities. Mungham's study also raises a plausible question that has implications for a rewriting of everyday youth cultural history: would a given young person during mid-1970s Britain have related more to the experience of dancing at a local Mecca hall[8] than, say, riding a motorbike or attending a rock concert?

Angela McRobbie (1984) also considered dancing as an everyday youth activity, engaged in by both 'mainstream' disco goers as well as post-punk subcultures. Everyday dancing served 'a function as both climax of the action and the necessary backdrop against which many [. . .] other "performances"' (1984: 139) such as fashion, music and style could be simultaneously enacted. Participant observation informed McRobbie that the major difference between female disco and post-punk dancers seemed to be their relationship to the parental culture. For example, while the latter group did not care about going out and returning home alone, the former group adopted 'a set of codes relating to "getting home"' (1984: 147) in terms of staying together in groups, as partly influenced by parental concerns. These mainstream female dancers conformed with the wishes of elders and conventional wisdom because they wanted to retain respectability, maintain same-gender friendship alliances and avoid the threat of sexual violence at night. Indeed, the experience of going out itself was not taken for granted by these females but was rather the outcome of some consideration and much preparation which itself was inseparable from the routines of going out. McRobbie's argument that academic writing on youth cultures and subcultures had been biased towards 'direct experience' in co-present consumer contexts rather than considering young people as 'viewers, readers, part of an audience' (1984: 141) was a novel and accurate viewpoint of its time.

Accounts of rock and pop youth cultures in the 1980s such as this one by McRobbie began to question the resistance thesis because no noticeable subculture had been conceptualised after punk in the late 1970s. Music as a force for political resistance was displaced to oppressive international regimes such as in the USSR (Street 1986), East Germany (Wicke 1992) and South Africa (Garofalo 1992). The 'New Romantics', who emerged as potentially the next subculture, were instead labelled 'post-punk'. Theorists of British and North American youth cultures became aware that the songs associated with subcultures like punk were as likely to be consumed for pleasure rather than protest. Dave Laing (1985) pointed out that

> While the subculture (or more precisely its interpreters) may pride itself on its ability to subvert dominant or established meanings, a listener to a manifestly punk song may be able to miss the point, and avoid reacting either as a punk initiate or as a shocked adherent of dominant social values. (1985: 56)

As such, a turn towards the study of fan cultures aimed to contextualise the pleasure as opposed to the politics of music consumption. Studies of fandom were pioneered by Ien Ang's (1985) analysis of letters written to her from viewers of the television serial *Dallas* – one of the first attempts to conceptualise the pleasure attached to being a fan of a media text. Her discussion of ideology in relation to active consumption contexts amounts to an insightful critique of the IRP. Those interviewees who disliked *Dallas* could comfortably adopt a critical stance from within the ideology of mass culture in their argument that the programme was a cynical appeasement of dominant, American cultural values.

However, those who were *Dallas* fans were without a similarly powerful ideological framework in which to explain their pleasure in watching the serial. Ang suggests that they could only articulate an ideology of populism – 'no one can account for taste' – which was often demeaned for pandering to the language of consumerism. What is actually more acutely evident from fan responses is that they were left without a powerful ideo-logical consumer position because they had no overriding perception of any ideological function in the product that they consumed. 'Pleasure eludes our rational consciousness' (1985: 84) and accounts for the difficulty in formulating a reasonable argument to justify feelings over thoughts. Ang has elsewhere advocated an approach to media consumption which she terms 'radical contextualism'. This approach enables temporal and spatial proximity to the social practices of media audiences so that these practices become interpreted by researchers before they become mytholo-gised through the media themselves in such forms as moral panics and political campaigns (Ang 1996: 81). A radical contextualist approach has certainly benefited studies on music fandom when it is considered how much popular music products are as disposable as those of the fashion industry. Moreover, this approach is not necessarily dependent on fandom contexts and I will apply the wider concept of radical contextualism to different levels of everyday audience involvement in music texts in later chapters.

Findings similar to Ang's in *Watching Dallas* (1985) have been made by Laurie Schulze, Anne Barton White and Jane Brown when they have inter-preted the 'resistive reader' of Madonna's songs to be someone who 'goes against the grain of dominant ideological meanings' (1993: 16). Contrary to 'authorised' textual readings of the powerful feminist values that Madonna's persona embodies, and her songs and music videos communi-cate (Fiske 1989a; Skeggs 1993; Kaplan 1993), Schulze et al.'s study of the responses of university students to a viewing of Madonna's video of her single 'Open Your Heart' did not show a correlation between intense levels of fandom and strong feminist views. The radical contextualism operated by soliciting responses from a media text such as a music video is associ-ated with creative methods of ethnography which provide data that can be usefully interpreted from information supplied by audiences *and* texts. Also, Barbara Bradby's (1994) analysis of girls' talk revealed how their dis-course on a popular cultural icon (again, Madonna) contradicted and was outside the dominant discourse of patriarchy versus feminism. Rather, the discourse used by one of these young girl fans was that of sexual autonomy and freedom, and she expressed her admiration for these Madonna quali-ties by extracting lyrics into conversations in a process of linguistic empowerment (1994: 88). Furthermore, the girls' secret group practice of dressing like Madonna in her music videos and films is considered by Bradby to indicate the significance of creative play away from parental con-trols on their public appearances. Again, radical contextualist accounts of fandom have escaped from the IRP by usefully theorising emotional responses to the pleasurable experiences of fan identification rather than the responses of survey questionnaires or secondary accounts in fanzines and other media that tend to rationalise such experiences in order to justify them.

Whilst sometimes wrongly assuming that the practices of fandom are reflected in mass music products such as magazines (see previous discussion of Frith and McRobbie 1990; Frith 1990), much of the research on music fan cultures has helped to revise the sensationalist nostalgia contained in many journalistic and biographical accounts of youth music (sub)cultures. Iain Chambers (1985) wrote the first of many subsequent histories of post-war Anglo–American popular music to try and contextualise the relationship between music and its consumers. The image of youth from historical accounts, Chambers noted, was metropolitan in character and inflated with regard to the ordinary daily experiences of most youth groups (1985: 16). But rather than revise pop and rock youth cultures against empirically uninformed assumptions about subcultures as presupposed, pre-structured, static, symbolic systems of signification, more recent accounts of club cultures and post-subcultures have often relied on postmodernist theories that remain unable to detail everyday youth interactions.

Club and taste cultures

Club cultural accounts may represent slightly different approaches to a revision of the subculture paradigm but I will argue here that they fail to move beyond such a paradigm. In this section I will assess the contributions of work on club and taste cultures (Thornton 1995, following Bourdieu 1984) and in the following section I will tentatively separate these contributions from those of the post-subcultures thesis, whilst maintaining that the two theoretical approaches share more similarities than differences. Following the pattern of previous sections, my assessment of much of this body of literature will situate it within the same structuralist framework that has prevailed in the European (particularly British) cultural studies tradition. I will conclude, however, by assessing more praiseworthy studies which have significantly revised – if only partially rejected – the subcultural model in favour of one that accommodates heterogeneous commitment to a given youth culture.

The ideology of populism and its definitive statement that taste cannot be accounted for (Ang 1985) receives its critique by Bourdieu, especially in *Distinction* (1984). His concept of the 'habitus' explains how taste is socially and culturally structured. The 'habitus' is a system of classification instilled in individuals at a young age 'which retranslates the necessities and facilities characteristic of class[es] of (relatively) homogeneous conditions of existence into particular life-style[s]' (1984: 208). The 'habitus' simultaneously produces and reproduces 'a stable and group-specific way of seeing or making sense of the social world; in other words, a *distinctive mode of cultural consumption*' (Lee 1993: 34). Operating below the level of individual consciousness, the 'habitus' is at work in taken-for-granted displays of consumers' tastes for food, cars and so on, as well as in their bodily expressions and dress (Lury 1996: 85). The 'habitus' is manifested in individuals by their characteristic proportions of cultural and economic capital. Those individuals with high cultural capital are likely to be well educated and to share tastes in classical art, while those with low cultural capital are mostly uneducated consumers of popular culture. By the same measure, individuals possess different levels of economic capital but there is no certain correspondence between their material wealth and their wealth of cultural resources.

Bourdieu's perspective, then, departs from the simple top–down continuum of structure versus agency implied by the IRP by arguing that the process by which consumers distinguish themselves from others is not wholly determined by conditions of capitalist economics because this process contains cultural codes that can be learnt and contextualised through educational capital (Lee 1993: 37–8). As such, consumer tastes in goods and practices enable groups to exclude and include other groups while at the same time being excluded and included by others. It is this universal process of distinction which explains why, in most cases, it is possible to classify an individual's tastes based purely on information about their economic status (including their occupation) and education history. Lee (1993: 38) argues that Bourdieu's perspective does not sufficiently account for the structuring properties of consumer goods inscribed at the production stage, but I would stress that a more vulnerable aspect of this social critique of taste lies in the realm of agency and the selection of stereotypical cases within a universal classification system which is still narrowly confined to dimensions of social class and cultural status. It can also justifiably be argued that the notion of different kinds of capital implies that there are finite resources which limit the capacity for individuals to conceal or manipulate their taste cultures in specific contexts of consumption for future benefit. Social climbers at evening dinner parties or middle-class ethnographers who attempt participant observation with the homeless would appear to have inescapable limits exercised on their performative mobility by the classificatory power of the 'habitus'. As Chapter 6 will reveal, the 'age play' resources used by young people to access certain public music venues may not be limitless but should certainly not be underestimated and would certainly escape straightforward classification, whether through self or society.

Nonetheless, Bourdieu's theories have been hugely influential to the sociology of consumption and his notion of 'cultural capital' as a resource for facilitating distinction through expressions of taste has helped to revise subcultural theories about cohesive youth cultural groups. His avid search for cultural distinctions, though, often distorts a situation in which such distinctions are slight between different social classes or barely exist at all. In the case of music consumers,

> 41 per cent of classical music albums are purchased by those in social classes AB, pointing in the direction of a Bourdieu distinction paradigm. However, only 17 per cent of the albums purchased by AB social classes are of this type. They are far outnumbered by the purchase of rock and pop albums which constitute 52 per cent of purchases. (Longhurst and Savage 1996: 288)

This example of how Bourdieu's survey data analysis can be interpreted with different outcomes underscores how this research method lacks a complementary ethnographic component to understand broader, more meaningful practices in the contexts generated by everyday consumer tastes and literacies. His operationalisation of social class can also be criti-cised on two accounts. First, the 'habitus' is premised on the notion of lifestyles that are determined by occupational status. Whilst occupations undoubtedly impact upon lifestyles, they do not necessarily determine class status, particularly for young people whose social class is dependent upon others (particularly parents). And second, recent findings from stratification studies that resemble long-established patterns of occupa-tional classifications problematise Bourdieu's citing of 'new middle classes' that possess occupational mobility and perform cultural distinction as a means of excluding and including groups with similar economic capital (Longhurst and Savage 1996). This idea of cultural distinction within relatively homogeneous social groups has been applied by Sarah Thornton to subcultural distinctions as performed by clubbers within a 'fantasy of classlessness' (1995: 12). I will now discuss her Bourdieu-influenced notion of subcultural capital alongside claims about omnivorous taste cultures within everyday life narrative analyses, followed by a discussion of neo-tribalist eclectic tastes.

Subcultural capital and omnivorous narratives

Club cultures are *taste cultures*. Club crowds generally congregate on the basis of their shared tastes in music, their consumption of common media and, most importantly, their preference for people with similar tastes to themselves. (Thornton 1995: 3)

Club cultures are thus contexts in which forms of subcultural capital such as 'hipness' are used by likeminded pleasure seekers to distinguish their tastes from others. Subcultural capital is both a source of material income for producers in these micro-economies of leisure – DJs, club organisers, journalists and so on – and a source of symbolic knowledge for consumers of these clubs and their affiliated micro-media networks. Simple and diffused consumer experiences interact in these taste cultures. Club cultures therefore operate outside the IRP to the extent that they are defined in distinction to other taste cultures within multimediascapes rather than against the mass media framework of power and resistance. As such, 'Subcultural capital can be *objectified* or *embodied*' (1995: 11) in practices of simultaneous performance and spectacle such as dancing and the communal experience of recreational drug use. Gay Morris (2001) has followed Thornton by applying Bourdieu's theories of distinction to the dancing body which remains grounded in social mores and conventions that problematise the aesthetic tradition of dance as an expression of individual ingenuity.

Thornton's participant observational approach to understanding club cultures comprises of the author's own and her respondents' inside experiences of a presupposed youth cultural world. Such reflexivity on the part of the researcher is invaluable as a means of providing insights into the research field as it is constructed by respondents and aiding the search for micro-social explanations of youth club cultures. However, Thornton constructed her research field in the same way that it was constructed in an extraordinarily meaningful manner by her small sample of respondents, all of whom replied to her research requests via the letters pages of magazines associated with clubbing and were therefore likely to be intensively committed clubbers compared to more representative club goers. Therefore, Thornton's construction of this club cultural world at no point differs from that of her respondents, so that her empirical accounts – which are also conspicuous by their scarcity – are prone to what some commentators consider to be the 'fallacy of meaningfulness' (Hermes 1995; C. Williams 2001). As such, her sympathetic and empathetic judgements on clubbers could easily be interrogated on the same grounds that Stanley Cohen (1980b) perceptively interrogated studies into subcultural resistance that adopted favourable value judgements on youth subcultures.

This presupposed youth cultural world also excludes any consideration of the everyday lives of clubbers, when they are not engaged in these context-specific taste cultures: 'We learn little of how these individuals interact with other forms of popular culture' (Carrabine and Longhurst 1999: 128). So whilst Thornton's concept of subcultural capital makes a valuable contribution to the argument that taste is socially and culturally performed through consumer practices, its presumed invisibility in everyday, non-clubbing contexts means that such a concept merely *revises* subcultural theory rather than systematically *reworks* it. It is her application of Bourdieu's (1984) concept of cultural capital that ultimately lends itself to culture-based distinctions between underground clubbers and mainstream disco goers rather than finer distinctions between extraordinarily and ordinarily committed participants inside the club cultures themselves. The term 'club cultures' would seem to better describe the plurality of youth cultural 'clubs' based around specific pockets of interest such as music and fashion tastes rather than ideological distinctions between high and low investors in subcultural capital. Detailing the different levels of investment and divestment in subcultural capital within these 'clubs' would have provided a more insightful reworking of subculture.

A consistent feature of club cultural – and, to a lesser extent, post-subcultural – accounts has been the argument that media and commercial organisations foster rather than threaten the survival of subcultural congregations. Thornton (1995) improved on Stanley Cohen's (1980a) application of labelling theory to mass media by interpreting the power of niche and micro-media texts to label clubbers advantageously and consolidate their underground ideologies. Likewise, Maria Pini's (1997) female interviewee respondents who were avid ravers felt like part of a team because of their intense engagement in the 'texts' of rave (club) culture – particularly music and dancing texts – as facilitated by the welcome absence of others' heterosexual motives. Beverley Best's (1997) Foucaultian reading of contemporary subcultural resistance has criticised traditional definitions of youth cultural empowerment in authentic as opposed to commercial music. She has argued that all cultural texts 'to reach an audience must negotiate in some way with the mass or micro media or the culture industry (i.e. with commerce)' (1997: 27). In this sense, club cultural or what Best refers to as 'over-the-counter-cultural' resistance redefines subcultural resistance to incorporate but then subvert the necessary evil of free-market forces. Two problems are evident with regard to this club cultural revision of subculture: first, the suggestion that media and commerce empower subcultural identities is biased towards small-scale, avant-garde producer networks when 'from a phenomenological perspective the apparent meaningfulness of much media use can be explained in terms of routines rather than resistance' (Hermes 1995: 21); whilst second and more importantly, empirical support is read in these micro-economic productions such as club flyers or through the responses of extraordinarily committed clubbing consumers rather than through the responses of more ordinary club cultural participants. This neglect of interest in the variable levels of commitment between clubbers seems to stem from a structuralist preoccupation with the IRP which necessitates that consumers remain relatively alike so as to be collectively differential from producers.

Studies of music taste that have considered its formation in personal histories rather than club cultural contexts seem to have more usefully avoided the stress on highly committed and emotional consumer 'moments'. Chris Richards's (1998) interviews with students and teachers of media studies in secondary school contexts are a good example. He draws on Bourdieu's (1984) social psychoanalytic biographical accounts of, for instance, the middle-class child whose relation to bourgeois culture is 'acquired, pre-verbally, by early immersion in a world of cultivated people, practices and objects' so that an object such as a piano produces a familiar relationship to music which gives the child a sense of superiority over others without a ' "musical mother" of bourgeois autobiography' (1984: 75). These biographical accounts, Richards argues, are an important improvement on the crude survey analyses that otherwise form the skeleton of Bourdieu's empirical frame. Biographies or life narratives were operationalised by Richards in a seminar in which teachers were asked to play music that reflected their past experiences in the same way that celebrities do on the BBC Radio 4 programme known as *Desert Island Discs*. Richards observed that

> even among consenting adults of similar educational background, already quite well known to each other, self-presentation through musical tastes was perceived to be more risky than a discussion in which selections of books, films, television programmes and even clothes might be the main concern. (1998: 146)

Such reluctance to discuss music as an expression of memories is considered by Richards to be indicative of how music is a distinctly personal resource and affective medium which articulates an 'interiority' of tastes. The advantage of life narrative over survey methods, then, is that the latter are generally ahistorical and impersonal, while the former afford greater attention to agent's everyday perceptions, 'drawing upon historically particular cultural repertoires' (1998: 149; see also Hermes's

(1995) definitions of 'repertoires' and 'repertoire analysis' as discussed in Chapter 5).

Closely connected with a concern for more personal taste formations within diverse everyday consumer experiences – that are not necessarily structured by the 'habitus' through flows of cultural capital – is the concept of the cultural omnivore (Peterson and Kern 1996). Cultural omnivores, often from middle-class backgrounds, express pluralistic consumer tastes for traditionally 'high' cultural forms such as classical music through to the latest chart music. Cultural univores, on the other hand, are taken to be mostly working-class consumers whose tastes are quite narrow and fixed (e.g. they might only ever like pop music). Middle-class omnivorousness, then, is an alternative to Bourdieu's notion of the new middle classes in late 1960s France who articulated distinct taste cultures as a means of defining their class status in relation to other classes. The middle-class students that Eamonn Carrabine and Brian Longhurst (1999) interviewed about their music tastes expressed a diversity of responses akin to omnivorousness. Rather than performing distinctions, for these respondents 'the most common way of expressing individual taste is *not* to appear exclusive [. . .] this may be part of a strategy to solidify a network on a non-exclusionary basis' (1999: 131). The authors, for instance, interpret a security of taste in the omnivorousness expressed by one male respondent who claimed that, 'I think I'm secure within myself of what is right and wrong and I'm certainly not going to hide all my tapes that you don't approve of before you come round' (1999: 131). A different interpretation of this response, however, would be that a possible scenario in which someone might hide their music collection to avoid censure or embarrassment was at least instilled in the consciousness of this late teenager. Like Richards's life-narrative experiment, music is at least potentially a personal, private resource for young consumers. What is undeniable is that such intricacies of expression of music tastes can only be interpreted through non-structured, radically contextualist interview methods: 'cultural omnivorousness is best understood in relation to the specific cultural context of its performance' (Carrabine and Longhurst 1999: 136). Intricate consumer taste cultures have also been conceptualised as contemporary mutations of anthropological tribes.

Neo-tribalism

In a foreword to Michel Maffesoli's *The Time of the Tribes* (1996), Rob Shields notes that 'our contemporary social life is marked by membership in a multiplicity of overlapping groups in which the roles one plays become sources of identity which, like masks, provide temporary "identifications"' (Shields 1996: xii). Maffesoli's neo-tribalist perspective is a qualification of

Bourdieu's overstated structuralist 'habitus' and its simplistic explanation of consumption as determined above all by social class:

> although *distinction* is perhaps applicable to modernity, it is by contrast totally inadequate in explaining the varied forms of social groups that are today at the forefront. Their outlines are ill-defined: sex, appearance, lifestyles [. . .] (Maffesoli 1996: 11)

These neo-tribal social groups do not react to political structures of domination but instead come together through localised collective sensibilities in contexts such as tourist resorts, festivals and through virtual community-based technologies such as the Internet (Maffesoli 1996: 23). Mass media messages are considered to be the present-day pretexts to communication once served by religious sermons and then political speeches. A renewed sense of 'neighbourhood' is thus pervaded by local cable television and radio channels, whose consumers perhaps share feelings of local communion similar to those felt by traditional tribal communities (1996: 26). Adopting Max Weber's notion of the 'emotional community', Maffesoli considers postmodernity to partly define a shift in emphasis in Western cultures from a rational model of civilised social relations to 'an empathetic "sociality"', which is expressed by a succession of ambiences, feelings and emotions' (1996: 11). Everyday life for Maffesoli is not adequately understood by the assumption that social groups always seek rational, self-serving taste judgements because human existence is motivated by 'rituals, situations, gestures and experiences that delineate an area of liberty' (1996: 21).

Maffesoli's tribes would presumably feel free to express their tastes through what would be understood as individualistic emotions that paradoxically 'deindividualise' the expresser and instead display personal roles within communal contexts of sociality: 'The tension between heterogeneities could be said to guarantee the solidity of the whole' (1996: 100). But the term 'neo-tribes' (Bennett 1999; 2000) clearly is at risk of overstating the capacity for individuals to create autonomous taste communities in contested public *territories* such as commercial nightclubs. Nonetheless, in the more specific communal settings of urban dance events – dance clubs and private house parties – according to Bennett's participant observations 'an area of liberty' is delineated by consumers with a variety of music tastes whose common desire is the search for eclectic experiences amidst conservative, mainstream nightlife found in Newcastle's city centre. Whilst certain subcultural responses might be gleaned from instances in which urban dance enthusiasts marked out 'spaces of defiance' (Bennett 2000: 87) against sexist and violent intrusions by minority groups at mainstream venues, inside these spaces

> the nature of the dance music event is becoming increasingly a matter of individual choice, the type of music heard and the setting in which it is heard and danced to being very much the decision of the individual consumer. (2000: 81)

Neo-tribalism in urban dance culture is, therefore, understood to involve highly localised, individualistic practices that construct – rather than are constructed by – a sense of collective identity.

The concept of 'neo-tribalism' clearly favours emotional agency above the rational structures implied by the 'habitus' in the social construction of taste. Maffesoli's theories about sociality and neighbourhood have contributed to a wider 'turn' towards the significance of localities in the formation of cultural tastes and identities which I will discuss in the next section of this chapter. However, as with Thornton's theory on subcultural capital, it is difficult to apply neo-tribes to the everyday contexts of consumers outside their specific leisure-time activities. For example, a group of office workers listening to music on the radio might have eclectic tastes in music but these personal tastes will almost certainly not also instil a feeling of collective taste sensibilities. Such a group is more likely to consist of cultural omnivores with their own historic repertoires of music tastes, some of whom will express these more conspicuously than others within the dynamic relations of power and status that typify office cultures. Two further criticisms of neo-tribalism are that Maffesoli's emphasis on free agency 'almost completely lacks empirical contextualisation'– particularly in non-leisure cases such as the example of working in an office – and that even in more apt neo-tribal settings such as nightclubs 'access to clubbing crowds is clearly not "open to all"' (Malbon 1998: 26). The choice restrictions and regulations imposed on clubbers which can exclude rather than include their presentation of personal tastes and identities – which still has its most rigorous examination in Mungham's (1976) account of door policies at a Mecca dance hall – is largely unaccounted for in concepts of neo-tribalism and subcultural capital. This book's wider concern with the accessibility of certain public music contexts will be explored in later analysis of fieldwork findings.

Post-subcultures

Some of the studies that can be loosely grouped together under a post-subculture umbrella manage to move away from the binary model of dominance and resistance, mainstream and alternative that plagues sub-cultural and club-cultural theories. And yet despite the apparent demise of youth subcultures since the punks of the late 1970s, several post(modern) revisions of subcultures continue to label marginal types of young people using terms that are neither novel nor indicative of subversiveness. Muggleton's (2000) interviews with individuals who appeared to convey subcultural identities, for instance, found that terms such as mod, punk, goth and hippy as well as their various permutations – hippy-punk, punk-hippy and so on – still held valuable currency. This study like many others, however, continues to construct its sample on the basis of respondents who display spectacular and stylistic features rather than on the basis of those who might cut inconspicuous subcultural identities in interaction with others in everyday contexts. Rather than investigate a broad sample of young people to identify subsequently those respondents with distinctive subcultural affiliations, then, the post-subcultures approach, as in the case of club cultures, tends to be guilty of a 'fallacy of meaningfulness' (Hermes 1995) in its construction of presupposed youth cultural worlds.

However, post-subcultures in some cases are conceptualised in terms that are even more sympathetic to subcultural resistance theories than are club cultures. This sympathetic stance is maintained by the possibility of authenticity in the activities of post-subcultures, albeit a shifting sense of authenticity in line with postmodernist perspectives on media-saturated simulations and ahistorical aesthetic sensibilities. Lawrence Grossberg has considered an 'ideology of authenticity [that] has determined the structure of the various histories of rock, whether they are produced by fans or critics' (1992: 207) to be in crisis from accounts of contemporary rock youth cultures 'where, for many fans, no single alliance, no single organisation of taste seems more authentic than any other' (1992: 237). Grossberg thus perceived 'a [postmodern] logic of "authentic inauthenticity"' (1992: 224) in the way that rock was no longer consumed as a realist youth cultural expression but instead had become a depoliticised, escapist and disposable commodity in times of popular conservatism. These claims are founded on a conventional historical framework of youth subcultural activity that, as Stanley Cohen (1980b) and Chambers (1985) have argued, pander to spectacular, news-worthy events rather than everyday experiences. Perhaps more telling, when Grossberg accounts for contemporary youth cultures, the absence of a his-torical framework excludes 'golden age' myths. It would appear, therefore, that Grossberg's notion of present-day inauthentic authenticity in relation to bygone realist authenticity in rock cultures is better explained by the mythologising tendencies of populist media historical accounts (Ang 1996) rather than by a cultural turn towards conservativist, postmodernist trends.

Postmodern subcultural authenticity has been read not only in rock but also in acid house rave cultures in late 1980s Britain. Particularly influenced by Jean Baudrillard's (1983) postmodernist theories of simulation and media saturation, Steve Redhead rejected histories of evolutionary youth music cultures in favour of a 'Pop Time' framework wherein 'the speed of what comes around again may change but the cyclical motion is embedded in pop's genealogy' (1990: 25). In other words, revivals of pop music sounds and genres are omnipresent but occur randomly. Youth cultures – merely marketing devices – therefore come to be associated with music that bears no relation to their social and historical contexts. Redhead then suggested that the cultural politics of pop music needed to interrogate the authentic originality of 'new' musical traditions such as US hip hop rather than 'the alleged importance of the appropriation of subcultural objects [. . .] to communicate fresh cultural meanings' (1990: 26):

> It does not mean that there are no subcultures any longer: these abound in youth culture today, but are frequently grounded in market niches of the contemporary global music industry – techno, bhangra, gangsta rap, ambient, jungle – even when they 'originally' came from the 'streets'. (Redhead 1997: 103)

The subject of this postmodernist perspective is cultural production rather than consumption, since Pop Time collapses these two processes and renders any original youth musical expression outside the confines of global music industry products to be implausible. However, relationships between music consumption and production are more dynamic and inter-active than Redhead's concept of Pop Time permits. As Brian Longhurst points out, 'he does not provide, or attempt to provide, a blueprint for how these relationships should actually be studied' (1995: 224). The latest thesis on youth 'pseudo-rebellion' through commercial music (Halnon 2005) similarly favours production over consumption analyses to present the flawed logic that Eminem or Limp Bizkit – or any other global act – say anything at all about young people's music consumer practices.

Muggleton (1997; 2000), by contrast, departed from conventional post-modernist assumptions by empirically testing a set of hypotheses (2000: 52–3) into whether or not postmodern, club cultural styles were evident in consumption practices. In general, he found that such styles concurred with postmodernist ideas about fluid, fragmentary, individualistic identities expressed through mixed-class membership groups. Despite Muggleton's claims that an 'Enlightened' modernity typically framed by CCCS theorists encouraged a false sense of subcultural style as homologous, his preference for framing subcultures with an 'Aesthetic' modernity more characteristic of postmodernity reworks rather than rejects the concept of subculture. Youth subcultures did and do exist but 'postmodernity entails an *intensification* of these aesthetic characteristics' (2000: 50) towards more partial, less collective subcultural identities that pre-date the postmodern epoch. Muggleton's subsequent formulation of post-subcultural style, then, facilitated by individuals' everyday mediated experiences of subcultural signs – represented, for example, in music videos – prior to 'inscribing these signifiers on their own bodies' (2000: 47) is an important interactionist insight into the changing surfaces of youth subcultures but cannot substantially break from the subculture paradigm towards a focus on everyday youth cultural identity formation. Moreover, it seems contradictory that the fragmentary tendencies of post-subcultures – rightly freed by Muggleton from the monolithic features of homology – nevertheless facilitate highly politicised networks of collective protest (Muggleton and Weinzierl 2003).

Post-subcultural approaches moreover account for youth cultural activity within a postmodernist perspective that shares many theoretical assumptions with the subcultures literature. For example, Rietveld conceptualised aspects of rave culture – intensive dancing, ecstasy drug use, music at 125 beats per minute, baggy cotton clothing, bum bags, comfortable shoes or trainers (1993: 53–4) – as parts of a youth homologous style, albeit reminiscent of escapist counter cultural rather than resistant subcultural expressions. Rave cultures did not subculturally oppose or club culturally breed on a dominant culture but aimed to remain elusive in the 'mad consumption race' (1993: 56–7) to prevent their styles being incorporated into the commercial fashion system through local entrepreneurial designers such as Joe Bloggs of Manchester. Nevertheless, the IRP that has been so prevalent in audience research following Hall (1992) is maintained by Rietveld in spite of this more promisingly localised contextualism. Further, her conclusion that 'the rave offered a release from day to day realities, a temporary escapist disappearance like the weekend or holiday' (1993: 58) is not far removed from the symbolic territoriality conceived by P. Cohen (1992) that denied examining interactions between different demographic groups within social worlds of restrictions, regulations and responsibilities. Similarly, the homologous bodily manifestations of Jonathon Epstein's (1998) crudely labelled Generation X are couched in the same characteristics as manifestations of subcultural style – tattoos, body-piercing, grunge music, drug use, long 'punk' hairstyles – without detailing any differential permutations in the deployment of these characteristics beyond their media-generated stereotypes.

Although post-subcultural accounts largely remain within a structuralist and constructionist framework that rarely probes into specific contexts of youth cultural consumption, there are a few examples of studies that have probed into the key issue of commitment in regard to consumer and producer activities. In a critique of *Rave Off* (edited by Redhead 1993) and other literature on rave cultures, Andrew Ward (1997) has pointed out that the most essential activity in raving (i.e. dancing) is rarely mentioned and certainly lacks conceptualisation. In Ward's opinion 'it would be quite possible to read most of the Redhead book and have no clear idea of what happens at raves' (1997: 5). This absence of concern with such a central facet of rave culture is endemic of a general avoidance of discussion about the ostensibly straightforward actions and interactions of dancing. An assumption made by much rave literature from both club cultural and post-subcultural perspectives, then, is that what the vast majority of rave consumers find most pleasurable about raving – the intimate co-presence of dancing in crowds – is ephemeral compared to the spectacular texts associated with raving such as drugs and the production of rave events themselves (an argument also made by McRobbie 1993). A further outcome of this assumption is the implication that rave dancing is enacted with more or less intense commitment by all ravers. As discussed in Chapter 4, Ben Malbon's (1998; 1999) interactionist insights into clubbing in part address the problems that Ward perceptively identified in many club-cultural and post-subcultural rave accounts. Still, Malbon's approach has remained biased towards a particularly intensive form of club consumer commitment of a 'remarkably emotional and sensual nature' (1998: 267) that overstates most clubbers' experiences.

Four further studies that have significantly revised subcultural assumptions about collective youth cultural commitment but continued to freely deploy the term 'subculture' to their respective objects of study are Robert Sardiello's (1998) examination of Deadhead, Paul Hodkinson's (2002; 2004) study of goth scenes and subcultures, Nancy MacDonald's (2001) ethnography of graffiti subcultures and Keith Kahn-Harris's (2004) research into the Extreme Metal scene.[9] Sardiello details three types of Deadhead based on different levels of personal and social commitment to the values and norms of the subculture: the hardcore Deadhead type that is highly committed across personal and social dimensions to the extent that it produces role models; the new Deadhead[10] type that is highly committed across social but lowly committed across personal dimensions and thus only identifies Deadhead associations in interactions with other Deadheads; and a stable Deadhead type that is moderately committed across social and personal dimensions. These different types of Deadhead were nevertheless combined into a coherent subculture by Sardiello when his insightful distinctions between Deadhead's cultural identities would seem to have better deconstructed claims about homologous styles within the so-called Deadhead subculture. As such, the author is guilty of universalising the spectacular features of Deadhead as evidence of its collective subcultural qualities. From an interactionist point of view, Sardiello's research exemplifies once again how 'researchers' desires to study the spectacular may simply reproduce, rather than deconstruct, the social processes that create the phenomenon of spectacularness' (Kahn-Harris 2004: 107). This flaw extends to post-subcultural studies that not only use the concept of subculture but advocate its applicability – with very few qualifications – to contemporary youth cultures associated with heavy metal (Brown 2003) and dance music (Carrington and Wilson 2004).

Hodkinson's conceptual reworking of subculture, on the other hand, ultimately reaches a set of indicators about subcultural substance – as opposed to style – that are so far removed from those that emerged within the Chicago School and CCCS traditions that his continual application of the term 'subculture' to goths is hardly justifiable. Goth subculture 'encapsulated significant elements of diversity and dynamism, its boundaries were not absolute, and levels of commitment varied from one individual to another' (2002: 29), which would surely suggest that goths were not uniformly bound to a particular subcultural way of life and so would have been more usefully studied as individuals in relation to others through an interactionist approach. At certain points Hodkinson's ethnographic interviews and observations succeed in detailing the dynamic relations between goth insiders and outsiders, but unfortunately details such as how goths learn to become goths are understated. MacDonald's (2001) discussion of the career paths taken by graffiti writers is more fruitful in tracing the processes through which writers enter graffiti subcultures, gain a reputation among members, move into different styles of writing and then perhaps retire or 'go legal'. Although her concept of 'career' – derived from Becker (1963) – is very usefully applied to the graffiti subculture, it is only ever closely applied to subcultural rather than extra-subcultural contexts. Like Hodkinson, MacDonald is critical of the CCCS's class-based assumptions about subcultures but still considers the label 'subculture' entirely appropriate for her interviewees. Regardless of these shortfalls, Hodkinson's and MacDonald's work has marked a necessary shift in emphasis away from postmodernist perspectives on youth culture as commodified, fluid and fragmented. Given an aim of this book to reject the IRP within which theories of youth music cultures mostly operate, though, I would argue that both accounts insufficiently problematise structuralist approaches to subculture as homologous style.

Kahn-Harris's (2004) approach to theorising Extreme Metal music cultures is perhaps the most convincing post-subcultural revision. He identifies a key problem with original methods of studying subcultures in that they were 'defined externally with little attention being paid to the meanings produced by the members themselves' (2004: 109). My argument about the self-fulfilling construction of presupposed club cultures resonates here. Instead, Kahn-Harris relocates the spectacular elements of subculture – in this case, the Extreme Metal scene – in the ordinary and everyday. This music scene is then usefully read as a performative space in which the scene's members interact with each other in spectacular ways such that they are simultaneously performers and audiences (2004: 110). Relocating spectacular moments in everyday experiences is partly embraced in this book by the concept of promenade performances (introduced in Chapter 3). Perhaps due to the transgressive extremities of this music scene, however, Kahn-Harris's research does better at revising the concept of subculture rather than rejecting it. Although he provides insights into the 'shock' processes involved in first becoming a member of the Extreme Metal scene, then, the author does not account for those (young) people who presumably move in and out of the scene, or how members of this particular scene interact with those of other music scenes. Delineating differences and similarities between numerous youth music cultures is a fundamental – and perhaps original – aspect of the research presented in Chapters 5 and 6.

Summary

Notable exceptions acknowledged, theories of both subcultural deviance and resistance have been mostly informed by a European tradition of structuralist cultural studies where textual have held sway over empirical analyses. Applied social studies of youth cultural activities more akin to the interactionist North American tradition are plentiful but they have not attained the weight of significance consequently bestowed upon structuralist – particularly semiotic – studies such as those associated with the CCCS. Consequently, these non-sociological conceptions of youth subcultures have not only set the agenda for a subcultural paradigm but have also stamped a huge impression on theoretical and historical accounts of youth cultural activities in general. Earlier interactionist accounts have done better to define subcultural deviance as an outcome of wider societal norms rather than the relatively superficial responses from within bohemian or marginal youth groups. On the other hand, subcultural resistance has been commonly understood as intra-generational and very often national (particularly British) resistance through a set of unifying symbolic artefacts and expressions. Whether intended or not, accounts of resistance associated almost exclusively with working-class youth subcultures implicate collective groups with shared demographic characteristics in the same structural relationship to the equally monolithic dominant/parent culture. An implication of this trend, for example, has been that sensationalist media reports of a youth subculture such as punks in which an impression is given that most young people belong to the punk subculture are not sufficiently deconstructed. The small proportion of punks among the youth population during mid-1970s Britain would better have been gauged by an interactionist approach to the dynamism of locations and generations than by a semiotic approach to the politics of spectacular artefacts such as that adopted by Hebdige (1979). Although Jenks's (2005) historical analysis of 'subculture' is sympathetic to the idea and its so-called 'modern' CCCS concept in particular, it reads like an obituary to the sociology of subcultures and the author even concludes: 'My sense is that the idea has run its course' (2005: 145). It is a diabolically pessimistic analysis that does nothing to inspire a contemporary study of subcultures.

Another implication of the trend towards structuralist models of youth subcultures has been that the study of young people's music consumption – as well as their consumption of fashion items, sports and other popular cultural artefacts – is still largely premised on unhelpful dichotomies between effects and resistance, dominance and opposition. The notion of (sub)cultural resistance in particular remains rife in studies of rock, pop and fan cultures where a bias towards very intense and emotional consumer practices, partly inspired by concept of homology (Willis 1972), continues to uncritically receive currency. By contrast, studies of youth music cultures grounded in ethnographic research methods (e.g. Frith 1978) that at the same time have avoided the excesses of what might be rephrased 'observer participation' have suggested that the syntagmatic analysis of subcultural style is an oversimplification of *actual* young people's cultural practices. Jones (1988), for instance, endorsed a more interactionist approach to researching reggae music by emplacing his sample of mixed race youth 'within the interlocking social networks and shared living spaces that have evolved between its black and white communities over the course of three decades' (1988: xiii). Situating youth music cultures in vivid social and historical contexts underpins both the archival and contemporary empirical research discussed later.

This chapter has also shown that notions of subcultural capital (Thornton 1995) and neo-tribes (Bennett 1999) that derive from critiques of taste (Bourdieu 1984 and Maffesoli 1996 respectively) are only part alternatives to subcultural models in the sense that they merely modify those models rather than devise new ones using other conceptual frameworks. Club cultures might differ from subcultures in the extent to which they are not clearly defined in terms of particular social classes, but they continue to describe 'members' who are collectively engaged in thinking and doing alike. An interactionist analysis of club cultures would examine in greater detail how subcultural capital is transmitted though individual clubbers, and how the consequences of these processes of social transmission impact upon the suggestion that individuals can be perceived to fit into the same (youth music) culture. Post-subcultures, on the other hand, are sometimes more successful at interrogating the idea of style as homology and departing from structuralist frameworks of dominance and resistance. Nonetheless, other assertions that post-subcultures exhibit many characteristics of subcultures and are even more politically resistant than their predecessors (e.g. Marchant 2003) do little other than prolong the inertia of the subcultures thesis in its misrepresentation of contemporary young people's recurrently diverse cultural identities and practices. Postmodernist sympathies that are expressed by a great many post-subcultural accounts furthermore lead to constructionist flaws – bracketing groups based on information gleaned from artefacts of commercial *production* such as clothes and magazines – in the absence of sound empirical information about both conspicuous and inconspicuous forms of youth cultural *consumption*. The wholly alternative conceptual framework that is to develop hereafter abandons universal models of power and resistance, and instead accommodates localised models of everyday interactions from which concepts of identification and presentation become central. As the next chapter unfolds it will become apparent that this alternative approach to understanding everyday cultures of music and youth gains its initial impetus not from present-day but from bygone contexts and practices.

Notes

1. According to Fornäs (1995: 6) 'the total dominance of structuralism' that occurred in British and much of continental European cultural studies never quite infected Scandinavian youth cultural research, thus 'avoiding the fetishism and reification of subcultural styles which characterised parts of the British 1970s tradition.' It is a shame that Scandinavian research did not have quite the same impact on subsequent ideas.
2. See Baldwin et al. (1999: 348–51) for a general review of the best-known subcultural critiques, which will be further discussed in this chapter.
3. The concept of homology as deployed by British cultural theorists is evaluated later, in the section on youth subcultures.

4. I will argue later in this chapter that Hebdige's treatment of ethnic-orientated youth subcultural identities lacked consideration of other social variables within these cultures that sat uneasily with a thesis about resistance and solidarity.

5. See Laing (1994), who argues that this European tradition of literary criticism significantly influenced later CCCS subcultural theory.

6. I would also acknowledge here an important point made by an anonymous reviewer that the relationship between youth and popular music is as much a cliché as the relationship between youth and subcultures that was problematised in the previous section.

7. The close alliance between theories of subcultural resistance, and of rock and pop youth cultural consumption, would appear to be partly explained by the fact that many of the authors discussed here who had connections to the CCCS contributed to both fields of enquiry.

8. Mecca dance halls peaked in number across Britain in the early 1960s and many are still used today even if no longer operated by Mecca. Mungham's (1976: 83) statement that 'most people still meet their eventual marriage partner at one' is testament to the mass activity that dancing was and still is.

9. There are numerous other examples of research that continue to apply a relatively orthodox concept of 'subculture' to their respective case studies (e.g. Richard and Kruger (1998) on German 'Techno subculture'; Verhagen et al. (2000) on Dutch gabbers, followers of hardcore house music) but I do not have room to discuss them all here.

10. 'Deadhead' refers to fans of the 1960s band the Grateful Dead, who shared similar characteristics to bohemian hippies of this period.

CHAPTER 3

Early Youth Cultures of Music and Dance

In this chapter I will consider both early and more recent accounts of youth cultures that consider such cultures to be intergenerational rather than intra-generational[1] – or counter cultural – units based in geographically and historically specific localities. As Karl Mannheim (1952, originally published in 1927) rightly proposes with regard to the social characteristics of a generational unit, 'At any given point in time we must always sort out the individual voices of the various generations, each attaining their point in time in its own way' (1952: 283). Furthermore, 'Mere contemporaneity becomes sociologically significant only when it also involves participation in the same historical and social circumstances' in which it is evident that 'constant transmission of the cultural heritage' (1952: 298 and 299) is a fundamental social process in the life course of a given generation. The possibility that the parent culture could transmit its heritage to youth subcultures or that transmission could be received in the opposite direction has been largely denied by structuralist approaches. Youth subcultures as well as club cultures and – to a lesser extent – post-subcultures have been portrayed as insular units that attempt to conceal and protect their cultural heritages from the threat of parental censure or media amplification.

An alternative portrayal of subcultures considers their transmission through interactions with dominant cultural forces to be a necessity for their ongoing impact: 'The diffusion may remain quite limited unless the information reaches wider audiences via the mass media' (Fine and Kleinman 1979: 9). The accounts discussed here set the agenda for my own interactionist approach to everyday youth cultural consumption and production of one such mass medium (i.e. music).[2] In particular, I will argue that an interactionist approach is better able to detail the people and places that surround youth cultures. By people, I mean not only the young people who live out youth cultures but the older people – parents, teachers, bus drivers and so on – who interact with youth on a daily basis. By places,

I mean concrete local and historical places rather than nations, anonymous spaces or needlessly pseudonymous places. The most significant source of information contained here on early youth music cultures derives from a team of researchers who, under the collective title Mass-Observation, observed people's everyday lives, as well as – more pertinently – young people's everyday music cultures, during late 1930s and 1940s Britain. Rather than merely try to discover what cultural changes have occurred to explain the decline of post-war youth subcultures (e.g. Chaney 2004), then, it might be better first to understand contemporary youth cultures in relation to a pre-war and intra-war generation of young people who ostensibly had no subcultural affiliations.

Contrary to the huge amount of literature on post-war youth cultures and their appropriation of music (e.g. Chambers 1985; Peterson 1990; Bradley 1992; Osgerby 1998; Bennett 2001; as well as the seminal youth subcultures literature), the period 1936–49 in Britain is rarely explored in any detail with regard to youth music cultures that might have prevailed at this time. Only relatively recently, for instance, has a book been published about popular music and dance in interwar Britain (see Nott 2002). Few attempts have been made to discover the use of leisure time by British youth cultures (see Fowler 1992, 1995; Davies 1992; Pearson 1983; Springhall 1998) and the characteristics of their music cultures (see Oliver 1995; Nott 2002) before the Second World War. As such, a false historical impression develops:

> From reading many accounts it is easy to get the impression that youth culture simply did not exist before the war, that it suddenly and spontaneously materialised in the 1950s amid a wave of rock 'n' roll records, coffee bars and brothel-creeper shoes. (Osgerby 1998: 5)

This chapter aims to build upon this dearth of social historical knowledge. In particular, I will interpret findings into youth and music cultures from the Mass-Observation (M-O) Archive.[3] An important methodological feature of the archival material that I have selected to interpret is that it concerns the activities and opinions of people within a certain locality. Together with local history books and material drawn from other local archives,[4] the findings here are almost entirely centred on the north-west region of England.

Furthermore, the local areas that are covered in most graphic historical detail here are geographically similar to those areas where I conducted my contemporary empirical investigations, as discussed in Chapters 5 and 6. So youth music cultures that were evident in the adjacent cities of

Manchester and Salford as well as the nearby large town of Bolton up to seventy years ago bear local historical comparison with today's youth music cultures in those places. I will also consider the importance of music to the seaside town of Blackpool,[5] hugely popular as a tourist destination for Britons in general and inhabitants of the aforementioned urban areas in particular during this period. The findings that follow, then, are not intended to preserve a picture of a bygone era that is scarcely painted in histories of popular music and youth cultures. The importance of social history to contemporary sociological research lies in how past observations in contemporaneous contexts can inform and contextualise present-day phenomena.[6] As such, these archival findings into early youth music cultures in tandem with my own empirical fieldwork findings will be used to evaluate theories about youth music consumption and production in everyday life as well as construct alternative perspectives. After introducing details about the social research that generated the archival data interpreted in this article, I will give a general overview of the everyday demographic and socio-economic characteristics of the urban areas that M-O visited as well as the north-west region in general during this period.

I will then discuss a counter tradition of thinking about everyday life which will inform what will be referred to as *promenade performances*. Such performances will be grounded in everyday, interactive scenes where highly localised regulations and motivations negotiate with wider, increasingly globalised influences. Evidence of this notion of promenade performances within youth music cultures is revealed in the various everyday music practices that M-O participants recorded, the main observed practice of which was public dancing. I will argue that the productive consumption of dance music by certain youth groups during this period to some extent resembles music's subversive function in the subcultures literature. However, I will advocate an alternative reading of these historic youth music practices as part of a wider set of promenade performances within localised and intergenerational contexts. Following on from these historical investigations, the next chapter will discuss the concept of performances – particularly with respect to the work of Giddens (1991; 1992) and Goffman (1963; 1969a; 1969b) – and relate this concept to research on music localities and scenes. Thinking of youth music cultures as contexts of performance will been seen to offer a bridge between pre-war and more contemporary examples, and the notion of promenade performances – rife in the streets and ballrooms of early youth music cultures – will be further explored in the later chapters on young people's music practices today.

Mass-Observation and the Worktown Project

To understand how mass-produced music was situated in young people's everyday lives during the first half of the twentieth century presents methodological problems. Without scope to draw on autobiographical material and faced with issues of memory recall when drawing on the biographies of others, how is the historian or theorist of everyday life able to grasp what it was *really like* during those bygone years? Fortunately, if not entirely satisfactorily, contemporaneous archival records offer alternative documents for interpretation. The applicability of the M-O archive to the study of early mass music and dance in everyday life was evident not only from M-O's wider methodological stance at the time to penetrate 'every part of local life' (M-O 1970, 'Preface': 8). On a purely historical basis, the period from the late 1930s to the late 1940s when M-O established and consolidated its main research activities paralleled an era of British music and dance that had remained largely unexplored by sociological and cultural studies. My search through the local history and archival holdings of several public libraries enabled me to identify jazz and dance halls in the USA and Britain as objects of study that had scarcely borne consideration in literature on *post-war* music cultures or youth subcultures. The M-O Archive now provided me with perhaps the richest source of detailed archival material on jazz and dancing that had foreran documentation by recorded music formats and television in the emerging age of mass communications which soon after instigated what is still widely regarded as the 'first' mass music culture – rock 'n' roll.

In a letter to the *New Statesman* in January 1937, the three founding members, Tom Harrisson, Charles Madge and Humphrey Jennings, stated that their 'science of M-O' developed 'out of anthropology, psychology, and the sciences which study man [. . .]. Already we have fifty observers at work on two sample problems. We are further working out a complete plan of campaign, which will be possible when we have not fifty but 5,000 observers.' These two sample problems paralleled distinct fieldwork concerns: the Worktown Project and the National Panel of Voluntary Observers. The Worktown Project was one of the first examples of participant observation research in British sociology. Worktown – named Northtown at first[7] – was M-O's pseudonym for Bolton, Lancashire. As well as assuring the anonymity of unassuming respondents, Bolton was referred to as Worktown 'because it is just a town that exists and persists on the basis of industrial work' (M-O 1970, 'Preface': 8).

There was nothing unique about Bolton and this was the reason why it usefully represented industrial, working-class Britain during the late

Figure 3.1 Inside 85 Davenport Street, Bolton, Tom Harrisson with local paper in the late 1930s. (Source: Humphrey Spender, Bolton Museums, Art Gallery, Aquarium, Bolton MBC)

1930s. Similar to today, the population of north-west England in the first half of the twentieth century was densely concentrated in several conurbations including the Bolton area, although significant rural communities have long since become established in more affluent areas such as Cheshire and the Lake District. Almost the entirety of M-O's data was accumulated from observations of urban life – the most familiar way of life for most of the population of Britain then as now, even accounting for the rise of suburbia in the second half of the last century (Cross 1997; Grossberg 1992). Comparing census figures is not necessarily useful because of the changes in metropolitan boundaries over these years. Nonetheless, an approximate assessment of these figures indicates that Bolton, for example, with approximately 177,000 inhabitants in 1931 compared to 261,000 (this figure is for the metropolitan borough) in 2001, was and is still a densely populated town.[8] What are commonly referred to as 'the Depression Years' in Britain from about 1929 to the outbreak of war were certainly felt by Bolton's local economy of 7–10,000 long-term unemployed people (Power 1980: 4 and 6). George Orwell in *The Road to Wigan Pier* (1937: 75) predicted that at least a third of the population in industrial areas such as Bolton were claiming the dole. Orwell also claimed that unemployment and low wages encouraged early marriages among working-class youths. Nevertheless, Fowler's analysis of young workers' earnings in late 1930s Manchester draws a different conclusion in which

> The standard of living enjoyed by teenage wage-earners was far higher than that enjoyed by the rest of the family [. . .] the interwar period [. . .] was probably the first time that a substantial number of teenage wage-earners in Britain found themselves with a significant amount of money to spend on leisure. (Fowler 1992: 135 and 150)

Moreover, Manchester marriage statistics indicate that these 1930s young people married later than subsequent youth generations in the 1950s and 1960s (1992: 149). Despite the spectre of poverty that haunted the everyday lives of many families during these Depression Years, young people at least had the potential to dispose some of their hard-earned wages on the consumption of leisure activities, many of which brought them in earshot of music.

After taking temporary jobs and visiting pubs in Bolton from mid-1936, Harrisson became the main instigator and organiser of the Worktown Project. From February 1937 he was joined by six full-time volunteers recruited from M-O's London headquarters, the majority of whom were university students on holiday (Cross 1990: 2). They took up residence at 10 Davenport Street, a terraced house close to the centre of Bolton (see Figure 3.1). They were encouraged to view before they interviewed; to overhear before they were heard; and to deploy 'inconspicuous recording methods' (M-O 1970, 'New Preface': 7). Whilst observers on the Worktown Project were based mainly in the Bolton and later the Blackpool areas of north-west England, the National Panel of Voluntary Observers were located throughout Britain, where they produced diaries and directive replies that they posted to M-O's headquarters on a monthly basis.

Theorising everyday life: a counter-tradition

Before being able to appreciate the value of the M-O Archive to an informed theoretical perspective on everyday youth music cultures during this period, it is important to outline key debates about the everyday. Everyday life is often taken for granted as a fundamental sociological concern[9] rather than explored as a concept. As such, the sociology of everyday life has emerged from related fields of enquiry such as anthropology, the sociology of time (Zerubavel 1981; 1991), Marxist sociology (Lefebvre 1984; Heller 1984) and – perhaps of most interest here – cultural studies of consumption (de Certeau 1984; Fiske 1989a; 1989b) rather than

Figure 3.2 Tom Harrisson fooling around in the late 1930s. (Source: Humphrey Spender, Bolton Museums, Art Gallery, Aquarium, Bolton MBC)

from its own frames of reference. Michael E. Gardiner (2000) has outlined a counter-tradition of thinking about everyday life that interrogates commonsense assumptions:

> such a counter-tradition evinces a pronounced hostility toward abstract social theorising (ranging from Saussurean-inspired structuralism to economistic Marxism and Parsonian-style functionalism), and a concomitant stress on the quotidian or non-formalised aspects of social interaction. (2000: 3)

One such exponent of this counter-tradition is the Russian literary and cultural critic Mikhail Bakhtin. In *Rabelais and his World* (1984), Bakhtin discovers qualities of originality and grotesque realism in the writings of the sixteenth-century French novelist François Rabelais. By appropriating the argot of the marketplace, Bakhtin argues that Rabelais's use of carnivalesque language and narrative vividly represented the mundane, material daily existence of ordinary folk. Rabelais partly achieved such vivid representations by being an active agent in the culture of the marketplace as both a young scholar and later a dramatist. Indeed, 'France's dramatic culture was at that time closely related to the marketplace' (1984: 157) and Rabelais needed to structure his writing activities around the tri-annual fairs that attracted people (i.e. potential theatre-goers) from throughout the surrounding communities to the urban marketplaces. So Rabelais's novels about the everyday lives of market-goers achieved a harmonious contextuality with this world through the author's empathetic imagination, and the material conditions of commercial promotion and opportunism in which they were produced.

The sixteenth-century French marketplace as depicted by Rabelais had all the hallmarks of a distinct social world in the epoch of modernity. A characteristic vernacular feature of this world known as 'cris' indicated its resemblance to later urban cultures. Cris were quite literally 'cries' in the English sense of messages spoken aloud (as delivered by a town crier). French 'cris' were specifically associated with oral advertisements called out by street vendors in Paris and 'each cry had four lines offering and praising a certain merchandise' (1984: 181). As Bakhtin points out, 'such have always been the announcements at the fair. They did not demand conventional forms or official speeches [. . .]. Popular advertising is always ironic, always makes fun of itself to a certain extent (as does the advertising of our own peddlers and hawkers)' (1984: 160). So here was an informal economy that operated with its own everyday commercial conventions (selling its own wares) more or less outside larger economic structures in which more formal retail and advertising operations, for example, would have demanded too greater capital. Carnivalesque advertising in the form of spectacular street theatre performances or stunts invited co-present spectators to suspend their disbelief for the sake of the conventions representative of a distinct – albeit informal – social world in which guile and cunning were attributes of everyday sellers *and* buyers.

These conventions representative of social worlds have been extended to the notion of art worlds (Becker 1982) in which patterns or networks of collective activity through routine cooperation are required for such worlds to survive. The collective activity of art worlds requires audiences as well as artists to follow certain oral and visual conventions of communication because 'the activity of response and appreciation must occur' for fundamental as well as economic reasons (1982: 4). Likewise, collective carnivalesque activities depended on conventions of oral and visual communication to enable creativity, response and appreciation. At the same time, cris were associated with sea-faring merchants from across the globe who brought exotic goods to marketplaces that vied for custom against local products: 'These utopian tones were immersed in the depths of concrete, practical life; a life that could be touched, that was filled with aroma and sound' (Bakhtin 1984: 185). In this sense, Rabelais's marketplace was a forerunner to contemporary, cosmopolitan city cultures in which the global and local intersect to generate spaces for a multitude of fluid self-identities (Giddens 1991).[10] British industrial and seaside towns such as Bolton and Blackpool would have likewise created an intersection between the locally familiar and – particularly while holidaying in Blackpool – the globally exotic in the days before mass tourism abroad.

Carnivalesque activities within formal urban structures are analogous to what de Certeau (1984) called the 'tactics' of consumers within formal structures of productivist economies. As opposed to 'proper strategies' in which space is successfully won over time, 'a tactic depends on time' (de Certeau 1984: xix) as it is a decision made within the complex ebbs and flows of everyday schedules. For example, while authors write books with the intention that their every word is read and preferably remembered, in everyday tactics such as speed reading there is a freedom of movement and 'an autonomy in relation to the determinations of the text' (1984: 176), only some of which is read and less still remembered in the long term. Indeed, de Certeau considers reading to be a prime example of an activity in which literal interpretations as authorised by professionals and intellectuals are *socially* legitimised rather than reflected in what are, in practice, pluralistic interpretations made by individual readers, each of which is a legitimate interpretation because 'the operation of encoding, which is articulated on signifiers, produces the meaning, which is thus not defined by something that is deposited in the text, by an "intention", or by an activity on the part of the author' (1984: 171).

It is clear from this statement how far de Certeau's understanding of the encoding and decoding practices of everyday life differs from that of Stuart Hall's (1992) classic structuralist model. Hall's 'Encoding/decoding' model presumed that the loaded encoding of media productions corresponded to decoded readings of these productions at the moment of reception. Media producers were therefore writing their own ideologies of professionalism and political inclinations on to their productions which functioned to communicate these ideologies to consumers, who either accepted, negotiated with or opposed these values, beliefs and opinions. However, this model lacked a pragmatic dimension for understanding how audiences decoded ideological content. Whilst Hall perceptively stressed that media productions generated polysemic readings at the point of consumption, this rather contradicted the simplistic Marxist framework in which three kinds of decoding tended 'to assume that audiences can *only* work within the false consciousness of the dominant frame' (Abercrombie and Longhurst 1998: 14). Nonetheless, the 'Encoding/decoding' model was hugely influential to – and influenced by – the European structuralist perspective on subculture discussed earlier. Indeed, de Certeau has stated that a turn towards studying everyday life was instigated by 'the necessity of not locating cultural *difference* in groups associated with the "counter-culture",' many of which were peculiarly privileged and amplified by social commentators despite being no more than indexes of society as a whole (1984: xii). As such, de Certeau moved beyond the tired Marxist framework of false consciousness by arguing that encoding is produced in the interaction between readers and the signifying properties of texts. The encoding intentions of authors or producers are arbitrary to how texts or products are read or consumed.

The argument made by de Certeau has been criticised for its extremity. Readers of texts are surely not entirely free to interpret any number of meanings divorced from those intended by authors. Nevertheless, the emancipation of readers and consumers from the ostensibly pragmatic motives of ideologically encoded mass media is a fundamental achievement of ethnographically informed research that has attempted to understand consumption practices in everyday life. This achievement is likely to have been propelled by the close association between sociologies of everyday life and the philosophical tradition of hermeneutics, and in particular Hans-Georg Gadamer's concept of the 'hermeneutic circle'. Gadamer contends that 'Not occasionally only, but always, the meaning of a text goes beyond its author. That is why understanding is not merely [. . .] reproductive, but always [. . .] productive' (1979: 269). So readers do not simply decode texts – whether with oppositional codes or otherwise – that are somehow loaded with encoded intentions, but they create new meanings that are never straightforward reactions or responses to what are intended or preferred meanings. Everyday life perspectives on consumption and production informed by perspectives on *texts as read* (Storey 1999), then, can no longer operate within the reductive hegemonic paradigm of struggles between dominant and oppositional codes, 'producerly' and 'consumerly' definitions.

How does this counter-tradition of thinking about everyday life map on to M-O accounts of youth music cultures in 1930s and 1940s Britain? First and foremost, M-O's objective to penetrate every part of local life grounded its observers in a situational contextualism comparable to that of Rabelais in relation to his carnivalesque marketplace (Bakhtin 1984). Therefore, M-O observers were bound to record music and dance practices that were most visible and commonplace in the communities where they temporarily lived and, in some cases, worked. Second and also in respect to the 'carnivalesque', public music and dancing at this time had not entirely broken free from their 'low culture' associations and – certainly in informal, working-class youth venues – were considered grotesque and transgressive according to elitist discourses of modernism.

Third, there was mounting evidence by the mid-1930s that music was becoming a feature of everyday experience for potentially everyone: a *mass* phenomenon:

> In the home, in the theatre, in the street, in (and on) the air, music now figures so prominently as a means of entertainment that it would be impossible to contemplate a world in which it no longer provided such a constant source of popular enjoyment. (Anon., quoted in Nott 2002: 1)

A justifiable definition of everyday music and dance practices, then, would be those modes of consumption and production in domestic and public contexts which each occurred on a daily basis and in combination created this sense of omnipresence. And fourth, the accurate use of the term 'practice' as a regular act of human agency such as the speaking of a particular argot (Bakhtin 1984) or the enacting of 'tactics' (de Certeau 1984) aids the formation of criteria for what might and might not construe music and dance practices of everyday life. As such, the everyday practices of music and dance recorded by M-O and detailed later in this article include those that occurred in sites that were regularly accessible for use by most people (e.g. public dance halls and domestic contexts via the radio) but omit those beyond the capabilities of the majority (e.g. 'producerly' broadcasting studios and record company offices).

Promenade performances

Early mass music and dance practices in young people's everyday lives certainly resonate with Bakhtin's notion of the 'carnivalesque' as well as de Certeau's tactics.[11] Linked to these two theoretical perspectives, what might be referred to as 'promenade performances' seem to capture best the common as well as incongruous features of mass music and dance vis-à-vis these theoretical models of everyday life. The promenade concert (prom), like the dance club or rock concert, is a self-serving everyday locale akin to the carnivalesque marketplace, characterised by a mix of global cultural influences or what Bakhtin termed a process of 'hybridisation'. Within formal structures of productivist economies, there is an informal economy of tactics at work during the prom wherein distinctions between producers and consumers become blurred. Promenade performances are thus highly interactive and localised phenomena that require a certain degree of learning through practices of bodily self-presentation (Goffman 1969a) in the form of demonstration and display, whilst at the same time such performances are moulded by processes of globalisation. Carnivalesque and promenade performances both enact everyday physical movement but situate this movement within those slightly more extraordinary interactions amid leisure that are nevertheless commonplace to work and other everyday contexts. Contemporary applications of promenading not only arise from physical or co-present communicative contexts, however, but are delayed through mediated communicative contexts whereby, for instance, a celebrity who models a particular item of fashion (along the promenade-like catwalk perhaps) transmits embodied resources to viewers who follow or modify this fashion trend in everyday relations with others, who in turn are influenced by such trends.

Although early mass music and dance practices arose largely through co-present rather than mediated communicative contexts, it was evident during the period in question that such practices were becoming increasingly disseminated through national and global communications networks. Americanised cultural influences were particularly prevalent in the popular music industries of Britain and other European countries during the mid-twentieth century (Hoggart 1958; Hebdige 1989). It is valid, then, to draw a distinction between co-present and mediated promenade performances at a point in time when globally distributed music and dance penetrated into localised contexts and became genuinely *mass*ive aspects of many (young) people's everyday lives. First, mediated promenade performances were demonstrated through the reception phase that provided knowledge about the latest tunes, dances and fashions to come on to the scene. Second, co-present promenade performances would be demonstrated and displayed through the exhibition phase that involved selection of this mediated knowledge. The extent to which different consumers experienced such performances varied considerably depending upon their level of involvement in and accessibility to mediated and co-present practices of everyday music and dance.

Co-present promenade performances on the dance floor were demonstrated and displayed in different ways. Imitation performances would be relatively informal attempts by single or partner dancers to follow visually the steps and moves of others as they rotated around the floor. On a more formal level, instruction performances would involve the instructor holding the learner and showing them how to dance through visual, verbal and physical means. Instruction performances in particular were engaged in by earnest, committed dancers such as a female respondent who wrote that 'more than physico-emotional pleasure is to be desired, although the majority fail to seek it' and who felt that 'The pleasure is enhanced by the knowledge of one's partner having interests in common with one's self' (DR 2312: July 1939). Imitation performances would be engaged in by all learner dancers but those less committed to dancing and more interested in striking up sexual relations would probably rely on such performances for longer spells of their youth, such as this male respondent: 'Feel self-conscious about asking young ladies to dance towards whom I have the strongest sexual attraction because I know little or nothing about dancing. Physical pleasure is the predominant attraction in dancing for me' (DR 1142: January 1939). Co-present dance promenading was clearly a part of some everyday consumers' lives more than others. Nevertheless, taking a walk or promenade down a city street, across a park or along the seafront was almost certainly a more *regular* everyday activity in an age shortly before the mass consumption of motor cars. Due to the portability of gramophones and wirelesses as well as frequent public performances by orchestras and brass bands, mediated as well as co-present music was often consumed while promenading.

What was different, however, about promenading as a performance by the 1930s and 1940s was the way in which it was enacted in a variety of leisure practices beyond those of walking outdoors. Promenading was part of dance-hall cultures where dancing became impractical. For example, at the Aspin in Bolton 'the floor is so crowded that those who cannot do dances like the foxtrot well are actually at no disadvantage, since even the good dancers can only promenade round in "crush" dance style' (WC 48d: July 1940). Another observation at the Blackpool Tower Ballroom on how spectators sit and watch as if on the promenade, and mostly 'play a passive role' (WC 60d), shows how spectators and performers at dance halls co-participated in a promenade situation. An observer at the Tower experienced at first-hand his promenade performance of display and demonstration: 'Look up and surprised to find dance floor is surrounded by a theatre-like double gallery full of people. Dance band takes other side.' Later, 'I suddenly feel I am being watched and look along balconies. I do not like the idea of all those eyes up there' (WC 60d). This account shows how the Tower Ballroom architecture catered for spectators as much as dancers but fostered demonstration performances to encourage collective involvement in an everyday activity that blurred distinctions between performers and spectators by incorporating dancing and promenading activities. But ballrooms were not the only places for promenading. As well as promenades per se (and promenades were not exclusive to seaside towns), parks, picnic sites, piers, country walks, swimming baths, shopping areas, train and bus stations all made excellent sites for promenade performances. What follows are more detailed archival findings into young people's early mass music and dance practices as they relate to the notion of everyday promenade performances.

Figure 3.3 Spectators overlooking dancers at Blackpool's Tower Ballroom during wartime in the early 1940s. (Source: Leisure Parcs Archive)

Music and dancing in Britain, 1936–49

Dance music and dancing in Worktown were certainly everyday music practices, particularly for the younger sections of the urban populace:

> In the life of its 180,000 inhabitants the dance hall plays a vital part, though their greatest significance is confined to unmarried youths of both sexes [. . .] In churches, pubs, political organisations and all other groups with social and co-operative interests, young people are today conspicuously absent in Worktown; the elder folk continually complain about it. In six main dance-halls on Saturday evening there are nearly as many young men as on Sunday evening in all the town's 170 churches. (Harrisson 1938a: 47 and 50)

Nonetheless, enthusiasm for jazz music abounded across the generations:

> When one remembers that only about 9% of the population goes regularly to pubs, and under that to churches; that under half the population is actively interested in the football pools, the tremendous power of the more than 75% pro-jazz public can easily be realized. (M-O 1940: 222–3)

Large-scale public dancing in Britain grew in popularity during the late nineteenth century. In Blackpool what were to become the town's three major dance halls in the 1930s and 1940s – the Tower Ballroom, the Empress Ballrooms and the Palace Ballroom – opened in 1894, 1897 and 1899 respectively. By 1933 J. B. Priestley (1934: 252) had formed the opinion en route through England that Blackpool's pioneering role in regard to dance entertainment before the First World War had resulted in such entertainment being made available throughout the country.

Prior to this growth in popularity, dancing in public was associated in the early nineteenth century with sexual immorality and working classness. Liz Oliver notes that at this time 'In Bolton [there was] a dancing hierarchy ranging from private dances in the homes of the wealthy to the dancing saloons of the working classes' (Oliver 1995: 18). These class distinctions in dancing practices were by no means as stark by the time that M-O entered Bolton in 1936 but they were still noticeable. Admission charges at Bolton's dance venues ranged from the cheap (threepence) at basic dance halls such as the Floral Hall, to the mid-market (one shilling) at ballrooms such as the Palais de Danse, to the expensive (two to three-and-a-half shillings) at dance schools such as the Premier School of Dancing. Which venue to choose, though, would perhaps have more bearing on levels of commitment to dancing rather than social class. For committed dancers in particular, the quality of floor, band and fellow dancers were paramount in their choice of venue. The notion of a more 'select crowd' was, then, by no means entirely synonymous with a more middle-class clientele and will be interrogated further as this chapter proceeds. The first part of this social-historical account of early mass music and dance in everyday life will examine evidence of co-present promenade performances of demonstration and display. These performances will be interpreted through the types of popular dances and the features of dancers during this period. The second part will account for mediated promenade performances of demonstration via the gramophone, the radio and magazines.

Co-present promenade performances

First, the types of popular songs played by dance bands in dance halls would be performed for and to a certain style of dancing such as the quickstep or foxtrot. Etiquette demanded that this dancing style had to be conventionally enacted by couples throughout the duration of a song and terminated by their walking off the dance floor in the silent pause between the end of that song and the start of the next one. Whilst Adorno (1991) considered dance music to be a standardised product of the culture industry, the manager of the Aspin referred to conservative dancers at his hall who favoured strict tempo[12] dances in which 'The speed of a quickstep must be standardised – the accepted number of bars to the minute' (WC 48d). A male directive respondent likewise stated: 'I like strict tempo without swinging' but he was not a fan of dancing per se (DR 1435: January 1939). Dance schools partly served a demand by dance-hall patrons to know conventional, standardised ballroom dance steps: 'It is now an essential part of any youth's social equipment that he or she may be able to go through two variations of these movements (waltz and foxtrot) with sufficient grace to avoid treading on a partner's toe' (Harrisson 1938a: 51). Despite the conservatism of most couple dancing styles, I will discuss two types of dances and their accompanying songs which grew in popularity during this period to the extent that they generated mass demand for their standardisation as well as demonstration in line with conventional dances, even when promenade performances of these dances – not unlike later accounts of youth subcultural activity – had disrupted the formal atmosphere of public dancing prevalent a decade or two earlier.

The jitterbug, or lindyhop, which would later mutate into the jive, developed in Britain around 1938 after its emergence as an African-American dance music practice in the USA (Gammond 1991: 298). It is worth quoting extensively from Adorno's tirade against this dance, its accompanying music and those who practised it in order to contrast his Marxist perspective on jitterbugging with that of contemporaneous conservative moral crusaders. He singled out for criticism

> the enthusiasts who write fan letters to radio stations and orchestras and, at well-managed jazz festivals, produce their own enthusiasm as an advertisement for the wares they consume. They call themselves jitterbugs, as if they simultaneously wanted to affirm and mock their loss of individuality, their transformation into beetles whirring around in fascination. Their only excuse is that the term jitterbugs, like all those in the unreal edifice of films and jazz, is hammered into them by the entrepreneurs to make them think that they are on the inside. Their ecstacy is without content. That it happens, that the music is listened to, this replaces the content itself. The ecstacy takes possession of its object by its own compulsive character. It is stylised like the ecstacies savages go into in beating the war-drums. It has convulsive aspects reminiscent of St Vitus's dance or the reflexes of mutilated animals. Passion itself seems to be produced by defects. But the ecstatic ritual betrays itself as pseudo-activity by the moment of mimicry. People do not dance or listen 'from sensuality' and sensuality is certainly not satisfied by listening, but the gestures of the sensual are imitated. (Adorno 1991: 46)

Adorno considered the jitterbug to be a marketing invention that had successfully duped its enthusiasts into embracing its pseudo-individualistic cultural effects to the point where they were deemed to have appropriated the dance to their own nomenclature. Jitterbug music is equated with regressive rather than sensual listening in which genuine passion can only be mimicked but never realised.

The point at which jitterbugging became a passive, stultifying practice for Adorno was its mimicry. Jitterbuggers' steps imitated the movement of the mindless, standardised music like the reactions of savages imitated the beating of war-drums. Interestingly, the mimicry of jitterbugging was observed in Bolton's Palais dance hall by an M-O participant who noted that, 'The newness of the craze here was shown by the strong vein of imitation in the jitterbuggers. They were following each other' (WC 48d: December 1939). He then described the jitterbug steps that were being imitated: 'feet together and feet shuffling sideways; hands clasped in front at waist and swayed in rhythm with body, which is swayed in opposite direction to feet turning; couple face each other and progress sideways' (WC 48d: December 1939). Even if this description reads better than the steps it actually describes, it tends to support a counter-action to Adorno's negative use of the term 'mimicry' that neglected to consider the athleticism and skill required of jitterbugging. Mimicry in this sense could be interpreted as a positive activity that enabled dancers to acquire some of the 'social equipment' (Harrisson 1938a) in relations with their peers so as to perform productive consumer selves. According to the Palais's manager the jitterbug 'is popular because you don't have to hold your partner in the correct dancing position. Now only a few couples do hold their partners in the correct dancing position. Some like to go round in promenade position. Well in jitterbug you can do this' (WC 48d: December 1939). Jitterbugging thus closely resembled promenading. Promenade jitterbug performances were breaking with established forms of standardised leisure practices through collective mimicry for means of everyday youth cultural – possibly even subcultural – exchange.

The rumba, on the other hand, was unconventional in the late 1930s both as a dancing style and because it tended to be popular among all-female couples and groups. One Worktown observer described it as 'the most deliberately active and distinctly "sexual" dance' (WC 60d). Moreover, female couples were more liable to smile, talk and treat dances like the rumba with fun than the sincerer, silent mixed couples: 'In the waltz and the veleta, with its tender romantic music as a background the girl prefers to dance with a man, but in the rumba, which is characterised by a more deliberately active step and a purer sex significance female

Figure 3.4 An MC moves to curtail jitterbugging at Blackpool's Tower Ballroom
during wartime in the early 1940s. (Source: Leisure Parcs Archive)

couples take the floor in greater numbers' (WC 60d). The male–dominated
characteristics of M-O personnel may account for why the appearance of
females dancing together was so noteworthy, but it would also be fair to
argue that public dancing during this period still operated under strict
taboos about sexual immorality and indecent public behaviour. Indeed, any

suggestion that female groups were engaging in collective leisure activities – largely dismissed in the literature on 1960s and 1970s subcultures (McRobbie and Garber 1993) – would have been even more radical and controversial in the pre-war years. Perhaps these strict taboos were a factor which influenced one group of young females to learn how to perform the rumba in an intimate, private context: 'Sometimes we dance, just 4 of us at my friend's house. But only because a visitor is a keen dancer, he teaches the rest of us rumba' (DR 1057: January 1939). Co-present promenade performances of the rumba here pervaded multiple contexts of everyday life through demonstration in the home (at the reception phase) and public display thereafter (at the exhibition phase).

Second, the features of dancers can be categorised into three themes: professionalism, appearance management, and social and sexual etiquette. Professionalism in dance-hall practices was personified by professional dance partners who demonstrated effective co-present promenade performances to customers. These dance partners were often male and female employees of equal numbers who reflected the demand from both genders for schooling in how to dance. The manager of the Aspin, for example, described changing trends in custom for his learners' nights: 'Girls start younger than boys and pick up quicker – for it is harder for a man to learn. But now we have noticed that there are more boys than girls some nights, which is very unusual' (WC 48d: January 1940). Meagre financial rewards suggest that professional dance partners adopted their teaching roles for pleasure rather than profit. Professionalism in dancing demonstration brought personal satisfaction by enabling committed dancers to engage in and exchange productive consumption practices through processes of imitation and instruction. Despite their more or less voluntary function as providers of consumer 'social equipment', professional dance partners were subject to much prejudice in some directive replies from M-O's national panel. A male respondent wrote that, 'If I could not find a partner I should not pay one to dance with me' (DR 2160: July 1939) and a female respondent considered their job to be 'a somewhat useless way of earning a living' (DR 1057: July 1939). Highbrow opinions aside, though, a Manchester schoolboy wrote: 'My 2 aunts who, being over 40, have little hope of securing partners otherwise make use of them and say how competent and pleasant they are' (DR 1375: July 1939). The professionalism practised in a range of public dancing contexts at this time enabled an inclusiveness of cultural exchange among promenade performers who demonstrated varying levels of competence and involvement in these early youth music cultures.

Appearance management as an aspect of self-presentation was an everyday concern for dancers then as clubbers nowadays. A female directive

Figure 3.5 Blackpool: girls dancing together on the Pier in the late 1930s.
(Source: Humphrey Spender, Bolton Museums, Art Gallery,
Aquarium, Bolton MBC)

respondent wrote: 'Preparing for a dance is half the fun, to my mind. Getting one's frock ready, wondering whether you should have your hair done, or whether it'll stick up by itself, hoping it won't be wet, or cold, for that matter' (DR 1040: January 1939). The care taken over physical appearance by dancers would seem to have been accentuated mostly in anticipation of choosing or being chosen by a dancing partner. It was rule of etiquette for a male to solicit a female dancer's company during 'excuse-me' dances in which an existing couple would be expected to split up or a single female dancer would be expected to submit after the tap on her shoulder by the enquiring male. Appearing courageous and confident were therefore necessary attributes of dancers and particularly male dancers. However, the fear of rejection when asking prospective partners for 'excuse-mes' or being prematurely split up in such dances was often experienced. Several instances of being snubbed at Bolton's Aspin persuaded a young male dancer that he should try the Floral Hall instead (WC 48d: February 1940). A female dancer clearly flouted etiquette by stating that, 'I do not excuse for a man I do not know' (DR 1057: July 1939) whilst for another 'The excusee must be tall' (DR 2312: July 1939). A male dancer accompanied by his partner used her to affirm an appearance of his own marital and social status: 'I occasionally attend a dance for the sole reason of showing the local society that my wife is desirable and attractive' (DR 1401: January 1939). So despite facilities to equip oneself with skills and professionalism, the competitiveness of appearance-management practices in dancing contexts clearly fostered everyday promenade performances of varying esteem and adequacy.

Practices of social and sexual etiquette in the dance hall overlap with appearance-management practices but warrant attention in their own right. The contradiction in couple dancing was that despite regulations on cavorting behaviour there was implicit opportunism for becoming intimate while holding a partner in the *correct* dancing position. Excuse-me dances were clearly the most likely contexts in which sexual relations might be developed but these were often assigned to particular songs at the discretion of the MC. Nevertheless, at the informal Spinners Hall on New Year's Eve Night much 'necking' was observed and 'each dance was treated as an excuse-me after about 10pm' (WC 48d: December 1939). Observation at Blackpool dance halls found that there was some leniency, with couples at the centre of dance floors who behaved promiscuously being only occasionally checked by staff (WC 60d). Furthermore, in the dance hall as opposed to more overtly public places 'picking-up' [chatting-up] and 'getting-off' [kissing] are accepted as normal behaviour [. . .] there is none of the preliminary manoeuvring seen on the Promenade. The method of approach is more confident, since prescribed by convention, and the chances of success are greater. (WC 60d)

Dance halls provided interactive co-present contexts for promenade performances of intimacy but the rules of etiquette remained the same across everyday contexts over the course of a typical day in a leisure resort such as Blackpool: 'At night, the focus of interest switches from the open air to the interior, roughly from the Promenade to the Ballroom. Sometimes the transition is made through the medium of the theatre and cinema' (WC 60d.). The rules of etiquette and conventions attached to promenading and dancing were learnt in public practice but the foundations for this learning could be built through the mass media reception phase.

Mediated promenade performances

The three main music media in Britain during the 1930s and 1940s were the gramophone, the radio and magazines.[13] I will consider each of these media in turn after outlining general characteristics shared by them. Mediated promenade performances in each case tended first to be enacted by enthusiasts of both music and the technologies that enabled that music to be mass communicated. These early adopters of media technologies were often middle class and self-taught. Issues of technological inclusion and exclusion were in many ways as prevalent then as they are today. Nonetheless, the demonstration of mediated promenade performances to others meant that certain exclusion barriers could be lifted through processes of social interaction. Like co-present promenading in the form of public dancing, therefore, mediated promenade performances required the honing of certain literacies in order for them to be successfully enacted in everyday life contexts. Indeed, it is erroneous to conceive of co-present and mediated promenading as mutually exclusive phases during this period. The distinction between music media and public music audiences had begun to blur even before the age of television. A striking example of this *massification* of music in everyday life was evident from the comments of a female dancer on how female factory workers collectively learnt lyrics via magazine excerpts: 'At the mill there are a lot of girls together. One will get one line and another another and they piece them all together [. . .] Now when the girls work in a shop – like I do – they don't get to know the words' (WC 48d: February 1940). Promenade performances of communal singing learnt through both the reception and exhibition phases appeared to consolidate important processes of social bonding.

The gramophone was the first consumer-based, mechanical music medium after replacing the piano in thousands of British homes during the late 1920s and early 1930s (Nott 2002: 101–2). Although mainly middle-class enthusiasts who constructed their own machines initially owned this earliest model of the future electronic record player, by the mid-1930s gramophones and gramophone records were affordable to working-class and young consumers too. These cheaper gramophones were portable so they could be moved around the house, between households or taken on holiday (2002: 37). Like the wireless that soon superseded it as the major domestic music provider, the gramophone had a public presence which also conferred social status. Furthermore, it was used frequently for domestic parties and soon gained favour over live music entertainment in homes because recorded music was less expensive to hire. Gramophones were to have a major cultural impact in that they encouraged American musical influences on British audiences and musicians with the mass importation of recorded popular music from across the Atlantic in the early 1930s (2002: 55). The globalising influence of the gramophone should not be exaggerated, though, given that highbrow classical music was and has remained mostly associated with this medium, particularly during wartime (e.g. DR 2413: February 1942). Mediated promenade performances in relation to the gramophone, then, incorporated global influences within highly localised contexts of social interaction around – often highly creative – enthusiasms.

If the gramophone became the first consumer-based, mechanical music medium, the radio that replaced it became the first mass music medium. In Britain by 1939 nine million wireless licences meant that 'the "friend in the corner" reached almost 34 million people – nearly three-quarters of all households' (Nott 2002: 59). Moreover, Harrisson noted the significance of music to radio programming in that it occupied 'well over half the [air] time in most lands' (FR 1637: 1943). Research in the mid-1930s found that 'over 75% of British wireless listeners spent an average 16% of their time listening to dance band music' (Greenwood 1986: 4). Although early radio transmitted national and global music products, it inadvertently served as a complementary promotional tool for local dance halls. A young male dancer at the Aspin told an observer 'that he used to listen to bands on the wireless and then thought he'd try dancing' (WC 48d: January 1940). Publicity material for the Tower Ballroom at this time described how 'Its famous wonder Wurlitzer Organ and Dance Orchestra are heard broadcasting throughout the Empire' and how residential organist Reginald Dixon was an 'all-year wireless hero' (WC 60d). Although the radio was essentially a domestic entertainment provider, its early usage – particularly by youth groups – was frequently in public contexts such as pubs, factories and milk bars because listening demand outstripped receiving supply. All factory managers who installed radios tuned to the BBC's *Music While You Work* programme, broadcast each weekday from 10.30 a.m. to 3.00 p.m., 'found the effects highly beneficial' in terms of work productivity (FR 1249: 1942). Another report on girls' leisure activities referred to 'a supper bar where they go to listen to the wireless and no doubt to meet the boys of their district' (Harley 1937: 103). The growth in presence of the radio during this period made it the forerunner to television as a mass entertainment medium infiltrating everyday consumer experiences as well as a musical resource for demonstrating promenade performances.

Last but not least of these early mass media, music and dance magazines emerged in Britain during this period. The *Melody Maker* was founded in 1927 but the clearest indication of a demand for dance-orientated magazines came in the shape of *Danceland*.[14] First issued in 1937 and closely associated with the Mecca leisure company, the magazine's banner line – 'Exclusively Reserved for the Modern Generation' – in part reflected its agenda to modernise ballroom dancing so as to incorporate new and popular dances like the jitterbug. *Danceland*'s campaign in support of jitterbugging included columns by professional dancers who favoured this new dance and wished to see it become a fifth standard dance after the quickstep, foxtrot, waltz and tango (November 1943 issue). A regular feature of the magazine was a series of diagrams that demonstrated the steps to the latest popular dance hit. It was clearly in Mecca's interests that the dances promoted across its nationwide ballrooms should also be promoted through print media. *Danceland* readers were encouraged to rehearse the dances at home through mediated promenade performances before publicly demonstrating and displaying such dances at the local Mecca branch: 'Directly you see it, you can do it. Dancer or non-dancer you can "step it" . . .' (February 1941 issue). One commentator even drew a contrived relationship between mass public dancing and experiences of stardom:

> The unique feature in comparison with the theatre, cinema and music hall lies in the fact that every [Mecca] patron, after the necessary visit to the box office, thereupon becomes a member of the cast, immediately steps on to the stage and in very truth becomes a performer. (July 1941 issue)

Given existing data, it is impossible to interpret the extent to which readers of this magazine were influenced by its market-driven editorials. *Danceland* like other magazines as well as other music media in general, though,

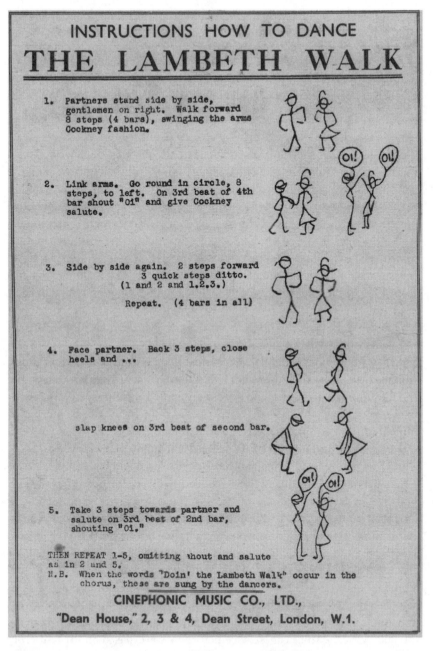

Figure 3.6 Instructions on how to dance the 'Lambeth Walk.' (Source: Music Sales Group, London)

appeared to supply an enthusiastic readership with knowledge that they could select and then demonstrate in closely juxtaposed, co-present everyday performances – as opposed to the spectacular, star-studded kind.

Localisation and intergenerational youth

The importance of mediated as well as co-present promenade performances is certainly evident during this period, and yet it would be inaccurate to assume that the rise of mass music media corresponded with a trend towards transnational (or even national) youth music cultures. On the contrary, early mass music and dance practices remained firmly situated in localised and – by extension – intergenerational frames of reference. Nonetheless, the outbreak of the Second World War brought a mix of cultural influences into Britain. Blackpool in particular became a temporary home to a transient population, and not just those seven million domestic tourists who visited the popular resort each year (Harrisson 1939b: 26). From 1939 to the mid-1940s nearly 770,000 RAF recruits carried out their basic training in the town, 60,000 of whom would have been there at any one time. By 1942 20,000 US servicemen who had arrived in Britain took over operations at nearby Warton airfield and over 18,000 Polish airmen were stationed in Blackpool after fleeing their war-torn country. Furthermore, 1,700 civil servants had migrated from London during the first four months of the war and effectively coined Blackpool as 'Whitehall-on-Sea'.[15] Clearly this seaside town had an immensely larger, more cosmopolitan population during the war years and was certainly a centre of greater activity and national importance than at any previous time.

In Blackpool as well as many other British towns and cities, US servicemen in particular introduced their own youth music cultures to 'the locals'. The jive (a faster variation on the jitterbug) together with the Latin-American samba, rumba and conga were ground-breaking developments in the gradual transformation away from rigid, professionalised ballroom dancing to 'a wealth of choice to suit all tastes and ages' during the 1940s (Rust 1969: 102). Whilst terms like 'Americanisation', 'negro', 'jazz' and 'Cadillac' have tended to be attached with negative connotations such as homogeneity by paternalistic European cultural commentators across the political spectrum (see Hebdige 1989), Les Back has argued that the 130,000 African-American servicemen who were based in Britain from 1942 until the end of the war contributed to the empowerment of youth cultures by forming swing bands and hosting dance events (Back 1997: 188). White English women dancing with African-American men would have certainly represented subversive cultural expression in this social and historical context, and it would appear that the destablising consequences of war paradoxically enabled the wage-earning female to experience greater independence: 'Along with their increased spending-power the wartime dances had allowed English women to explore areas of self-expression and autonomy that had been previously unthinkable' (1997: 195). These English women were engaged in processes of cultural exchange very much in keeping with the notion of promenade performances.

Although US servicemen expertly displayed the jitterbug, jive and boogie-woogie crazes that had grown so popular at most British dance halls during this time, these dancing styles were not directly introduced by the Americans. Rather, these dance crazes had peaked in popularity circa 1938, prior to mobilisation (Gammond 1991: 71 and 297). Rust also presents three reasons to explain how the Second World War in general – not merely the American involvement – afforded a change in British popular dance culture:

> Evacuation mixed up the population and tended to spread knowledge of different kinds of dances throughout the country, the 'black-out' and the absence of transport facilities meant an increased emphasis on the 'locality' and on the provision of one's own amusements and, finally, the greater feeling of diffused warmth and friendliness always manifested in times of war and danger could be much better expressed in the group dance-forms than in the isolated 'couple dance'. (Rust 1969: 103)

Each of Rust's three explanations for the growing expression of youth cultural coherence through dance, therefore, surely adds weight to a localisation as opposed to an Americanisation thesis. The localising effect of the war was also felt by the manager of Bolton's Palais de Danse who said that attendances were 'up above pre-war, owing to the fact that at the weekend people are not able to travel out of town [. . .] Monday, Wednesday, and Saturday are well up – I should say 50% above pre-war level' (WC 48d: December 1939). Heightened consciousness of being part of a local community was clearly evident from notes taken by several M-O participants during this time.

A localisation thesis on early mass music and dance is closely tied to the significance of intergenerational relations for youth cultures of this period. This close association between the local and the intergenerational finds further support in Hoggart's (1958) concept of generational transmutation as applied to working-class communities in northern England and a Mass-Observation report into 'doing the Lambeth Walk' in London (Madge and Harrisson 1939). These two accounts reveal some important local historical insights into youth as an interactive phenomenon that have since been largely dismissed by youth cultural studies. Hoggart adopts the term 'transmutation' to define the rigorous and hard-fought process by which new replace old cultural products across time and place. Writing about an era that extended across the period in question, he observed that the prevailing influence of older cultural forms served an important conservative function for controlling the 'shiny barbarism' (Hoggart 1958: 193) that characterised many youth cultural practices. An archetypal example of transmutable conditions observed by the author was the unwritten rules by which a pianist who participated in a Working Men's Club

> must know the exact idiom in which to play. This involves not only knowing the established songs and how to play them, but which of the new songs are catching on and, more important, how to play them so that, though their main lines are kept, they are transmuted into the received idiom. (1958: 155)

Similarly, a Mass-Observer at a private house party in Lambeth noted 'certain rules, like keeping silence during solos' (Madge and Harrisson 1939: 146). It follows that live-music audiences who preceded the onset of recorded music consumption seem to have demanded some alterations in the form and content of mass distributed sheet originals to create versions flavoured with certain localised features. This hypothesis is borne out in the case of the 'Lambeth Walk', which had a slight yet fundamental alteration to its lyrical content whilst being appropriated as the 'Blackpool Walk' among other versions. Hoggart goes so far as to suggest that strong melodic and sentimental values in new club songs lent themselves to canonisation depending on communal consent. Working-class groups were actively critical in democratically judging what mass-produced music could and could not be appropriate for their local clientele.

Despite Hoggart's insights on generational transmutation, he perceived numerous symptoms of degenerational transmutation which he blamed on the Americanised 'glorification of youth', particularly influenced by Hollywood films and Tin Pan Alley songs, and personified in juke-box boys. However, the cynicism prevalent in Hoggart's mostly textual analyses about the Americanisation of British (youth) culture is called into question by Mass-Observation's fieldwork report. By contrast, the 'Lambeth Walk' was found to have provoked a 'Britishised' effect: 'It spread to New York and thence right across America; to Paris and thence to Prague' (Madge and Harrisson 1939: 139). As a well-known Mecca instructress said about dances at its halls in reference to discussions with the management, '[we] want to keep them all English now and they'll be simple' (1939: 161). Although the 'Lambeth Walk' may have represented a less than typical pro-Britishness in mass-produced music of its time, its national and international popularity together with the localised imitations it gave rise to are significant rejoinders to Hoggart's assumption – shared by subcultural theorists (e.g. Hebdige 1989) – that cultural imperialism only flowed from west to east across the Atlantic. Comparisons of these two classic accounts of cultural activities engaged in by but not exclusively associated with youth groups reveal that local contexts of interaction (working men's clubs, house parties) transmitted distinctive meanings on to music texts independently from how these meanings were potentially controlled by national or global structures of dominance. Such informal, localised networks of argot and appropriation resonate with Bahktin's (1984) 'cris' and de Certeau's (1984) tactics of everyday life.

Whilst most of the youth cultural literature discussed in this chapter has lacked an interactionist sociological framework to evince what Mannheim (1952) referred to as those historical and social circumstances in which generational values and traditions are transmitted, the small proportion that has accounted for intergenerational relations has tended to stress their harmoniousness. Mungham (1976: 90) noted the 'largely non-mobile' characteristics of youth groups that attended a Mecca dance hall a generation or so after those Mecca dancers studied by Mass-Observation (Madge and Harrisson 1939). He argued that this predominantly working-class youth 'comes to share many experiences and problems with the generation of their parents' and 'becomes a carrier of their prejudices and insularity as well' (Mungham 1976: 90). In stark contrast to ideas about symbolic spaces of defiance or territories, the territory shared by two generations of local people is given a historical and social materiality or sense of place. Frith's (1978; 1983) study of youth music consumption similarly provides a vivid sense of how the structures of interaction evident in a local community shaped opportunities for social progressiveness among its younger members. Carole Pegg's (1984) survey of music users in an area of southern England usefully sampled a broad age range and found that – particularly in relation to young male respondents – 'some of the state [school] boys might have been influenced by their parents' choice of rock 'n' roll and the same might be said of the public school boys with respect to classical music' (1984: 67). Paul Corrigan's (1979) ethnographic study of a group of schoolchildren revealed that 'usually the music as experienced at school bears little relationship to the music that they experience at home' (1979: 104). This finding was based on observations of a school concert in which the classical music section was greeted with enthusiasm by teachers in contrast to students (including the musicians) and parents, whilst the later 'sing-along' section found willing participants among students and parents alike in contrast to its reticent reception by teachers. When the relationship between youth and other brackets of people is analysed through an interactionist approach, then, intergenerational relations are often noted at least for their complexities and at most for their stark correlations.

Summary

Contrary to the widely held assumption that youth music cultures only developed after the age of television and rock 'n' roll, this chapter has interpreted valuable archival research to explore how a national and increasingly global network of mass music dissemination already pervaded young people's everyday lives in Britain as well as other Western countries by the 1930s and 1940s. Mass music and dance entertainment was accessible to a vast majority of the British population at local dance venues or through media such as magazines and the radio. Whether consumed and produced in co-present or mediated contexts, the notion of promenade performances neatly captures the significance of demonstration and display in leisure practices during this period. For instance, 69.4 per cent of young females in Manchester went for 'evening walks' – often with boyfriends – and 'There are nearly always certain streets in every district which are used as promenades by the young people of the locality' (Harley 1937: 102). Promenade performances are thus enacted in interactive, familiar contexts where young people transmit to others (not just their peers) certain tastes, styles and values for particular kinds of music and dance – among other cultural practices. All performances require audiences, though, so rather than merely understanding promenade performances as enactments (displays) it is important to also understand them as instructions (demonstrations). Moreover, promenade performances are very often learnt through intergenerational relations in which certain rules, conventions and skills – such as how to play a piano, what song to play and how best to sing it – are necessarily mastered.

Akin to informal economies of the carnivalesque marketplace (Bakhtin 1984) and of productivist consumer tactics (de Certeau 1984), everyday promenading and dancing blurred the distinctions between consumption and production; spectacle and performance; the local and the global. The case of jitterbugging was a prime example of a promenade performance. Quite apart from Adorno's tirade against the mindless mimicry inherent to this dance, jitterbuggers and sympathetic dance musicians alike engaged in highly localised cultural exchanges of demonstration and display whilst simultaneously engaging with the wider global (particularly Americanised) cultural implications that jitterbugging practices provoked. These cultural exchanges thus occurred in contexts of 'hybridisation' (Bakhtin 1984). Global cultural imperialism was certainly not a dominant structural force with respect to early youth music practices but might be better understood to have enriched the diverse mix of local music activities through military immigration into Britain generally and north-west England in particular (especially Blackpool). Even less committed dance consumers experienced promenade performances – usually mediated ones – that demonstrated the pervasiveness of music in everyday life during this period. The young male dancer who had 'used to listen to bands on the wireless and then thought he'd try dancing' (WC 48d: January 1940) was a late adopter of promenade performances who could fully participate, nonetheless, in self-presentations of social equipment through the exhibition of knowledge about dancing first learnt at a media reception phase. The next chapter will keep the idea of promenade performances firmly planted in this remarkable period of youth cultural history but locate it within a more contemporary theoretical discourse.

Notes

1. 'Intergenerational' units are defined as networks of relationships between people from different generations (e.g. between young and old); 'intra-generational' units, on the other hand, only comprise relationships between people from the same generation (e.g. between one young person and another).
2. I will develop this interactionist approach further in Chapter 4.
3. I visited the Mass-Observation (M-O) Archive at the University of Sussex, UK, on four separate occasions between March 2001 and June 2002.
4. As well as the M-O Archive, I examined material from the Bolton Local History Archive, the Manchester Local Studies Archive and the Blackpool Leisure Parcs Ltd Archive.
5. See Walton (1998) for a comprehensive social history of Blackpool, justifiably thought to be 'the world's first working-class seaside resort' (1998: 172).
6. A classic sociological perspective would critique a modern sociology that is preoccupied by field research methods or universal theoretical models and is not 'thinking in terms of societies as developing structures' (Goldthorpe 1977: 184). John Goldthorpe has defended the relevance of history to soci-ology by arguing that 'according to the classic tradition, sociology is in effect a historical discipline' and that 'the comparative method, which more than any other is fundamental to the classic tradition, is also in large measure dependent upon history' (1977: 184). A thorough hermeneutic understand-ing of society and culture would show that interpretations of the past are dependent upon the social and historical contexts within which the reader is positioned, in the same way that present-day interpretations are dependent upon these extra-temporal contexts. By extra-temporal contexts, I mean contemporaneous interpretative positions that are informed not only by immediate social conditions but also by previous experiences and insights

that might consequently acquire the form of conventions, stereotypes, traditions and so on.

7. I assume that Northtown was abandoned because it might have been decoded by readers as a name that described its geography within Britain rather than its universal culture.

8. 2001 census information: http://www.statistics.gov.uk/census2001/downloads/pop2001ew.pdf

9. 'Sociology is the study of everyday life' according to countless university prospectuses.

10. The concept of self-identities is further discussed in Chapter 4.

11. I will only suggest a few parallels in this section but intend to marry gradually the ideas of Bakhtin and de Certeau to everyday youth music cultures as this chapter and others develop. See Tony Bennett (1986) for an account of how carnivalesque elements were particularly rife in Blackpool until the early 1960s when tradesmen and showmen would 'set up shop in the forecourts of houses on the promenade' and when 'a transgressive discourse embodied the practices of the popular classes and their preferred entertainments' (1986: 139 and 147). Bawdy music, singing and dancing in this 'promenadesque' context intermingled with more overtly carnivalesque practices, including excessive eating and drinking, fortune telling, quack doctors, mock auctioneers, peep shows, unlicensed stall holders, gypsies and other migrants, ventriloquists, phrenologists, astrologists, lay chiropodists and even sociologists (thanks to M-O), and then there was the 'screaming, flailing, bumping, crushing, vertigo and bodily exposure' (Walton 1998: 94) associated with Blackpool Pleasure Beach, consistently one of the most popular British tourist attractions over the past one hundred years.

12. Strict tempo was a 'dedication to metronomic exactitude' (Thomson 1989: 150) associated in particular with the music of Victor Sylvester and his dance band, as advocated by Sylvester in his well-read training manual *Modern Ballroom Dancing*.

13. Another important music medium at this time was, of course, sheet music. Some magazines included pages of sheet music for the latest popular tunes.

14. *Danceland* briefly changed its name to *Dance News* between 1941 and 1942 before reverting to its original title thereafter. Unfortunately, many issues were destroyed during the Second World War so that existing British Library records are incomplete.

15. This information is drawn from Stan Rowland's 'Memories of Wartime Blackpool' (available from Blackpool Central Library) and the *Blackpool Evening Gazette VE-Day Supplement* (May 1995: 19).

CHAPTER 4

Towards Everyday Consumption and Production: Approaching Music Audiences and Performances

In the previous chapter it was argued that de Certeau's (1984) 'tactics' and the idea of *texts as read* provided an alternative framework to orthodox structuralist accounts of dominance and resistance, as typified by much of the subcultures literature discussed in Chapter 2. In the context of audience research, the classic 'Encoding/decoding' model (Hall 1992) and the semiotics which informed it have been challenged by more detailed ethnographic investigations of everyday life. Abercrombie and Longhurst (1998) contend that these audience ethnographies reconfigured previous models of simple and mass audiences to those of diffused audiences. Simple audiences are co-present at live events such as theatre productions. Mass audiences consume events through media of mass communications, some events of which are simultaneously consumed by simple audiences. The BBC's *Top of the Pops*, for instance, is consumed by both a studio (simple) and a mass (television) audience. By contrast, diffused audiences are not party to any singular event but consume several via 'a fusion of different forms of the media' (1998: 76). Being a member of a diffused music audience is not like the spectacular experience of being a committed member of a youth subculture or other constructed youth cultural world. As Ulf Boëthius (1995) argues in relation to youth music and media consumption, 'Engagement has decreased; we do not listen or watch as attentively as we used to [. . .] the need for all-absorbing aesthetic experiences has diminished' (1995: 151). Rather, being an audience member in modern societies is 'constitutive of everyday life' and at the same time a performative experience because the media 'provide an important resource for everyday performance' (1995: 68 and 74). As such, diffused audiences can be situated within a 'Spectacle/Performance Paradigm' (hereafter SPP) – they engage in interactive processes of spectacle and narcissism because 'the aim of modern life is to see and be seen' (Abercrombie and Longhurst 1998: 81).

The SPP, then, considers spectacle and narcissism as processes in which diffused audience members play at being spectators *and* performers in multimedia contexts. John Urry's (1990: 16) analysis of how the tourist gaze constitutes 'gazes of taste' in the formation of a 'resort "hierarchy"'' is indicative of the spectacular gaze which is a more pervasive feature of everyday life beyond the contexts of tourism. Debord's spectacular society (1995) is simultaneously a narcissistic society in which individuals perceive reflections of themselves through interactions with others. Thus, the self is actively constructed and managed within diffused audience contexts where 'An adequate performance demands attention to the outward face, and the management of appearance is therefore a major preoccupation' (Abercrombie and Longhurst 1998: 93). Moreover, contemporary diffused audiences highly skilled in multimedia literacy are less constrained than previous generations of mass audiences by the potentially ideological functions of singular media texts such as television programmes. Rather than form subcultures in resistance to dominant ideologies, diffused consumers tend to group around networks of enthusiasms which are collectively honed and enacted outside of wider formal structures of power and ownership. Everyday diffused consumer practices are more complex than could ever be evinced by hegemony. In the shift towards an SPP, 'the *ordered* structure given by the IRP [within which Hall operated] is being undermined by the *disorder* of actual audience response – a disorder of *unpredictability* not of *resistance*' (1998: 32). Fragmented consumption experiences such as viewing the television while listening to music on the radio or surfing the Internet render theoretical accounts centred on a particular medium (such as Hall's model, which was applied specifically to television) to be artificial representations of these complex everyday contexts of consumption.

Despite this tangible shift in emphasis in audience research from the IRP to the SPP, Hall's 'Encoding/decoding' model was hugely influential in early media consumption research (Morley 1980; Hebdige 1979) and still sets the agenda for much debate in media and cultural studies to the present day. The rest of this chapter follows on closely from the previous one by seeking to conceptualise music consumption and its necessary 'other' – production – within a paradigmatic framework that suspends orthodox structuralist models of hegemony polarised by dominant and subordinate socio-economic classes, in favour of dynamic interactionist models that systematically explore concrete, everyday cultural practices. These dynamic interactionist approaches to cultural practices do not all neatly fit into the same 'spectacle, narcissism and performance' framework but they necessarily contain elements of the SPP in their movement away from structural Marxism. After first evaluating the most ground-breaking theories into everyday consumption and production, I will apply those theories of greater usefulness for the aims of this research to the relative merits of studies into audiences and – more pressingly – performances.

Everyday consumer and producer practices

A distinct consumer culture complete with imagination, choice and emotions has only recently warranted study in its own right, freed from the dominant Marxist paradigm of 'almighty production' (Adorno 1991) prominent within sociology for most of the twentieth century. As Peter Corrigan (1997) points out,

> now the majority of the populace have access to the ever-growing consumerist fruits of the productivist tree, and so perhaps it is time to stand Marx on his head and claim that consumption, and not production, is the central motor of contemporary society. (1997: 1)

Whilst the sociology, media and cultural study of consumption has justifiably become a significant concern for contemporary research activities and funding, the most fruitful studies have attempted to map consumption on to different modes of production to show that 'Consumption is not the end of a process, but the beginning of another, and thus itself a form of production' (MacKay 1997: 7). As a result, the Marxist framework of mass capitalist production has been problematised by a shift in focus to modes of production independent of commodification that often emerge as a consequence of consuming commodities.

Before consideration of these studies that explore the relationship between everyday consumer and producer practices, a clearer definition of what I mean by 'practices' should be outlined since the term will be repeated frequently hereafter. Bourdieu (1977) has considered practices to be produced by the 'habitus' or 'strategy-generating principle enabling agents to cope with unforeseen and ever-changing situations' which is 'laid down in each agent by his [sic] earliest upbringing' (1977: 72 and 81).[1] Becker (1953; 1982) equated a practice with a process of learning to carry out an action such as smoking marijuana or playing the piano. Similar to Becker's notion of practice is that of Stephen Turner (2001), who has drawn an analogy between learning practices and learning languages:

> we communicate by virtue of sharing in the possession of this highly structured whole, a language, including the non-linguistic learned conditions for the use of the language, the practices. (2001: 121)

Like languages, practices needed to be learnt before they can be shared through contexts of social interaction. A cultural practice according to Pierre Mayol is thus bound to the concept of propriety; of knowing how to behave and act properly as judged by society. As such, a practice emerges from a family or social tradition and is 'reactualised from day to day across behaviours translating fragments of this cultural device into social visibility, in the same way that the utterance translates fragments of a discourse in speech' (de Certeau et al. 1998: 8 and 9). Theodore Schatzki (1996: 89) has suggested an alternative albeit related notion of social practice as 'a temporally unfolding and spatially dispersed nexus of doings and sayings' that involves three processes: first, understanding what to say and do; second, following instructions and rules on how to say and do it; and third, engaging in 'teleoaffective' structures such as emotions, tasks and moods during the saying and doing. The second process is aligned to the discussion in the previous section about conventions that are routinely required to be followed in carnivalesque and art world contexts. All these definitions of practices stress the requirement of learning but Schatzki's third process of social practice extends these definitions to include the consequences of having learnt what to say and do. As teleoaffective structures of practices change, grow or decline, so in turn occur changes in how those practices are understood and learnt (and taught). This definition of 'practice' is endorsed here in considering how consumer and producer practices affect changes on each other.

Following de Certeau (1984), John Fiske (1987; 1989a; 1989b), Paul E. Willis et al. (1990), Roger Silverstone (1989; 1994) and Mike Featherstone (1991) have all argued that everyday consumptive practices are to some extent also productive practices. Everyday life is understood to be an important site for articulating creative human agency. Fiske shows that consumers are able to radically reinterpret media texts by experiencing subversive pleasures in oppositional meanings. As discussed in Chapter 2, young female fans of Madonna can gain empowerment over their male peers by using the lyrics in her songs to express their superiority in everyday social contexts. A 'culture of things-in-use' with which Celia Lury (1996: 10) defines the materiality of contemporary consumer culture is close to Fiske's examples of how media products are appropriated – in ways akin to the youth subcultures theorised by the CCCS. Indeed, Fiske ultimately grounds his arguments in the same simplistic dichotomy between dominant and subordinate classes that I argued earlier to be the structuralist flaw of subcultural theories.[2] Willis et al.'s *Common Culture* (1990) also ultimately operates within this structural Marxist IRP but is better grounded in cultural practices than Fiske's text-based studies.

The authors' notion of 'the symbolic creativity of the young is based in their everyday informal life and infuses with meaning the entirety of the world as they see it' (Willis et al. 1990: 98). Outside the boredom and routine of paid work, young people throw increasing impetus behind organising their leisure activities to create their own cultural forms, spaces and identities. The role of music within this informal economy of symbolic creativity warrants further discussion here because Willis et al.'s ethnographic findings can be applied to an alternative paradigm closer to the SPP.

Home-taping, for example, is an act of collective symbolic creativity partaken in by a group of record collectors who compile tracks on cassette tapes from the radio or a record collection for purposes of exchange. Social networks develop from these exchanges to form common cultures of creativity (through tape editing and selecting practices) and appreciation (through collecting and compiling). Another example of symbolic creativity is music-making in the form of DIY (Do It Yourself) recording and mixing. Tracks played simultaneously on two decks are mixed together to create a new cassette or Compact Disk (CD) recording from a combination of existing vinyl recordings. As such, 'the hardware and software of consumption have become the instruments and the raw materials of a kind of cultural production' (1990: 77). DIY mixing is one of several 'grounded aesthetics' of youth music-making that bypass orthodox classical training in instrument playing, performance and composition. Instead, music-making begins during the phase of pleasurable music consumption and fandom (1990: 79) in which particular styles of popular music are sampled or imitated. Music provides a resource that transcends everyday banalities such as insecure employment and boredom at school or work. If Abercrombie's and Longhurst's model of the diffused audience continuum within the SPP is applied to these two forms of cultural production, home-taping might be akin to the knowledgeable media productivity gained through immersion in particular kinds of music 'within the network of the enthusiasm' (1998: 146), while DIY mixing might be positioned further towards the extremity in this continuum, in the realm of petty production. Both practices would be at least equivalent to enthusiasms in the sense of highly organised networks of specialised media users who engage in collective activities rather than shared individual tastes.

Silverstone's (1994) consumption cycle usefully attempts to understand how consumers feed back to producer practices, which are in turn fed back to consumers. This model of mutually dependent consumption and production as informed by everyday life – and particularly domestic – economies is situated firmly outside an IRP which assumes that producer and consumer practices are arbitrarily related. Thus the initial phase of commodification in material and mediated products both influences and is influenced by five 'dependent moments of consumption' termed imagination, appropriation, objectification, incorporation and conversion (1994: 123–4). The moment of consumer imagination can occur either before or after the purchasing of a product. Anticipation of the pleasure that might arise from a prospective purchase as well as the work of attaching pleasurable meanings on to the purchased product 'either as a compensation for disappointed desire or as a celebration of its fulfilment' (1994: 126) are compared by Silverstone to those productive, imaginative tactics outlined by de Certeau and typified by speed readers. Following imagination, the phase of appropriation occurs when consumers transform the mediated and public meanings of products – that are initially consumed via advertisements or supermarket shelves – into their personal and private meanings in post-purchase contexts such as bodies and living rooms. Objectification then occurs through the embedment of new in relation to existing products into everyday domestic consumer lives. Television, for instance, becomes objectified in everyday household interactions: 'accounts of television programmes, the characters in soap operas, or events in the news, provide a basis for identification and self-representation' (1994: 128–9).

Following objectification, incorporation occurs when household products become 'a part of the furniture' and float freely among the ebbs and flows of everyday life, such as 'the use of radio as a companion for the tea-break' (1994: 129). The final moment within the consumption cycle involves the conversion of products with everyday personal and domestic meanings into products that are capable of conveying meanings outside the home, in public contexts such as offices and cafés. Television programmes thus become topics of conversation with friends, colleagues and even strangers, having already become topics of conversation with family members or stimuli for individual thoughts and feelings. Consumption has now turned full circle to inform the phase of production or commodification that initiated its cycle:

> The consumption cycle, perhaps more of a spiral in its dialectical movement, acknowledges that objects not only move in and out of commodification as such [. . .] but that their status as commodities (and their meaning as a commodity) is constantly in flux. (1994: 124)

To question the emphasis on the commodity values of material products associated with the Marxist paradigm of commodity fetishism expounded by Adorno (1991) among others is the most telling contribution by this cyclic model. However, there appears to be a fundamental limitation to Silverstone's model. This cycle or spiral rotates unidirectionally based on assumptions about the transitions of a purchased product's meanings from public to private (through appropriation) and later from private to public (through conversion) contexts of consumption. Although the purchasing of mediated products such as television programmes or music on the radio never strictly occurs – and Silverstone acknowledges this point about non-material products – there is still the suggestion that both mediated and material products go through some sense of personal embodiment or private ownership within this consumer cycle of transitions. Silverstone's model therefore seems to accommodate tentatively both mediated and material consumption but ignores the obvious differences between public and private consumer practices that do and do not involve purchase. Non-purchasing consumer practices such as listening to music in shops or watching televised football in pubs, for example, would seem capable of being initiated during the public as well as mediated moment of *commodification* and bestowed with social meanings via everyday public interactions during the moment of *conversion* without necessarily passing through those private consumer moments of *appropriation* in-between.[3]

A different perspective on cultural consumption and production is suggested by Mike Featherstone's (1991) discussion of the aestheticisation of everyday life, which in part finds ethnographically informed support from Willis et al.'s (1990) notion of grounded aesthetics. Grounded aesthetics are honed and produced *in* consumption contexts, so that 'messages are now not so much "sent" and "received" as *made* in reception' (1990: 135). Similarly, one indicator of the aestheticisation of everyday life is the consumer experience of making meaningful 'the rapid flow of signs and images which saturate the fabric of everyday life in contemporary society' (Featherstone 1991: 66). MTV, for example, subtly targets music videos – which function as low art forms like advertisements – that pastiche forms of high art such as film noir to youth audiences who are required to acquire skills in detecting these intertextual moments (1991: 69). Although everyday life as a constructed aesthetic consumer experience is often associated with postmodernism, Featherstone suggests that such an experience is encapsulated by the fictional figure of the *flâneur* – often regarded as a phenomenon of modernity and early metropolitan cultures. Charles Baudelaire's pioneering depiction of the *flâneur* is of 'an "I" with an insatiable appetite for the "non-I"' whose 'passion and his [sic] profession are to become one flesh with the crowd' (Baudelaire 1964: 9 and 10). The figure cut here contrasts starkly with the objective detachment personified by Georg Simmel's (1971b) 'stranger', in that it actively lives to be observed and attended to by its community, and to gain a fleeting identity among individuals it can know only fleetingly. The visual pleasure felt by 'the painter of modern life' is in observing while being observed in the crowded, impersonal context of the city.

Featherstone perceptively argues that a real-life *flâneur* who strolled around the crowded cities of the eighteenth and nineteenth centuries would not have maintained – nor sought to maintain – anonymity, particularly if their deportment and fashions embodied the wealth and intellect that they invariably enjoyed vis-à-vis the impoverished urban masses (Featherstone 1991: 75–6). Simmel (1971a) observed how the cosmopolitan attitude exercised by the higher social classes fuelled a fashion system that enabled them to differentiate their identities from those of the lowly majority in fleeting interactions within contexts of metropolitan impression-making. The bohemian *flâneur* is considered to have taken

> over in a displaced form much of the symbolic inversion and transgressions which were found in the carnival. It may be possible therefore to trace back to the carnival of the Middle Ages many of the figural aspects, the disconnected succession of fleeting images, sensations, de-control of the emotions and de-differentiation which have become associated with postmodernism and the aestheticisation of everyday life. (Featherstone 1991: 79)

The strength of Featherstone's argument is this reading of historical trends as informing social constants as well as changes. By associating *flânerie* with the 'carnivalesque', he is able to suggest a common theme running through modernity in which city streets and marketplaces become sites where different types of people and cultural objects interact to construct Bakhtin's (1984) previously discussed 'hybridisation' of everyday identities. Featherstone thus associates the aestheticisation of everyday life with Victorian Britain's carnivalesque music hall practices – laughter, sensationalism, melodrama and spectator participation – compared to the formal aesthetics of the proscenium arch theatre, wherein performers and spectators were kept at a comfortable distance. By extension, it seems plausible to associate aspects of *flânerie* and the 'carnivalesque' with the informal music consumer and producer practices of contemporary everyday networks of young enthusiasts such as those observed by Willis et al. (1990). Such concepts might also account for how shoppers interact with music that functions to reflect seasonal variations in retail sales, such as Christmas songs at Christmas and faster music during the January sales

(DeNora and Belcher 2000). I will explore these two social historical phenomena further in evaluating how research into diffused music audiences
and performances has shifted debate in the sociology of everyday life
towards alternative paradigms such as the SPP.

Diffused audiences and performances

So what implications might a diffused contemporary audience have had
on recent theories into music audiences and peformances? First in relation to audiences, ethnographic research into music consumption –
although growing – continues to be sparse compared to the weighty body
of television audience research, so popular music is relatively untested as
a series of dynamic, diffused consumer media. The need to resolve this
absence of empirical information is particularly acute given that popular
music pervades everyday experiences across various media and cultural
contexts (radio, cars, shops, television, the Internet, gyms and so on), and
not just for young people or necessarily when it is welcomed. Anahid
Kassabian (2002) has convincingly argued the case for the 'ubiquitous listening' of music in contemporary public and private places: 'whereas we
are accustomed to thinking of most music, like most cultural products, in
terms of authorship and location, this music comes from the plants and
the walls and, potentially, our clothes' (2002: 137).[4] The research presented later will reveal how the omnipresence and mobility of the various
media through which music is aired serve to produce regular contexts of
youth cultural exchange as well as conflict. Sara Cohen (1993: 127) has
pointed out that the important role of music in everyday life must be
gleaned from a 'focus upon people and musical practices and processes
rather than upon structures, texts or products', which is more or less the
motive behind this book and other attempts to reject a structuralist theoretical framework.

Another implication of the diffused audience model is the significance of
what might be called visual culture or more specifically the 'theatricalisation
of culture' (Kershaw 1994) in contemporary life. Baz Kershaw states that 'in
consuming theatre as a service we are more or less implicitly consuming the
ideologies of the society which built it' (1994: 177). Not dissimilar to the
argument about how carnivalesque aspects of everyday culture were imbued
in nineteenth-century music hall practices (Featherstone 1991), Kershaw
shows how the Victorian proscenium arch theatre reflected everyday capitalism, wherein the elite from the capitalist classes would have been the only
audience members able to afford seats in the stalls and upper circles while
the humble labouring classes made do with the galleries. Theatres built

today, however, no longer are designed with hierarchical seating arrangements and instead tend to charge the same price for all seats. Contemporary society is thus read as finer divisions of social classes that operate in more democratic conditions. Kershaw also considers the simple audience experience of live theatre to be a collective resistance to attempts to commodify consumption because such an experience has a creative use-value (in which audiences become co-producers of a temporal, non-material commodity) and denies an exchange-value (in which a material commodity is purchased under the false pretext of empowerment).

This method of interpreting consumption in everyday societies through aesthetic experiences such as theatre productions clearly resonates with Featherstone's (1991) perspective on the aestheticisation of everyday life. I would argue that recent changes in the theatrical experience against the backdrop of what have developed to be dominant mediated forms of entertainment have wider relevance to everyday consumption and production in general. Howard Barker's (1989) argument for a contemporary theatre that distinguishes itself from television has stressed the need to disrupt conventions of audience–actor separation:

> The audience will no longer sit in tiers. It will not be encouraged to think itself a jury [. . .] The actor will dominate the audience, not only by his [sic] performance but also by his elevation above the audience. (1989: 86)

One such style of production which has significantly impacted upon the theatrical experience is borrowed from British conventions of classical music promenade concerts or 'the proms'. Promenade theatre characterised the original production at London's Royal Court Theatre of Jim Cartwright's play *Road* (1986). In this production the actors were freed from the restrictions of the stage to perform within spaces conventionally reserved for spectating, whilst seats were allocated in such a way that many audience members were left without them and encouraged to mingle around spaces also used for performance. Whilst *Road*'s overt theatricality might seem unconventional in relation to the predominantly naturalist style of most contemporary drama, it nevertheless shared traits of what is known about Greek epic drama and Elizabethan theatre. These theatrical traditions resemble the carnivalesque sixteenth-century French marketplace and the *flâneur*'s vivid paintings of metropolitan life. Later in this chapter I will apply these ideas about diffused audiences in further developing the notion of promenade performances evident in relation to early youth music cultures. What is suffice to note so far is that these historical examples of everyday life aesthetics equate to interactions between simple and diffused audiences but appear not to accommodate the abstract, invisible mass audience configuration.

Second, the diffused audience model has had implications for a revised conceptualisation of music performances. Far from the orthodox view of performances as contexts solely of production, diffused music consumers perform tastes and identities through everyday producer *and* consumer practices. Much of the debate about tastes is important to the discussion of identities, and how individuals and groups perform these identities through everyday consumption and production. Specifically, the literature on omnivorous life narratives of cultural consumption reviewed in Chapter 2 can be centrally located within the SPP. For instance, the notion of 'emplotment' (Somers 1994) – a process by which individuals construct present identities from past biographies – has been applied to a reworking of the 'habitus' which recognises

> both individual as well as social dynamics [. . .] consumption practices are driven by performative processes directed at impressing others, processes directed at reassuring oneself, and also processes forming links and bonds with significant others. (Abercrombie and Longhurst 1998: 293 and 296)

This articulation of 'the self' to others through narratives is fundamental to an understanding of diffused, complex music performances that can be generated both through short-term and long-established consumer practices.

The argument that consumers enact performative identities both as a constitution of the self and of relations with 'significant others' is echoed by some of the literature on the broad sociological theme of everyday life. The following two sections on localities and scenes, then, resonate with Featherstone's (1991) association between metropolitan *flânerie* and the aestheticisation of everyday life, and Bakhtin's (1984) depiction of the carnivalesque marketplace. The figure of the *flâneur* and similar historical figurations are also cited as an influence on theories of self-identity (e.g. Giddens 1991; Bauman 1996) which I will evaluate thirdly. In the final section of this chapter I will apply consumer and producer practices to theories of self-presentation particularly informed by a dramaturgical model of everyday life (Goffman 1969a; V. Turner 1987). Focusing on young people's music consumption and production in everyday contexts, I will suggest that the most valuable concept to underscore this field of sociological enquiry is that of individual and group *performance*. The concept of performance has its indicators in practices of inconspicuous as well as conspicuous consumption, appearance and impression management, play and story-telling to name but a few. I will explore these indicators and the problems they pose to methods of researching performances. Earlier discussion of the notion of promenade contexts for performance will be developed more thoroughly by drawing an analogy between the promenade and carnivalesque practices of youth music cultures.

Localities

Localities as resources for as well as sites of performative identities have grown in conceptual significance in correspondence with the popularity of ethnographic audience research methods. One of the most comprehensive ethnographies of a cultural locale has been Ruth Finnegan's (1989) study of music-making in the large English town of Milton Keynes. Rather than focus upon a particular music activity or scene within this locality, she participated in several musical worlds, each with 'its own contrasting conventions about the proper modes of learning, transmission, composition or performance' (1989: 6). For example, whilst local orchestras retained the orthodox performance principle whereby musicians were trained to read conventional music notation, many local rock bands learnt to perform music through group experimentation and self-teaching. Finnegan draws on the previously discussed concept of art worlds (Becker 1982) wherein art is produced through collective practices rather than individual authorship. Art worlds, she argues, have 'successfully drawn attention to the interacting elements that enable the continuance of specified musical traditions' (Finnegan 1997a: 128). These art worlds or collaborative networks of enthusiasts include both performers and spectators. Indeed

> the audience in a live musical event are themselves part of the performance,
> playing the role (or range of roles) expected of audience participants in the
> appropriate music world – or, perhaps, disrupting the event by refusing to
> follow the conventions. (1997a: 137)

However, the conventions of these music worlds are rarely disrupted by unexpectedly spectacular, subcultural audience or performer roles, which accounts for the emergence and maintenance of local music traditions. Finnegan, then, considers localised art worlds to be almost entirely self-contained and sealed off from wider structural forces. Local music cultures – participated in by young and old – possess unique historic traditions of ritual enactment and performance that are largely untouched by global consumption patterns and mass media power.

Finnegan's study of Milton Keynes as a music locality can be situated within a wider field of sociological and geographical debate around changes in suburban and urban leisure cultures (e.g. Chaney 1994: 139–78;

Silverstone 1997; Chatterton and Hollands 2001; 2003). Whilst Paul Chatterton and Robert Hollands (2003) argue that urban nightlife in British cities like Newcastle, Leeds and Bristol has become increasingly exclusionary, privatised and regulated in the interests of national pub and bar operators, Frith (1997) supports Finnegan's argument that suburban people's leisure activities need to be taken as significant regardless of their workaday employment routines and regardless of their lack of power in relation to corporate entertainment industries. He considers suburbia to have provided the location for radical creative forces in post-war music and other art-school movements (see also Frith and Horne 1987). Not only have the suburbs of large cities such as London and Manchester become products of mass planning and mass media since their growth from the mid-twentieth century onwards, but they have also provided 'the setting in which art is most important as a mark of social difference' (Frith 1997: 278). Gary Cross (1997: 117) likewise points out that, 'The suburb was always as much a consumer market as a refuge from production,' the latter of which has tended to be of the industrial or commercial type located in urban centres. Suburban cultures, then, are generally represented as localities where leisurely cultural or artistic performances are enabled and enacted in stark contrast to the work-orientated routine and commerciality representative of urban cultures. In relation to localised *music* performances, at least, it would nevertheless be a mistake to suggest that suburbia has been the only place for creativity and enactment. Sara Cohen has shown how local music production and consumption in central urban areas of Liverpool 'reflected not only characteristics of the music business in general, but those of Liverpool itself' (1991: 19).

This celebration of the local and suburban as a kind of romantic refuge has been attacked by some commentators for constructing worlds in which the perceptions of agents are preferred to the structural conditions of a highly concentrated music industry dominated by international entertainment conglomerates. Dave Laing (1986) has argued that conditions are often favourable for Western cultural imperialism to disseminate into poorer countries through the uncontrollable business of music piracy. Whilst Western music companies do not directly profit from pirated sales of their artists' records, in the long term such music grows in popularity, which leads to increased quantities of legally imported records to the overall detriment of local and national music traditions. Furthermore, developments in digital technologies 'only make the distribution of music more flexible and efficient, and further eradicate the distance between, and cross the borders of, musical practices' (Fenster 1995: 84). If local music traditions can still emerge such as 'Seattle Sound' and 'Madchester', they are

'immediately and intimately articulated within a flexible international corporate structure or institutional grid' (1995: 85). Mark Fenster's argument
might be applied to many independent or 'indie' record labels during the
1990s that distributed grunge and indie sounds with financial backing from
their 'sister' US-based majors (i.e. one of the five major record companies).
However, this perspective leans too far back into the IRP by ignoring local
influences in favour of abstract economic statistics and functionalist analyses of capitalist production. An attempt to reconcile local with global cultural practices has been made by Will Straw (1991) in his comparison
between communities and scenes.

Scenes

A music scene might be defined as a pool of musical tastes and values that
are constantly susceptible to change; a 'cultural space in which a range of
musical practices coexist, interacting with each other within a variety of
processes of differentiation' (Straw 1991: 373). The same author contrasts
the *scene* with the more stable music *community* who are understood by
sociological variables (e.g. age) and are involved in 'an ongoing exploration
of one or more musical idioms said to be rooted within a geographically
specific historical heritage' (1991: 373). This transition from sociologically
measurable communities to less tangible cultural scenes has its symptoms
for Straw in changing trends in the Anglo–American music industry. These
changing trends are typified by the relatively steady popularity of mass
music movements such as stadium rock – for example, the defection of
Bruce Springsteen's male-dominated, worshipping concert community –
compared to the simultaneous rise of more localised, disposable music
scenes, such as the various ones that might be listed under the heading
'Dance Music'. Indeed, the term dance music is necessarily broad
and abstract but encouraged by marketers because it is one of the few
remotely adequate terms for branding a range of scenes – house, garage,
hip hop, trance, techno, R 'n' B and so on – not to mention the local
nuances within each of these scenes (in the case of house: acid house, old
skool Chicago house, Italian house, new skool house and so on). This
fusion of local and global influences within cultural scenes produces 'new
forms of the universalism of the diffused audience' (Abercrombie and
Longhurst 1998: 160) and provides a framework for analysing consumer
performances by relating the local to the global influences that shape these
scenes.

There are problems with the notion of music scenes, however, which
centre on the suggestion that they are at once defined by their places (or
localities, such as 'the Austin scene' (Shank 1994)) *and* spaces such as clubs,

record shops, old warehouses and so on. The conceptualisation of space is particularly problematic because it is usually theorised as that realm of musical activity which escapes global cultural influences. As such, these spaces within scenes smack of the semiotic 'spaces of symbolic defiance' practised by subcultures of resistance within a dominant-oppositional dichotomy that I have argued has hindered theoretical insights into young people's everyday interactions with music texts. Barry Shank's (1994) discussion of the rock 'n' roll scene as a 'signifying community' uses similar vocabulary to that found in definitions of youth subcultures:

> Such scenes remain a necessary condition for the production of exciting rock 'n' roll music capable of moving past the mere expression of locally significant cultural values and generic development – that is, beyond stylistic permutation – toward an interrogation of dominant structures of identification, and potential cultural transformation. (1994: 122)

Spaces are therefore conceived to be lived in by avid fans or alternative musicians rather than by less committed music consumers and producers: 'In fandom, identifications and investments with particular scenes are continually shifting, in flux, never forever in place or emplaced' (Olson 1998: 284). Perhaps this focus on 'that intensity of fan commitment and cultural production known as a scene' (Shank 1994: 122) explains why 'The term "scene" is usually deployed interchangeably with the notion of a music subculture' (Olson 1998: 270). The most recent contribution to the 'scenes' literature (Bennett and Peterson 2004) is a collection of studies, most of which continue to be biased towards intensive music practices such as music-making and fan networks. By contrast, analysis of research findings in Chapters 5 and 6 will conceptualise processes of casual as well as intense youth music consumption and production.

An improvement on the application of scenes which combines insights into emplaced localities is Bennett's epistemological view on the local as 'a series of discourses' rather than 'a definite space' (2000: 63). This view aptly illustrates the way in which local contexts have been conceptualised as politically charged, structuring contexts in much the same way as national and global contexts. Referring to David Chaney's (1993) work on the interplay between real and fictional narratives in 'lived out' contexts which are locally and globally fused, Bennett explored his fieldwork locations as sites of 'contested space'. In one instance, he suggested that hip hop-associated graffiti might represent – as well as be a visual realisation for – a way in which 'young people can negotiate those aspects of the local that they find least appealing' (Bennett 2000: 69). Similarities can be also usefully drawn between a record shop in Newcastle that specialises in hip hop and the music shops identified by Shank (1994) in ethnographic observations around Austin, Texas, with youth groups in both cities 'positioning themselves in relation to other music scenes located in the same city or town' (Bennett 2000: 154) rather than in relation to other national or world music cultures. Where scenes are closer tied to specific localised contexts rather than set against global trends, then, they would appear to offer more promising research routes and disprove the otherwise convincing argument that 'the concept of "scene" is not fundamentally concerned with audiences, and is unlikely to inspire empirical studies of them' (Hesmondhalgh 2002: 128).

Rob Drew's (2004: 77) study of karaoke is one of the few attempts to understand how 'casual public participation' might be accommodated by a music scene. Drew shows how karaoke differs from other music-making scenes in being more accessible and demonstrating different levels of involvement among its participants. Unlike the exclusivity associated with the typical notion of a scene as a network of committed members, karaoke in public entertainment venues is a relatively democratic, even apathetic pastime that nonetheless plays an important role in the local lives of those who come to sing or just listen. Quite simply, 'It is always possible to perform' (2004: 77) and this is why karaoke is more deeply embedded in everyday (public music) life than any other music-making scene. Drew's account is actually more in keeping with Bennett's (2000) focus on place and locality than the idea of scenes as cultural spaces. Becker's (2004) autobiographical discussion of socially and economically defined 'jazz places' together with Whiteley's (2004: 15) discussion of how hip hop expresses 'personal and group histories [. . .] that resonate with the formation of ethnic and geographic identities' are two further accounts which problematise the idea of spaces without localised roots. In Chapter 6 I will show how my sample of young people tended to perceive music practices – karaoke included – in concrete, local places that in turn provided the reference points for perceptions about the extent of scenic spaces within these places. An outcome of these perceptions of scenes within clearly defined localities was that the strength of music scenes was thought to differ from place to place.

Self-identities

Stuart Hall's post-structuralist claim that 'identities are constructed through, not outside, difference' (1996: 4) and therefore function ideologically by including and excluding other identities can say little about how agents come to perform identities and understand them outside wider structural relationships of power. In his work on authority contexts, Abercrombie has noted that, 'Many sociological accounts make it difficult to get at the idea of resistance to *authority* because they are more usually concerned with resistance to *power*' (1994: 48). Authority contexts provide useful examples of how consumer self-identities are performed and constructed because their various forms are rarely deemed to be bound together by unilateral motives akin to a hegemonic bloc (1994: 49). Consumers are therefore related to producers in contexts of authority whereby producers try to control what meanings can be ascribed to their products, whilst consumers resist producer authority by assigning new meanings to those products. Abercrombie has further suggested that consumers have a strategic advantage over producers in the ways that they can play with products in pleasurable ways that conflict with the sincerity with which producers ply their trade. Within these authority contexts, then, consumers have freedom to perform identities through the meanings that they appropriate to products that they consume. Contrary to Hall's (1996) claim which is closer to the IRP, consumption in authority contexts can enable the internal construction of self-identities through playful pleasures that mass producers cannot determine.

Furthermore, Abercrombie states that 'an apparent transfer of authority to consumers' (1994: 56) can occur for short periods when producers are competing with each other for the market share of a given industry. It could be argued, then, that the current fragmentation of the popular music industry indicated by the multitude of music genres in marketing currency amounts to such a period of consumer authority to dictate subsequent market developments. The self-identities thus played out by consumers in seemingly empowered authority roles can temporarily lead to contextual changes in the resources made available to meet their desires. Grossberg (1984; 1994) has argued that everyday consumer empowerment is exactly what rock 'n' roll music has authorised through the production of an organised network of practices and events (1984: 227). Rock 'n' roll's 'power lies not in what it says or means but in what it does in the textures and contexts of its uses' (1984: 233). However, the empowered self-identities of rock 'n' roll fans which perhaps represented genuine authority roles in the early post-war period can now 'provide no challenge to the dominant organisations of desire' (1984: 257) because everyday life contexts can only be pessimistically conceived to be 'daily life becoming routinised [. . .] Everyday life is predictable, and, paradoxically, that predictability is itself a kind of luxury and privilege' (Grossberg 1994: 51). This pessimistic conception of everyday life is shared by Michael Bull's study of personal-stereo use in which 'The everyday is defined critically as being unable to provide the significance or meaning desired by users' (2000: 165). Management of the mundanity of everyday life through mobile music technologies, however, is an oversimplified interpretation of the intricacies of everyday consumer and producer practices which this book aims to explore. Despite the relative impotence of contemporary rock culture, Grossberg (1994) is more optimistic about how it can still suggest an alternative to the routinised aspects of everyday life where authority and empowerment might be possible.

Anthony Giddens (1991) also refers to 'authorities' as increasingly diverse together with a 'pluralisation of contexts of action' in a late modern age when 'lifestyle choice is increasingly important in the constitution of self-identity and daily activity' (1991: 5). Self-identities in these diverse 'contexts of action' are performed by flexible and 'reflexively mobilised' bodies that are constructed and try to be controlled by the self through processes that are sometimes associated with narcissism (making-up, styling hair and so on). One interpretation of these lifestyle choices might be that 'the body plays a mediating role between consumer activities and the cultural constitution of the self' so that 'cultural goods are consumed not merely for their use-value (their material utility), but for their sign value (for what they signify)' (Jagger 2000: 46). The constitution of self-identities through the signs of consumption is close to the postmodernist Baudrillardian view that 'individuals use commodities and their random, open-ended meanings to continually reinvent themselves' (2000: 52). This notion of the mobile consumer self-identity as a *process* rather than an expression or what Frith refers to as 'a becoming not a being' (1996: 109) has implications for homologous youth subcultures (Willis 1972; 1978) and ostensibly homologous taste cultures (Bourdieu 1984; Thornton 1995):

> What I want to suggest [. . .] is not that social groups agree on values which are then expressed in their cultural activities (the assumption of the homology models) but that they only get to know themselves *as groups* (as a particular organisation of individual and social interests, of sameness and difference) *through* cultural activity, through aesthetic judgement. Making music isn't a way of expressing ideas; it is a way of living them. (Frith 1996: 111)

Consumer self-identities, then, are simultaneously constituted and performed through social and cultural practices that can reflexively change or even reinvent the identities of individuals within groups, and therefore the identities of the groups themselves.

The 'reflexively mobilised' constitution of everyday music consumer self-identities is nicely demonstrated by Sloboda and O'Neill (2001), who argue that music in everyday contexts has certain emotional functions rather than being central to people's lives or significant for its own sake. Using an 'experience sampling method' in which respondents carried electronic pagers with them to record their music experiences every few hours, they found that few respondents considered their music listening to be concentrated or focused during daily activities. Rather, music consumption in public places functioned to enable certain self-presentations – as a soundtrack to prevent other people overhearing intimate conversations – and it was only in the private arena 'where emotional work of one sort or another could be accomplished with the help of music' (2001: 421). Self-presentations of music consumption and production will be considered in more detail in the following section but the emotional qualities of music – at their most revealing in highly personal, private contexts such as moments of grieving – should not be underestimated in the constitution of self-identities. A further analysis of music and self-identity (Hennion 2003) has perceptively argued that any musical work only exists in the act of it being performed and consumed because music – perhaps more so than any other cultural form – lacks a material dimension and the performance of music expresses its immateriality.

Zygmunt Bauman (1996) states that the postmodernist 'problem of identity' is not how to construct one but 'how to avoid fixation and keep the options open' because the lack of a historical sense of progress means that, 'No consistent and cohesive life strategy emerges from the experience which can be gathered in such a world' (1996: 18 and 25). The modernist figure of the pilgrim whose single-mindedness and sense of linear direction was unwavering, then, has been replaced by four postmodernist figures: the stroller, vagabond, tourist and player. The stroller is similar to the *flâneur* but is as likely to stroll around multimediascapes by 'zapping' remote controls as around shopping malls and city streets. The vagabond in a postmodernist sense is the stranger who never acquires a local identity 'because of the scarcity of settled places' which requires him or her to have mobile careers and lifestyles (1996: 29). The tourist seeks out the novel and new in an escape from mundane daily experience. And finally, the player is the figure that is willing to embrace the rules and outcomes of a series of life-games or life-chances in the pursuit of promotion and success. These four postmodernist life strategies may not be easy to measure empirically but they provide an analytical framework for comparing self-identities in different everyday consumer contexts, as I will attempt to do in Chapters 5 and 6. As was noted earlier about the features of *flânerie* and the carnivalesque in specific portrayals of everyday social worlds, their historical figurations – whether fictional or not – are important 'products of their time' in concrete, interactive contexts.

In reference to Bauman's ideas about consumer freedom (1988), however, Alan Warde (1994) has usefully problematised how lifestyles are conceived:

> The notion of life-style indicates constraints, imposed by group belonging, on individual choice [. . .] the consumer chooses the group as much as, and probably more than, the style; and membership of the group commands a certain path through the enormous number of commodities on sale. (1994: 69–70)

An instance of how group belonging potentially constrains individual freedom to choose their own identities through consumption is the context of peer group dynamics in the policing of what is 'good' and 'bad' music. The youth cultural omnivore who expresses eclectic tastes in group interviews, as Frith (1996) suggests above, may actually be 'living out' the values of expressing eclectic tastes within everyday activities such as informing adult researchers in educational settings. Christina Williams (2001), for example, in interpreting whether or not her student interviewees used music to construct personal identities concluded that, 'It may be that they do use music in this way [. . .] but what is interesting is that they were extremely reluctant to admit to it' (2001: 233). The performance of self-identities, therefore, seems to be constrained by the maintenance of a sense of group belonging in fluid, mobile contexts such that, 'people move in and out of subcultures and in and out of fandom, and that popular music is integrated into everyday life where its significance shifts according to different situations' (2001: 225). The maintenance of a sense of group belonging perhaps explains why Williams's respondents like some of my own (as discussed in the following chapters) generally claimed that other people's identities – particularly younger than themselves – rather than their own were influenced by particular types of music.

Self-presentations

Self-presentations can be distinguished from self-identities as the more elusive practices of consumption that enable performers to guide impressions that others make of them and be guided by expressions of them made by others. As such, self-presentation conceptualises simultaneous relations between consumers and producers along an ever-moving continuum through simple audience interactions. It might be considered, for instance, how the process of 'disclosive communication' outlined by Erving Goffman (1969a) applies to club cultures and more specifically the everyday club cultural activity of courting:

> When individuals are unfamiliar with each other's opinions and statuses, a feeling-out process occurs whereby one individual admits his [sic] views or statuses to another a little at a time. After dropping his guard just a little he waits for the other to show reason why it is safe for him to do this, and after this reassurance he can safely drop his guard a little bit more. By phrasing each step in the admission in an ambiguous way, the individual is in a position to halt the procedure of dropping his front at the point where he gets no confirmation from the other, and at this point he can act as if his last disclosure were not an overture at all. (1969a: 189)

Those who participate in club cultures may share homologous tastes and values but the feature which they are most likely to share – their sexuality (Thornton 1995: 112) – ironically engenders differences between masculine and feminine performances. One of the earliest studies to adopt a Goffmanian perspective on consumption contexts observed a variety of techniques that dancers deployed to manage the stigma of being seen to actively seek sexual relations. 'Coming with friends' or 'coming late' were techniques used by actors to express their limited involvement even when courtship was their secret intention (Berk 1977: 534). Similarly, 'Becoming overly involved in side events such as music or drinking or in conversation with one's companion are other ways of escaping' (1977: 540). If the club cultural world is constructed as an intensely involved community whose subcultural capital is shared and circulated among its members, different music consumers in perhaps more mainstream clubs and discotheques could be argued to invest different degrees of involvement in the courtship performance.

Self-presentation theory not only highlights differences between the discourses of club cultures and individual clubbers, but also between these discourses and groups of clubbers, or what Goffman refers to as 'teams'. He states that, 'if performers are concerned with maintaining a line they will select as team-mates those who can be trusted to perform properly' (1969a: 95). As such, teams will generally be formed by a team director who disciplines their team-mates when they perform to audiences and allocates roles to each team member from the various characters, sign-equipment and props that are conventional to the social context (1969a: 102–3). This theatrical model of team performance and management is clearly applicable to young people's peer and friendship groups. It helps to explain how club cultures can provide a sense of membership and belonging, but also how constraints within and between friendship groups are created by the tense relations between different performing roles. Further, Goffman's account of regionalisation in the performance of self-presentations lends itself to a convincingly micro-social perspective on nightclub environments. In 'front region' performances such as dancing on dance floors, focused social interactions tend towards politeness and are relayed by conversation. However, 'back region' performances are perceived through the eyes of any beholders, so unfocused interactions such as glances tend towards decorum and are relayed by comportment as well as conversation. Goffman notes that, 'Performers can stop giving expressions but cannot stop giving them off' (1969a: 111), so the first-time clubber who controls their 'front' to impress hipness or coolness will probably be unable to conceal the eccentric 'back' that they express to regular clubbers. Regions within club cultures might also serve to exclude audiences from actors, as Berk observed at the singles' dance: 'Individuals may physically locate themselves in such inaccessible places as behind a door, in a dark corner or wedged behind a group of tables' (1977: 536).

Malbon's is the most recent study of youth cultural consumption to deploy Goffman's self-presentation thesis. He draws on Judith Butler's notion of how gender identities are constructed rather than innate to such an extent that *acting out* gender is akin to 'performative acts within theatrical contexts' (Butler 1990: 272) and 'notions of identification are always performative' (Butler 1999: 136–41). Malbon (1999) contends that

> through alloying together these two approaches to performativity we can improve our understandings of how the consuming experience of the [clubbing] crowd can be simultaneously expressive (Goffmanian) and constructive (Butlerian) of self. (1999: 29)

The benefits of combining these two approaches include a focus on the significant dynamic between self-investment in bodily presentation and reinforcement of group identities; on the relationships between the different spaces of performative consumption (e.g. back and front regions) and how the experience of these spaces are impinged by structural powers; and on performativity as a process of everyday life rather than a political standpoint within the IRP. Malbon argues that the playful vitality of clubbing consumer performances is a celebration of 'being together' in crowd contexts where 'There is a collusion between the clubbers as audience and the clubbers as performers' and clubbers 'can slip between consciousness of self and consciousness of being part of something much larger' (1999: 83 and 74). The clubber in the crowd starts, then, to resemble the man of the crowd (Poe 1967) and the painter of modern life (Baudelaire 1964) who performs an everyday identity within a particular milieu or even, perhaps, neo-tribe.

It is Malbon's apt example of a non-clubbing music crowd comprising individuals who perform both consumer and producer roles that provides useful empirical support for the concept of promenade performances introduced earlier:

> The annual Proms Concerts at the Royal Albert Hall where 'revellers' (never merely 'listeners' at the Proms – a notion that is interesting in itself) traditionally not only stand and dance (if somewhat minimally), but even 'dare' to cheer, shout and sing – they actively embody the performance in many ways as much as the orchestra on the circular stage. (1999: 84)

The promenade concert, like the dance club or rock concert, is a self-serving everyday locale akin to the carnivalesque marketplace and the nineteenth-century music hall. Self-presentations are simultaneously performed and constructed; expressed by and impressed upon the identities of individuals and groups as a whole by 'living out' their cultural practices. The notion of 'promenade' in a wider sense, therefore, can serve to diminish effectively the perceived separation between everyday consumption and production practices. By definition, promenade performances are thus highly interactive and localised phenomena that require a certain degree of learning through practices of demonstration and display, whilst at the same time such performances might be indirectly moulded by national and global influences.

Interestingly, several parallels can be drawn here between promenade and Bakhtin's (1984) carnivalesque performances. The 'cris' of cosmopolitan street traders selling worldly goods could apply to either the sixteenth-century marketplace, the twentieth-century seaside resort or the more contemporary thoroughfare. Highly visual as well as oral communication practices are conventional to both contextual frameworks too and therefore also tend to parallel performance practices as conceived in art worlds (Becker 1982; Finnegan 1989). And just as the Edwardian 'promenades' referred both to acts of walking and the scenic walkways themselves, so the 'carnivalesque' encapsulates both acts of street theatre and a description of where they were placed. Furthermore, carnivalesque and promenade performances both enact everyday co-present movement but situate this movement within those slightly more extraordinary interactions amid leisure that are nevertheless commonplace to work and other everyday contexts. As discussed in the previous chapter, though, contemporary

applications of promenading not only arise from co-present communicative contexts but are delayed through mediated communicative contexts
whereby, for instance, a celebrity transmits embodied and performative
resources to viewers who follow or modify this fashion trend in everyday
relations with others, who in turn are influenced by such trends.

Self-presentations as consumer performances need to be understood
through the methodology of radical contextualism suggested by Ang
(1996) – as discussed in Chapter 2 with respect to fan cultures – so as to
enable researchers to solicit more detailed information on how such
processes of everyday promenading are enacted. Tia DeNora's (1999; 2000)
suggestion that music can both reactivate and construct personal memories,
for example, is grounded in interpretations of radically contextual biographical accounts:

> The telling is of course part of the presentation of self to self and other(s).
> Such reliving, in so far as it is experienced as an identification with/of
> 'the past', is part of the work of producing one's self as a coherent being
> over time, part of producing a retrospection that is in turn a resource for
> projection into the future, a cueing in to how to proceed [. . .] Musically fos-
> tered memories thus produce past trajectories that contain momentum.
> (1999: 48)

Central to DeNora's argument here that music can become a technology
of the self is the metaphor of personal maps on which music within everyday contexts might serve as a structuring force of human agency (1999:
54). If music has the power to structure personal histories, as has been
suggested elsewhere (Richards 1998; Bourdieu 1984; Abercrombie and
Longhurst 1998), it might be proposed that music can also structure local,
regional and perhaps even national identities. Hollands (1995) has claimed
that the demise of industrial production in Newcastle has meant that

> if young adults can never be Geordies in a true occupational sense, such an
> identity can be derived from a selective borrowing of historical images and
> traits, which are then combined with present day experiences and realities in
> other spheres. (1995: 20–1)

Consumer self-presentations, then, can be performances of a particular
historical archetype such as the proletariat 'Geordie hard man' or the carefree 'mod' as well as performances borrowed from more contemporary
figurations such as – in present-day 2005 – the 'garage MC' or urban
rapper. How consumers make sense of the everyday promenade performances that they enact and observe may require a retrospective search for

presentations of themselves and others in past experiences which they can comfortably interpret from hindsight to be a golden age in their lives.

Summary

The aim of this chapter has been to evaluate the usefulness of perspectives on consumption and production informed by theories on everyday life as applied to literature about audiences and performances. Particularly useful to thinking about how music can be conceived as an everyday consumer and producer practice has been perspectives on the carnivalesque marketplace (Bakhtin 1984) and the productive tactics of consumers/(speed) readers (de Certeau 1984). These perspectives typify a fundamental shift from the IRP to an SPP or some similar paradigm which avoids situating all acts of human agency within dominant cultural or hegemonic struggles. The IRP within which is situated subcultural and other prominent youth cultural theories – critiqued in Chapter 2 – still also situates much contemporary research into everyday consumption and production, particularly with regard to enduring concepts such as the homologous taste arbitrator known as the 'habitus' (Bourdieu 1977) and scenes that overcelebrate fandom (Shank 1994; Fiske 1989a; 1989b). There is, though, a convincing counter-offensive in evidence from approaches that emphasise the localised and self-contained enactment of cultural practices (Becker 1982; Finnegan 1989; 1997a) informed by radically contextualised narratives (Hermes 1995; Ang 1996; Richards 1998; DeNora 1999). If cultural practices are defined as processes of learning what and how to say and do certain activities so that they become familiar and routine, the usefulness of approaches that detail the everyday interactions between practitioners who engage in what might be construed as 'teleoaffective' structures of thoughts and feelings (Schatzki 1996) becomes clear. Learning how to consume and produce music on an everyday basis, for example, occurs in localised contexts such as schools and homes, and is articulated through personal narratives either about the self or significant others in which – even if global media appear to dominate the agenda about what is available – co-present influences ultimately shape literacies and tastes.

The notion of performances in everyday life has suggested the most fruitful line of enquiry to employ in relation to the empirical data that I will analyse in the following chapters, although aspects of fan and taste cultures will be employed too. Ideas about the collusive relations between consumption and production in diffused audience contexts where local and global influences often intersect have been particularly enlightened by the notion of promenade performances. By favouring the conception of spaces within emplaced localities rather than constitutive of autonomous scenes for the enactment of music practices, I have tentatively proposed some characteristics of promenade performances that are shared with the carnivalesque practices of Rabelais's marketplace (Bakhtin 1984). Promenade performances are evident in the formation of self-identities and self-presentations that develop within everyday contexts of demonstration and display. Moreover, promenade performances share facets of both highly localised and global meanings that are perceived in relation to the former contexts. Everyday consumption and production is thus performed in Goffmanian (1969a) teams through impression management and identity playing, where agents tend to draw on cultural repertoires to frame or 'emplot' a temporarily extraordinary role for themselves other than that routinised one which they ordinarily occupy. Later chapters, then, will build upon an understanding of how young people interact with music in their everyday consumer and producer practices rather than construct a music subculture or movement around such practices.

The research methodology deployed hereafter broadly supports the ethnographic turn in audience research – particularly with regard to individual and group interviewing methods – that has improved upon research dependent upon surveys or purely textual analyses. Nonetheless, this research is informed by a methodological pluralism. It disassociates itself particularly from positivist perspectives without wishing to advocate a wholly constructivist point of view. So my role as the sole researcher tended to position me closer to the hermeneutic tradition of phenomenology (Schutz 1972) than to Simmel's classic portrait of the objectivity of the stranger (1971b). According to Alfred Schutz's phenomenological methodology,

> sociology has to employ 'constructs of the second degree', whereas everyday actors operate with 'constructs of the first degree'. Sociology's concepts are produced and used for scientific purposes, but they refer to phenomena – human actions – which already have meaning in common-sense terms, that is, as first-degree constructs. The sociologist must clearly relate these two levels of concepts. Only in this way can sociology attain its scientific goal of formalised knowledge of social life without losing contact with the everyday world. (Cuff, Sharrock and Francis 1990: 172)

The spirit of phenomenology, then, is very much in keeping with approaches to the sociology of everyday life where at least as much attention needs to be applied to first-degree constructs (i.e. concepts used by respondents in their own perceptions of everyday contexts) as to second-degree constructs (i.e. concepts used by the researcher in response to perceptions of respondents' own perceptions of everyday contexts). The three methods deployed here provoked both first-degree and second-degree constructs in various relationships. Simple observation[5], for instance, provided my second-degree with first-degree constructs by importantly adding a visual dimension to the other, mostly verbal forms of data retrieval. Survey[6] and particularly interview[7] accounts, by contrast, enabled first-degree and what at times approached second-degree constructs by reflexively informed everyday actors, as well as my own second-degree constructs that similarly were informed by reflexive responses.

Notes

1. Bourdieu's notion of the 'habitus' is based on the conviction that 'although diverse and varied, consumption practices are socially structured' (MacKay 1997: 5). I have argued earlier that the structured and structuring principle of the 'habitus' denies the performative power of everyday consumer and producer practices.
2. Although Fiske (1996) has since retracted from the argument that everyday consumption is radically subversive, his argument has continued to situate consumers in relation to mass media institutions by calling for the increased availability of alternative audiovisual productions, which hardly inspires the gathering of adequate empirical information to fill a major void left by his semiotic approach.
3. In Chapter 5 I apply Silverstone's consumption cycle to the music media practices talked about and enacted by the young people whom I interviewed and observed.
4. Closely associated with the contemporary notion of diffused music audiences is Ron Moy's (2005 forthcoming) argument that the active, close 'listening' of the 'hi-fi generation' during the 1960s and 1970s has been replaced by a mode of ambient 'hearing' among today's youth music consumers.
5. Simple observation as defined by Eugene Webb et al. is where 'the observer has no control over the behaviour or sign in question, and plays an unobserved, passive and nonintrusive role in the research situation' (1966: 112). In this sense, simple observation is an alternative to the practical complexity of assimilation associated with participant observation. Citing Naroll and Naroll (1963), Webb et al. discuss the problem of 'exotic data' which tend to be generated by participant observers who accord to anthropological conventions: 'The observer is more likely to report on phenomena which are different from those of his [sic] own society or subculture than he is to report on phenomena common to both' (Webb et al. 1966: 114). This problem of overemphasis on the extraordinary and spectacular has been a flaw of several subcultural accounts. A cautious approach to analysing 'exotic data' was thus deployed.

6. Data from 232 questionnaire replies were inputted into and analysed using the statistical software package SPSS for Windows Version 10. Respondents were aged between fifteen and thirty years.

7. Fifty-two semi-structured group (32) and individual (20) interviews with a reasonably random selection of the survey respondents (138 from 232) occurred in three stages at schools, colleges and universities in Manchester, Salford and Bolton from September 2001 to May 2002. Interview respondents voluntarily formed groups based on either friendship or classmate ties. Some respondents were revisited in later interview stages on the basis of their representing a range of different findings from questionnaire replies and first-stage interview transcripts. The intention behind returning to interview particular groups – and later individuals – was reflexively to probe into themes that arose from previous findings by tailoring questions accordingly, as well as to account for the changes in tastes for and uses of music in the social and cultural everyday lives of interviewees.

CHAPTER 5

Music Media Uses and Influences

Following on from the broad divisions drawn in Chapter 3 between mediated and co-present youth music practices of promenade performances, this chapter will focus on the former and Chapter 7 will examine the latter. There are three reasons why I have chosen to distinguish mediated from co-present music practices. First, the distinction between these sets of practices is qualitatively defined by the specific contexts in which music is consumed and produced. Thornton's (1995) distinction between mass, micro and niche media as resources for subcultural capital may be insightful textual analysis but it ultimately ignores how such resources are experienced within the contexts of club cultures. As Phil Jackson rightly observes, 'you can pick up most of what Thornton defines as "subcultural capital" from the clubbing media without ever learning how to really party' (2004: 96). Second, these two sets of music practices provide a framework for probing into important thematic issues about the relationship between young people's private/domestic and public consumer lives. And third, content analysis of thematically coded interview transcripts and field notes found that instances of mediated and co-present music practices were divided reasonably equally in number. Therefore, to afford equal weight to either set of practices by discussing them in distinct chapters appears to be a valid strategy for writing as well as reading ethnographic research (see Hammersley 1990), not least because this avoids overemphasising one over the other.[1] Despite the adequacy of this distinction it should be stressed that the two sets of practices are not mutually exclusive. Indeed, uses of music media frequently occur in public places, and public music consumption and production is almost always mediated in some form. As this research unfolds, the synchronicity between mediated and co-present practices will be shown to be as significant to contemporary youth music cultures as their separability.

In this chapter I will describe and explain how music media are used and become influential in various everyday contexts. I will differentiate between types of media use in terms of degrees of consumer involvement. Interpretations of empirical findings will reveal that different media are consumed along different points of an involvement continuum from intensity to detachment. Contrary to the majority of studies into youth subcultures (e.g. Hebdige 1979; Willis 1978), I will detail the profound extent to which domestic, family experiences are reported by respondents to have influenced their music consumer choices. Having outlined these media uses and influences, the implications of a paradoxical trend for growing public uses of music media which wield their strongest influence in the privacy of young people's domestic lives shall be assessed. The growing public presence of non-terrestrial music television channels and the Internet across young people's everyday educational, work and leisure contexts seems to be stimulated by a desire to consume mediated technologies that might be excluded from domestic settings at the will of parents. Discussion will then turn to the extent to which media consumer literacy is able to be productive and even innovative in the formation of music tastes and practices regardless of ostensibly omnipotent global media influences. The final section of this chapter will consider the importance of everyday life narratives to youth music practitioners' immediate but also embedded identities and presentations of themselves and significant (familial) others.

Uses

Conceptualising media use has been an objective of audience research approaches at least since the 'uses and gratifications' model (see Katz et al. 1974). This model assumes that needs generated by social and psychological circumstances are expected to be gratified through use of media and other sources. Subsequent use of these sources at different levels of engagement generally results in need gratifications. Hall's (1992) 'Encoding/decoding' model, on the other hand, and its subsequent application (Morley 1980) suffered from a producer-led, institutionally deterministic theory of use which assumed that media texts were always decoded in contexts of political engagement vis-à-vis their ideological functions. Where these models have failed in practice to provide insightful evidence are not so much around consumer need gratifications or ideological interpretations stimulated by media but around consumer uses of media at the assumed stage in which gratifications are met and ideologies are read (i.e. during or after reception). Later studies of media use by fans of certain media texts (e.g. Ang 1985; Fiske 1989a; Schwichtenberg 1993) and by families in specific media contexts (e.g. Morley 1986) have dealt more acutely with the complexities of audience reception. However, because of their narrow focus on fandom and tendency to read media consumption as a reaction or resistance to dominant ideologies, these studies along with their predecessors – subcultural consumer models of spectacular appropriation included – have been prone to the 'fallacy of meaningfulness' (Hermes 1995). The uses of music media by the young people in my sample were not always meaningful and rarely perceived by these consumers to meet some social or psychological need. What follows is an attempt to understand different types of music media use in the contexts in which they are received. Of paramount importance to understanding how music interacts with young people's everyday lives is an analytical framework that differentiates intensive media use from casual media consumption along a continuum of consumer involvement. The complex relationship between young consumers and music media stars/genres tends to endorse the rationale behind conceptualising a continuum rather than a dichotomy.

Intensive media use

Respondents tended to consume more recorded music than music transmitted through the media of radio or television. As Table 5.1 shows, more than half the sample (51 per cent) consumed nine or more hours of CDs, tapes and other recorded formats on average each week. By contrast, distributions of respondents across the time categories were more evenly spread with regard to levels of music radio and television consumption. Only 32 respondents (14 per cent) consumed nine or more hours of music radio or television weekly.

Intensive music media users, it would seem, were more likely to consume high levels of recorded music than music radio, television or any other medium. Nevertheless, interview findings suggest that music television channels – often in conjunction with other media – were used intensely by many of the respondents who were also heavy users of recorded music. Heavy users of one music medium were therefore likely to be heavy users of other media that complemented each other in their contextual closeness across a selectively trodden mediascape (Abercrombie and Longhurst 1998). The formation of music tastes and practices for intensive media users appears to follow three phases of consumption: previewing, purchasing and appreciating.

Before considering each of these phases it is important to stress that the second phase of purchasing music products can often be surplus to the requirements of appreciating them. Silverstone's (1994) allocation of the moment of imagination to his six-phase consumption cycle (as discussed in Chapter 4) seems to understate its greater significance when applied to

Table 5.1 Recorded music consumption on average each week (hours)

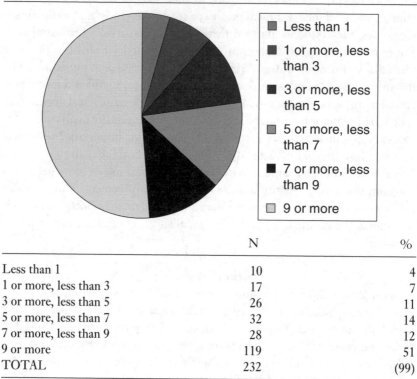

	N	%
Less than 1	10	4
1 or more, less than 3	17	7
3 or more, less than 5	26	11
5 or more, less than 7	32	14
7 or more, less than 9	28	12
9 or more	119	51
TOTAL	232	(99)

intensive music media consumers. This moment when 'goods are imagined before they are purchased, prior to any loss of illusion that comes with ownership' (1994: 126) parallels the extensive previewing phase of intensive music consumption that I will detail below. Previewing techniques used by respondents can similarly be mapped along with Silverstone's imaginative moments on to de Certeau's (1984) tactics for everyday living. However, intensive music media use could be perceived by these young people to not only allow for significant delay before the phase of purchasing but to do without the purchasing phase altogether. Therefore, the imaginative tactics deployed by respondents – facilitated by the omnipresence of music in their everyday life contexts – could precede and indeed override those moments of imagination which Silverstone also situated after purchasing. As such, Silverstone's next phase when an appropriation of a product's meanings relocates it in private contexts might not be experienced by intensive music users who rely on means other than purchasing in order to listen to, borrow or copy. 'Ownership' of music goods in a legitimate sense is not necessary to the attainment of intensive use. Home-taping and CD-writing certainly seem to be tactics that de Certeau would associate with subversive consumer practices. The redundancy of appropriation in certain cases therefore means that Silverstone's cycle breaks down and that those remaining moments of consumption are rendered problematic. This ultimately means that the dialectical relationship between consumption and production implied by a cycle is fractured by disruptive, tactical consumers. However, in the next section I will return to assess how these other moments can parallel young people's casual music consumption.

Previewing mediated music is a means both of forming expectations about a possible purchase and searching for knowledge about prospective consumption opportunities. Gareth used MP3 files from the Internet to preview albums which he would then look for in an independent record shop:

> Gareth: [. . .] I'd start off, like, me friend would lend me a CD that I want.
> DL: Yeh.
> Gareth: And I started listening to the stuff.
>
> . . .
>
> DL: So where do you go to find these CDs then? Is it, like, record shops?
> Gareth: What I do, you get, er, an MP3 first. [. . .] you can, like, hear three songs off the album or go out and buy the album.
> DL: Right. So you get it off the Internet?
> Gareth: Yeh. Or if I feel lazy I'll just get the whole album off the Internet.
>
> . . .
>
> Gareth: I go in Vinyl Exchange.
> DL: Is that in Manchester, is it?
> Gareth: Yeh, they have all, like, you know, promotional copies of CDs.
> DL: Yeh.
> Gareth: [. . .] go in HMV and you see the album for 16.99, go in there it could be 8.99 so=   (Pollington College A1)

Another interviewee, Gaz, also shopped for promotional copies of albums at Vinyl Exchange prior to their retail release date (University of Salford 3). These promotional copies are mainly used by DJs aware of the credibility that comes from playing unreleased music at clubs. Such credibility is similarly sought by everyday intensive media users. Justin's use of artists' websites enabled him 'To see what they're gunna release and/it just gives you the added edge on what you know' (Scarcroft College 3). Sophie's use of magazines similarly enabled her to 'keep up' her knowledge about the latest metal-music releases:

> Sophie: [. . .] there are a lot of bands that don't get in the charts, you know, and just release albums all the time so you have to buy magazines and you have to, you know, look.   (Scarcroft College A1)

Sophie and Justin transferred their intensive personal media use on to their everyday social media use at college:

> *Justin: [. . .] we do it every morning.*
> *DL: Oh right.*
> *Sophie: Right, what we usually do is, erm, we sort of log in on the Internet and/ we usually get here – get here quite early. We'll go on the Internet and, like type in, like, music [. . .] type in a band and it will come up with everything.*
> *DL: Yeh.*
> *Sophie: And a lot haven't – a lot of other bands are on there.*   (ibid. A2)

'A lot of other bands' here referred to metal bands that had not previously appeared with releases in the UK Top 40 Chart. The Internet in particular was used as a source of fandom activity for consumers with more alternative music tastes than those available from chart-orientated music media such as radio and terrestrial television.

Purchasing recorded music for intensive media users was very much informed by previewing media like the Internet. Expenditure on recorded music was reasonably but not unsurprisingly high. The modal category was '£20 or more, less than £100' in the past year (i.e. 2000–1), which accounted for 106 respondents (46 per cent). Only 23 respondents (10 per cent) who spent £300 or more in the past year on CDs, tapes and other recorded formats might be regarded as exceptionally heavy buyers of recorded music.[2] When it is considered that over half of the sample listened to nine or more hours of recorded music each week it might be assumed that much of this music was not purchased by them but perhaps borrowed or copied on to blank cassettes/CDs from others' record collections. The progression from previewing to purchasing, as already discussed, might often be bypassed en route to prospective appreciation of mediated music. Where purchasing does occur this is likely to follow exposure across a mediascape:

> *Dave: I've got, erm, MTV2 on Sky Digital.*
> *DL: Right.*
> *Dave: Like introduced me to, like, loads of new bands and stuff like that. A band called Everclear – they're, like, massive in America but like=*
> *Vicky: I know.*
> *Dave: Not very well known over here at all – I've got three CDs by them now and I only heard them, like, six months ago.*
> *. . .*
> *DL: And er – so you saw them on MTV2?*
> *Dave: Yeh, I saw one song on MTV2 and loved it.*
> *DL: Yeh.*

Dave: They've got it on the Internet and I played it to death and bought three CDs after that.   (Richmond High School C1)

Here Dave's use of cable television channels and the Internet combined to form his tastes for a particular band that were 'massive in America' but yet to break the UK market. Intensive media use extended to purchasing imported albums and singles that are generally more expensive than those mass distributed in the UK. Kevin ordered a US-imported CD for his girl-friend from the HMV website (Richmond High School 3). R 'n' B fan Gaz bought HMV imports of recorded music on the mid-week release date that he obtained from websites as well as the US-imported hip hop and R 'n' B magazine *Vibe*. He also bought four Mary J. Blige singles for about £70 from a private seller in Canada via the eBay auction website 'which is a lot but I'm a hardcore fan and they're mine' (University of Salford 3). What Gaz termed 'fan base importance' appears to extend to other respondents who engaged in intensive music media use. Although he was the only respondent to claim openly to buy singles and albums in their first week of release to 'kind of help sales' (ibid.), there was an implicit desire among fans of alternative bands and artists to gain credibility among other young music consumers if that with which they were long familiar became the latest popular soundtrack.

Appreciating music that has already been extensively previewed across various media and perhaps purchased represents the final phase of inten-sive use. However, the sense of appreciation meant here is that of acquir-ing a taste for music through repetitive listening rather than through an educated understanding of its formal aesthetics. Becker's (1953) account of the 'learning process' required to appreciate the social use of marijuana resonates with the ways in which respondents perceived formations of music tastes within familiar interactive consumption contexts. Chris and Nicky found that repetitive consumption provoked certain changes in response to mediated music:

Chris: [. . .] After you've listened to a song for a certain amount of time or what-ever, and it starts, like, getting drummed into your head and sometimes – most of the time it's, like, either it gets to a point where it's really annoying to hear the song again or it gets to the point where you end up liking the song / and that's hap-pened a couple of times. It's like, I'm not into that sort of music at all but I do like that song.   (Scarcroft College 3)
Nicky: [. . .] if it's something that you keep hearing, then they come on a lot anyway – if you listen to the radio them kind of songs are always on, and you won't think, you know, but then one day you listen to it and you start humming along.   (Natton College A1)

Jen was a heavy viewer of the cable music television channel Kerrang! and aware of how her evolving tastes were instigated by watching the older metal bands like Guns 'N' Roses that appeared on this channel alongside her contemporary preferences like Korn (Scarcroft College 3).[3] Louise was one of a minority of respondents who had been exposed to MTV from an early age. She considered that her use of the channel at a younger age had to some extent formed her music choices (Richmond High School A1). Heavy purchasers of recorded music such as Craig learnt to appreciate investments through a process of episodic consumption whereby for a given CD he would 'listen to it for a bit, then not listen to it for a bit, then listen to it again' (Scarcroft College 3). Songs that Andrew liked while previewing them on television gained appreciation on further hearing through remembrance of that initial pleasure: 'you hear it [. . .] and you think it's quite good and next time you hear it you're, like, just thinking of it/sometimes' (Wilson High School B1). That tastes can be formed through intensive processes of previewing and appreciating music without always creating a desire for its material purchase is testimony to the pervasiveness of music media in young people's everyday lives.

Casual media consumption

Although a notable proportion of respondents could be described as intensive media users – of recorded music in particular – there remained a significant number who consumed little music other than that direct from CDs and other record formats. Indeed, 48 per cent (111) of respondents consumed less than three hours of music radio and 52 per cent (120) consumed less than three hours of music television each week. Music was rarely if ever consumed on the Internet, which was used less than one hour each week by 73 per cent (169) of the sample. Purchasing of recorded music and merchandise by no means equated to consistently high expenditure and was not even an inevitable facet of intensive media use. However, low levels of media consumption are not deemed to be synonymous with the term 'casual consumption' as it is applied here. Whilst Internet music was rarely used by the sample as a whole, those 6 per cent (13) of respondents who spent seven hours or more surfing the web were involved in intensive consumption akin to enacting their fandom by searching for alternative tastes, specialist knowledge and rare artefacts. Casual music media consumption, on the other hand, was particularly evident through the uses of radio to expound populist tastes for music that was common knowledge. Definitions of alternative and populist music tastes as they are applied to intensive and casual media uses respectively share parallels with those of Thornton (1995: 87–115) in exploring how the meaning of mainstream discotheque music asserts the authenticity of club cultural values and beliefs.[4] Respondents' perceptions of alternative and populist tastes rather than my own or anyone else's perceptions are deemed adequate as definitions. Populist mediated – like mainstream co-present – music practices, such as listening to the Sunday afternoon Top 40 Charts on BBC Radio 1, provided sufficiently wide frames of reference *against* which some young people asserted their different (i.e. alternative) tastes or *within* which others placed their resemblant (i.e. populist) allegiances.

In spite of the uniform alternativeness that Thornton bestows on clubbing and dancing activities, she nevertheless suggests a gendered distinction between 'the femininity of representations of the mainstream' (1995: 103) and the masculinity of alternative music cultures. Gender differences within the frames of reference of casual music media consumption point to the wider significance of this distinction beyond its co-present consumer application. As Table 5.2 shows, the casual consumer medium of radio was used for listening to music more by female than male respondents.

Only 18 per cent (21) of female respondents listened to less than one hour of music radio weekly. This figure was approximately half that of the proportion of male respondents who perceived themselves to fit into this lowest category of radio consumption. Further multi-variate analysis found that gender differences in music radio listening were starkest among the 15–16 age band, where 36 out of 57 (63 per cent) males compared to 20 out of 54 (37 per cent) females listened to less than three hours per week. At the start of a first-stage interview with an all-female group Hilary immediately revealed omnivorous music tastes formed by coincidental exposure to songs and artists broadcasted on radio:

DL: [. . .] it doesn't matter who starts – what music do you like at the moment?
Hilary: Anything that's on the radio, really.
?: Emm.
DL: Right.
Hilary: I don't have a particular music. I just listen to it and if I like it, I like it.
(Southwell College C1)

If the three phases of intensive media use are mapped on to this respondent's casual consumer practices, Hilary's mediated music tastes are evidently formed through disorganised previewing practices via a single broadcast medium rather than through those organised practices of engagement in knowledge-searching facilitated by other media such as the Internet. Casual music radio consumption for Claire was a pleasurable

Table 5.2 Gender and music radio consumption on average each week (hours)

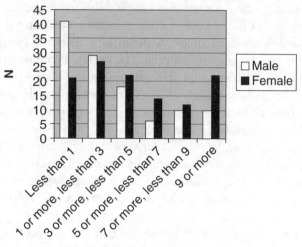

Time each week (hours)

	Male		Female		AVERAGE	
	N	%	N	%	N	%
Less than 1	41	36	21	18	62	27
1 or more, less than 3	29	25	27	23	56	24
3 or more, less than 5	18	16	22	19	40	17
5 or more, less than 7	6	5	14	12	20	9
7 or more, less than 9	10	9	12	10	22	10
9 or more	10	9	22	19	32	14
TOTAL	114	100	118	(101)	232	(101)

activity freed from the firm expectations about personal tastes formed by intensive media users:

> *Claire: [. . .] I like things that are on – I listen to the radio so/ I don't think it's certain types of pop that I like, it's just things in – in the charts, like – Linkin Park I like – I quite like them=*
> *Karen: [Yeh, I do.*
> *DL: [Yeh.*
> *Claire: [. . .] and they're not pop.*   (Richmond High School D2)

Again, a taste for music defined by its broadcast medium rather than by other criteria such as its commerciality (i.e. whether or not it is chart music) or associative genre (i.e. pop, rock, etc.) frames the omnivorous tastes of many casual music media consumers.

The casual consumption of music radio can be explained by its solely audio reception. Music on the radio can serve as a background soundtrack to other everyday activities such as washing clothes in such a way that consumers might easily become unconscious or only semi-conscious of its presence. This is literally manifested in its consumption by some respondents as an aid to falling asleep. Craig claimed that, 'I usually fall asleep when I'm listening to it [. . .]' (Scarcroft College 3) and Gaz went to sleep on Sunday nights during or after Trevor Nelson's *Rhythm Nation* programme on BBC Radio 1 (University of Salford 3). Claire's domestic radio consumption is dependent on specific contexts: 'if I'm in my room I'll put the radio on, if I'm downstairs and there's no one in I'll put the music [television] channel on' (Richmond High School D2). However, if she has the house to herself she prefers to do homework over the audio transmissions of music television rather than radio:

> *Claire: I watch it in the background, if you know what I mean. Like, if I'm doing something and I'll have, like, my homework I'll turn that on cause/it's like, the radio's got loads of talking in it, but music TV – most of it, it doesn't. It's music after music apart from the adverts. And you do – I don't always even watch it, I can listen to it and it's just all different types of music.* (ibid. 3)

Here is an instance of how consumers can selectively receive different communicative properties of media during other everyday activities akin to the speed-reading tactics identified by de Certeau (1984). These tactics of casual media consumption apply to those moments in Silverstone's (1994) consumption cycle that were rendered redundant by certain intensive media users who could appreciate music without needing to purchase or privatise its meanings. Domestic music technologies and products that go through the phases of objectification and incorporation along this cycle can be read, for instance, in Claire's casual consumption of music television as a companion for homework or the bedroom consumption of music radio as a facilitator of sleep. Yet certain domestic music media will not necessarily begin or end their casual consumption cycle outside these privatised contexts for young people who have grown up with their elders' or siblings' technologies and products. Silverstone's phases of product appropriation from public to private and subsequent conversion from private to public contexts remains as uncertain for casual as intensive music-media consumers. The extent to which the cycle can continue to feed back private and personal consumer practices to the commodification phase of production is once again problematised. Whilst tactical, intensive music-media use is plausible without ever becoming purchased or personally contextualised, it would seem that the tactics of young, casual music-media consumers enable them to

Table 5.3 Gender and music media consumption

	Distribution	
Even		**Skewed**
Television		Radio
Magazines and newspapers		Internet
Music merchandise		Recorded music

permanently locate the meanings of their aunt's vinyl record collection or elder brother's MP3 player within familial contexts.

Overall gender differences in the use of intensive and casual media are illustrated in Table 5.3. Solely audio media – radio and recorded music – were favoured by female and the more visual Internet attracted male respondents, whilst the other visual media attracted either gender to a similar degree. By extension, music media that demanded less consumer involvement and were more likely to function as a background soundtrack to other activities were generally favoured by females. Those music media that involved the consumer in more intense interactions which rendered other activities redundant operated in a more male-centred domain together with – as can be assumed from countless studies – computer and video games. As is shown by Claire's selective reception of music television though, it is not so much the case that different media engender certain types of (casual or intensive) consumption but that the *uses* of these media seem to be divided along gender lines. Nevertheless, certain properties of different music media are attached with casual (populist) and intensive (alternative) uses. It would seem that the broadcast properties of music television and radio that ultimately lead to narrowly commercial offerings by way of maintaining audiences and pleasing advertisers are attached to casual uses that can only form populist tastes. The narrowcast properties of Internet music or certain music magazines, on the other hand, are attached to intensive uses that can potentially hone alternative tastes. I will explore respondents' reflexivity with regard to the attachment of meanings on to media later in this chapter. How they attach meanings on to media content in the shape of stars and genres will now be considered.

Relating to stars and genres

How respondents related to the stars and genres produced by and through music media tended to situate them at various points along an involvement continuum between intensive and casual types of consumption. Different perceptions of what constituted appropriate levels of involvement in music consumption could lead to peer group conflict. In the following interchange, tension surfaced between Gary, who liked the metal band Linkin Park, and Conor and Rick, who dissociated themselves from such fake pop tastes in favour of what they perceived to be alternative metal bands like Slipknot (described by Gary as 'stupid'):

> DL: Gary. What are you into?
> Gary: Er, same as Conor really, Linkin Park and things that.
> Conor: [I'm not into Linkin Park.
> DL: [Quite heavy stuff.
> Rick: Linkin Park, heavy. {Laughs}
> Pause.
> Gary: What? Linkin Park are not heavy, are they?{Ironically}
> Rick: Jumped-up pop where they don't play their own instruments.
>
> . . .
>
> DL: Quite, sort of, heavy – who plays that at the moment, Linkin Park? Stuff like that.
> Rick: No, they're nu-metal.
> DL: New metal.
> Rick: Yeh, which is all pop-inspired.
> DL: Right.
> Rick: But, like, it mixes, like, loads of different kinds of music together like hip hop and soul.
> DL: Em, but stuff that plays thrash is what – sort of,/Slipknot or something like that.
> Rick: No, Slipknot are kind of/
> Gary: [...] stupid.
> Rick: Yeh. {Feigns laughter to mock Gary's retort}
> {Holly laughs}   (Richmond High School B1)

Along an involvement continuum, then, the search for non-pop, heavy (thrash) metal genres by Conor and Rick relates to their intensive music-media use in the search for alternative taste formations. Their criticism of what they perceived to be Gary's populist tastes and Gary's counter-criticism represented positions at different ends of this involvement continuum. Whereas Gary dressed for school in conventional jumper and trousers, Conor and Rick both displayed their intensive, alternative music affiliations by wearing black, hooded Nirvana tops and thick metal chains attached to loose-fitting pants. Whereas Gary went out on Friday night to a local pub where he preferred to refrain from dancing in the disco area, Conor and Rick sought out goth clubs and thrash-metal gigs – although they lamented their scarcity around Bolton and instead searched them out in Manchester (a thirty-minute train journey).

The interchange above importantly indicates how some young music consumers perceive the involvement continuum as a measure of evolving appreciation for specific stars and genres. So consumers who purchase lots of recorded music and merchandise might appear to be intensive users but until they are able to express appreciation for what they have purchased through verbal and bodily communication, they may remain excluded from others in groups formed by shared musical tastes. This sense of exclusion from others who share intensive appreciation for a specific music genre or star was experienced by myself while in conversation with a group of garage and R 'n' B consumers: Gavin who was mixed white and black Caribbean and Nicky who was black Caribbean:

> *DL: So can you tell the difference between, sort of, R 'n' B, garage, house and all that?*
> *Nicky: Yeh, totally.*
> *Gavin: It's different.*
> *Nicky: It is different.*
> *DL: Because for me, I find it a bit hard sometimes trying to work out, you know, if that music's=*
> *Gavin: But you know what we'd probably, we'd find it hard, or what I'd find hard, if you told me something different like indie music and, sort of like/*
> *DL: Indie music and what?*
> *Gavin: And say, like/*
> *DL: But indie music has got its own sound, hasn't it, like=*
> *Nicky: But we don't know it. {Laughs}*
> *Gavin: What's he called? Cocker, what's he called. Jarvis Cocker.*
> *DL: Yeh, yeh.*
> *Gavin: All that sort of music.*
> *DL: Well, that's distinctive isn't it, that sound? It's like=*
> *Nicky: That's what it means for you but not to us.*
> *Gavin: Yeh, but to us, it's all the same to me.*
> *DL: {to Gavin and Nicky} Right, so you would say – what is me and what is you? How are you comparing me with you?*
> *Nicky: Um?*
> *DL: How are you comparing me with you? In terms of age, you mean?*
> *Nicky: No.*
> *Gavin: No.*
> *Nicky: You said like, everything's the same, but to you it is but to us because we listen to, like, garage and R 'n' B and stuff like that, to us it's not cause we don't really listen to that sort of music and come across it*
>
> *[. . .]*

DL: So it depends what you listen to as to whether you can pick out=
Nicky: Yeh, cause you don't really pay attention much to that sort of music so
you don't think, 'oh, that sort of music's that', you just know what you like [. . .]
(Natton College A1)

During this conversation I was aware that assumptions drawn by Gavin and Nicky about my music tastes in relation to their own had created a perception about the gulf in appreciation of particular genres dependent on personal choices and identities. My suspicion at the time was that differences in ethnicity partly explained this comparison between music tastes, particularly as the discussion immediately prior to this interchange focused on how successful R 'n' B stars such as Craig David were capable of attracting a 'middle' ground that included diverse ethnic followings. The explanation for this comparison of tastes articulated by Nicky, on the other hand, pointed not towards differences in personal identities along ethnic or age lines but towards differences in personal choices around what was listened to with more and less attention. This explanation for differences in genre appreciation also indicates how involvement continua are always applicable to specific youth music cultures rather than popular music in general, the latter of which invariably fits for all youth music cultures without detailing the practices of exclusion and inclusion that occur in each of them.

Relating to stars as well as genres in the formation of music tastes and identities mostly served to position respondents towards the intense end of an involvement continuum in relation to others who were less interested in and knowledgeable about a given star's career and catalogue. For example, an all-female group began to show their appreciation of the recently deceased black female R 'n' B artist Aaliyah in terms of her singing, dancing and attractive image. Later in the discussion more profound bounds of appreciation for lyrics that Aaliyah sang as well as the star's resemblance to them in terms of age and gender are collectively expressed:

Melissa: And some of the lyrics they put in the songs as well. {Various 'yeahs'}
DL: Right, so how does it influence your thinking?
Zahida: You relate, you know – like Aaliyah, she was just about our age group.
Melissa: Yeah.
Zahida: Whatever she sang, whatever she did, it related to us.
DL: Right.
Zahida: You know, if we – if we were like heartbroken or [. . .]
(Natton College B1).

Another star who had died recently, the male rap artist 2Pac, was the subject of intensive consumption by several respondents including Jolene, who stated that 'you get to know about the person as well [...] it defines the hard times that he went through and everything – he brings that out in his music and everything [...] you respect him' (ibid. D1). Searching for knowledge about the 'person' behind the star persona involved a variety of media, including books and magazines. Some stars had been consumed by respondents over considerable periods of their life, such as Hayley's relationship to Michael Jackson who 'liked him when he was young' (Pickles High School A1) before the cosmetic surgery that he underwent, and Matthew's following of singer Sean Ryder from the band Happy Mondays to his second band, Black Grape (Scarcroft College 3). Gaz (University of Salford 3) retained a loyal, intimate relationship to female soul and R 'n' B vocalists whom he had followed since their career beginnings during his early teens and whom he now referred to on first-name terms – Beth (Beth Orton), Mary (Mary J. Blige), Missy (Missy Elliot) – as if he knew them personally.

This process of relating to the genre and star constructions of the music media industry mostly indicated intensive use of the products associated with these constructions but could also indicate distaste for and detachment from such products. Sam, for instance, responded to my use of the term 'band' to refer to Blackstreet with the retort that 'It's a/ – a group, I hate band [. . .] you say Oasis is a band or something' (Natton College D2). Similarly and from the same group of black Caribbean female respondents, Tanya said that she would never listen to 'bands and pop and classic' (ibid. 3) where the term 'bands' again becomes synonymous with the rock music genre. Another group of minority ethnic respondents debated the qualities of ostensibly 'black' (R 'n' B, hip hop, jungle) compared to ostensibly 'white' music genres:

> Shauleen. Rock 'n' roll. {Expressing disgust}
> DL: So what's wrong with rock 'n' roll then?
> Shauleen: Oh, it's old.
> ?: Old.
> DL: It's out of date, is it?
> Raja: No, it's alright you know – it's alright.
> Anicea: You're not betting.
> Raja: It's good you know.
> Shauleen: That is dirt, that is nasty.
> Raja: Only because it's white, only because it's white. That's why you don't=
> Jab: No.
> Shauleen: No. It's not because it's white but just, er – I mean it's=
> Ruth: The music, yeh – we like black music.

> ...

Ruth: [...] Rock 'n' roll is rubbish. That's not talent – I don't think that's talent, music has to be talent.
Shauleen: Some of it is, like, noisy.
Ruth: The way they dress and men putting (?make-up) and that's errrr.
{Expressing disgust}   (ibid. C1)

In this discussion music genres were closely related to ethnicity and therefore to personal ethnic identities. Thornton's claim that 'The ideological categories of "black" and "white" define the main axes of authenticity within dance music' (1995: 72) appears to apply to youth music genres in general here. Shauleen, Jab and Ruth were cousins of black African descent. Faced with Indian respondent Raja's belief that they disliked rock 'n' roll 'because it's white', Shauleen and Jab refuted the accusation but Ruth immediately reinforced her and her cousins' ethnicity-based affiliations by stating that they 'like black music'. White rock 'n' roll music was deemed to be old and lacking talent compared to up-to-date black music genres. Detached positions as well as positions of distaste along the involvement continuum either related to very broad definitions of genres and stars (e.g. pop, chart, rock 'n' roll, men in make-up) or omitted relating to them by name: 'I listen to (music) but I've not got really a, sort of, style really' (Ryan, Scarcroft College 3).

Figure 5.1 summarises the main characteristics of an involvement continuum applicable to young people's uses of any specific mediated music culture as gleaned from interview discussions. The closeness with which respondents related to stars and genres would dictate where they might be positioned along this involvement continuum. Jolene's (Natton College) dedicated following of 2Pac's rap music and other artefacts such as biographies of the rapper positioned her considerably towards the intensive-use end of the continuum where a sense of alternative taste for as well as a specific relationship to the star would be consolidated. On the other hand, Shauleen, Jab and Ruth (ibid.) distinctly positioned themselves as casual consumers – perhaps even non-consumers – of rock 'n' roll by broadly

Intensive use	**Casual consumption**
Taste-group exclusion	Taste-group inclusion
Alternative tastes	Populist tastes
Specific relationships	Broad relationships
Male-orientated	Female-orientated
Publicised realm	Privatised realm

Figure 5.1 An involvement continuum for music media uses.

relating to negative stereotypes about the music genre but nonetheless articulating no alternative tastes to such 'white music' beyond that equally
populist genre known as 'black music'. Heterogeneous involvement in music
media use begs the question that I will now address about from where
different types of influences are exerted upon young people that result in
such unpredictable levels of consumer involvement.

Influences

Buckingham's point that, 'Media research has often sought to remove television from its social context, as if this were some unnecessary "mediating
variable" that could be deducted from the process, leaving us with the
"pure" act of viewing itself' (1993: 103–4) informed the kind of questions
that I addressed to respondents about those social contexts in which they
consumed and produced music. Interviewees were asked if they listened to
music with friends or family and who influenced their music preferences as
well as if they felt music influenced them in various personal contexts such
as their choice of physical appearance. Focusing on the contexts as well as
the texts of media consumption has marked a relatively recent paradigmatic
shift in audience research from diametrically opposed 'effects' and 'resistance' models to those of 'influences' (see Gauntlett 1995). Influences of
mediated consumption from intersecting local and global sources are fundamental to previously discussed formulations of the diffused audience, cultural localities, scenes and performances. Two limitations of the subcultures
literature – ethnographic neglect of *localised* (as discussed by Bennett 2000)
and *globally* mediated (as discussed by Hodkinson 2002) music media practices – are likely to be explained by an overarching emphasis on homologous
political resistance premised on *national* scales. The rest of this section will
consider how a combination of local and global influences on young people's
everyday music media uses in family and peer group contexts interact.

Family influence
The romanticised portrayal of some youth subcultures in symbolic opposition to their elders but motivated to recapture those qualities of the parental
culture destroyed by housing policies and unemployment (see P. Cohen
1992 in particular) left little scope for the possibility of any significant interactions between older and younger family members around everyday contexts such as those of music media consumption. A powerful stereotype is
still represented by situations in which children scorn at parents' music
tastes. It was not surprising during interviews, then, when respondents
abruptly denied that familial elders had influenced their music preferences.

What did prove to be more surprising were the far more frequent moments when these young people openly acknowledged the interactive processes by which their elders had influenced their tastes and had been influenced by their children's own tastes as formed by respondents in extra-familial contexts. A less surprising but only occasionally more pervasive influence on respondents' music choices was that exerted by siblings, cousins and other family peer relations. Before interpreting some important associations between the concepts of 'family' and 'culture' drawn by several respondents, I will outline instances where family influences on mediated music uses and preferences were understood through everyday life narratives.

One female respondent who lived with her father – her parents were divorced and her mother lived elsewhere with a second partner – shared an appreciation of what she perceived to be his 'broad range' of music tastes:

> *Claire: I think that's why I've been like that, cause I've grown up listening to, sort of, such different – like Paul Simon and all the Simon and Garfunkel stuff, he's got all that [. . .]I've always listened to loads of different music. It's always like – since I was born he's always influenced me because my dad loves music as well/ and so does my mum so, like, when they was together he used to always play loads anyway and now he plays even more, like. When we have tea/ he'll switch the television off and put the CD on [. . .] we always have the CD on when we're having tea/ and in the morning as well cause we have the radio on and in the car we always have the radio on. {Laughs}* (Richmond High School 3)

Claire thus respected and adopted the different types of music enjoyed by her dad across different media such as CD recordings and the radio, and in different everyday contexts such as at home and in the car. Her father's increasing music media use was cited by his daughter to have stemmed from the domestic absence of her mother, to whom he used to enjoy playing music to as well. Differential levels of domestic music use here frame a biographical trajectory of family life for this young person. Domestic music media use also influences how different family members are identified by young people through wider historical frames of reference. Ryan's current taste for 1980s music at the time of interviewing (March 2002) was borrowed from both his father's record collection and a historical image of his father as a younger man during Ryan's early years:

> *Ryan: Mostly my dad used to play (eighties) as well as dance music when I grew up as well and my mum's not a great fan of it but she'll listen to a bit of it, but my dad was more the eighties kind.* (Scarcroft College 3)

This 'selective borrowing of historical images and traits' as applied by Hollands to the young 'Geordie hard man' (1995: 20–1) interpreted previously as a performance in self-presentation here seems to influence performances presented by familial others. The very personal and privatised meanings that Ryan attached to a record collection which he had listened to in domestic contexts since he could remember supports a point made previously in response to Silverstone (1994) with regard to how casually consumed music media can be objectified and incorporated into young people's everyday lives without being appropriated from or converted to the public realm of production and promotion through a cycle or spiral.

Such performances perceived through life narratives typified the interactive local and global influences of several respondents' families on music media tastes and practices. In each case a nostalgic affiliation to the music of their youth provided the stimulus for elders who seemed to have significantly influenced the music uses of younger family members. Jen's father's collection of 1970s music – accumulated from his past hobby as a DJ – served as the resource for how his daughter had 'got into listening to Queen' (Scarcroft College 3). Tanya had 'grown up with' bashment music[5] which her father and uncles played at home and Stacian's preference for gospel music derived from attending church at the will of her grandparents, who clearly held firm religious beliefs (Natton College 3). Hilary 'was brought up with' the pop music liked by her parents which was 'stuck in my head now' but 'they like me to be up-to-date with everything else – they don't want me to just act like them' (Southwell College 3). In all four examples above the personalised and localised meanings of music media collected by familial elders intersected with the globalised properties of these mass-reproduced and distributed media. On considerably fewer occasions, respondents acknowledged the music influences of brothers, sisters and cousins. There were also fewer occasions when elder family members were perceived by respondents to be influenced by their tastes. On these occasions one parent tended to be more tolerant and appreciative of their children's music choices than the other (if another was present in their everyday lives). Claire's single-parent father, for instance, watched less music television than her but 'if I've got the music channels on he'll hear a song that he likes and he'll go out and buy the single' (Richmond High School 3). Matthew's parents would allow him to play his indie music in the car but 'My dad prefers it more than me mum' (Scarcroft College 3). Whether or not these young people's parents shared their music tastes did not receive a carefree response but rather created a desire for knowledge on a personal front.

Familial interactions through music consumption and production practices manifested such a degree of depth in respondents' recalled memories that the use of the terms 'family' and 'culture' became interchangeable at times. Leng from Singapore had experienced what Bourdieu (1984: 75) referred to as the ' "musical mother" of bourgeois autobiography':

> *Leng: I was, sort of, made to learn the piano when I was a child by my mother [. . .] it was more because of, like, [. . .] you know, the norm, it is, like, a good thing to make your child do it, OK. [. . .] I would put it down, like, to cultural, erm/how would you say, you know, the culture started it.*
> (Manchester Metropolitan University 3)

The piano in this sense became a status symbol and an ability to play the piano became of socio-cultural as well as musical value to the family. The following discussion with a group of Indian students indicated the powerful cultural and ethnic associations of music to their families:

> *DL: [. . .] Is there any kind of music that your – your parents liked that [. . .]=*
> *Farnaz: Indian music.*
> *Mo'aaz: Indian.*
> *DL: Yeh.*
> *Farnaz: When you watch Indian films and, like=*
> *Sohel: [. . .] films.*
> *Farnaz: And listen to Asian Sound Radio all the time we're [. . .] in the kitchen.*
> *{Rafiqa laughs}*
> *. . .*
> *Farnaz: Now and then I listen to Indian music.*
> *DL: Yeh, yeh. Do you listen to it with ya – ya mum?*
> *Farnaz: Yeh – she'll be often in the kitchen cleaning or cooking or something – she'll have Asian Sound Radio on*
> *. . .*
> *Sohel: [. . .] I don't listen to Indian music that much – they do go listen to a lot of Indian music, our parents, because they've been brought up in India, that's what they instead listen to but we've been born in Britain and=*
> *Farnaz: We want [to listen to our own music.*
> *Sohel: [Yeh.   (Northborough College A1)*

Towards the end of this discussion resistance to Indian elders' music preferences was expressed but respect for their parents' cultural background was manifested in acknowledgement of the importance of Indian music to these respondents' domestic, everyday lives. These young people apparently were influenced to some extent by their parental and ethnic cultures in their preference for bhangra club nights: 'where there's bhangra doing, you find out when it is and then you go out that night' (Farnaz, ibid.). When Gavin suggested that culture influenced music tastes, I asked him what he meant by 'culture' and he replied: 'Who you grew up with. If your mum and dad listened to, sort of, what sort of music they do, I don't think you – you drift off from it but you still, sort of, stay with it' (Natton College A1). Culture in this sense appears to combine two mutually dependent influences: family members' – particularly parents' – music choices and the music texts themselves. Uses of music media texts in familial contexts, therefore, are often closely aligned to a combination of local and global cultural influences – akin to the hybridised contexts of the carnivalesque (Bakhtin 1984).

Peer group exchange

Issues around the intersection of local and global influences in diffused audience contexts are as central to peer group exchanging as to familial influencing. Peer group exchanges as such could be interpreted as analogous to promenade performances of demonstration in early youth music cultures (see Chapter 3). Music exchanging was evidently quite a frequent activity in contemporary young people's everyday consumer lives: 96 respondents from the total sample (41 per cent) engaged in this activity, mostly using the CD format (45 out of 112 replies or 40 per cent). The greater number of references to MP3s (29 or 26 per cent) against cassette tapes (26 or 23 per cent) indicates that the Internet had become a familiar format among some young consumers and producers for exchanging music. Most exchanges were carried out between friends (50 out of 70 replies or 71 per cent). 'Family' exchanges (10 replies or 14 per cent) were entirely amongst peers – brothers, sisters and cousins – as opposed to between young people and their parents, although presumably there tends not to be a need to exchange music between family members in domestic contexts where products can easily be borrowed or subtly possessed. Peer group exchanges as social contexts for music media influences will be considered first before the significance of the Internet as a medium of exchange and influence is assessed.

During one group interview I asked respondents if television was the main influence on their music tastes. One response suggested that radio was more influential and another respondent stated: 'First it's the radio, then it comes on to your TV and then newspapers' (Helen, Natton College E1). However, Helen did not feel that her preferences for garage music emanated directly from music television channels because this music was rarely played through the medium. The formation of such preferences was 'more inspired by your friends [. . .] if your friends make a tape and you hear it and you like it then it's inspired by that, innit' (ibid.). Borrowing or copying friends' recordings to preview music otherwise inaccessible through solely broadcast media is seen as influential in the excerpt below too:

> *Ian: Well, I think it depends on friends as well because if you've got friends who listen to a certain type of music and then you lend a tape from them – say, you might want to be liked by them so there might be that, sort of – that peer pressure going on so you might lend a tape and that's how you get into it.*
> *DL: Erm, yeh.*
> *Ian: Like, I got into Smashing Pumpkins by getting a tape off Steve, so that's how I first liked them, so if I – like, if I didn't know him I wouldn't like that and that was, like, the first sort of band I liked [. . .]*
> *. . .*
> *It's kind of – if you've got friends who like it, I think it just opens up that, sort of, opportunity to listen to it.*
> *Claire: Yeh, cause sometimes you don't hear it until your friends, like=*
> *Steven: Listen to it.*
> *Ian: [Because=*
> *Steven: [On the radio you get a lot of [. . .] {Laughs}.*
> (Richmond High School D1)

Steven's laughter here perhaps expressed the absurdity with which music radio could be considered as an influence on the shared music tastes which he, Ian and Lindsay (in this same group) perceived to be alternative. These three students and some others who were not interviewed certainly appeared to form friendship ties around exchanges of music tastes and practices. Steven and Ian played guitars in the same band and later interviews found that Ian and Lindsay had attended several concerts with other friends in this same network. Conor and Rick from the same school but in the lower sixth form identified themselves with a similar friendship network of exchange based on perceptions of alternative music tastes in relation to other peers' populist choices (see previous section). These alternative tastes were displayed to others through these music consumers' unconventional clothes and hairstyles in ways akin to promenade performances.

The Internet was certainly used to a large extent by respondents as a means of copying and exchanging (i.e. not only downloading) music. Although Internet usage was greater among male respondents,[6] a small but notable proportion of females were at times intensively involved with this relatively recent music medium. Gemma downloaded MP3 files and burnt them on to CDs which she gave to friend and fellow respondent Rachel in return for a small fee to cover the cost of the blank CD (Southwell College B2). Indeed, one male respondent learnt from a female friend that he could play Internet music directly from his computer hard-drive rather than needing to burn it on to a CD (Dave, Richmond High School C3). Copying and exchanging music downloaded from the web on to a blank CD was possibly the cheapest means of offering the pirated product as a gift to friends:

> *Kevin: I've got twenty albums all from the Internet.*
> *DL: Alright.*
> *Kevin: I just downloaded them on to a CD. And do that. Cause you can, like –*
> *you can get, right, about twenty blank CDs for eight pound.*
> *DL: Right.*
> *Kevin: And if someone wants an album I just do it for them – I'm not really both-*
> *ered about paying fifty pee for it.*   (ibid. C1)

Ian had become more influenced by music searched for on the Internet because 'it's the easiest way to get something' and 'as you grow older maybe you want to find new things' (ibid. D1). He wanted to be introduced to new music which he would then potentially recommend to or exchange among his network of friends who shared an appreciation of alternative tastes. Similarly, Gemma claimed that the web was 'the best way of getting music you don't know' (Southwell College B2).

There were indications from survey data that despite the generally low levels of Internet use which tended to suggest it as a medium of casual consumption, websites as sources of information and knowledge served a niche previously worked only by certain music magazines and newspapers. Only 64 respondents (32 per cent) read music magazines whilst a mere 44 respondents (19 per cent) read newspapers for music news. These low consumption levels are perhaps a knock-on effect of more up-to-date music news and gossip websites such as popbitch.com, which features 'hot' news exclusives derived from non-libellous sources (i.e. Internet users as a whole). A rare instance of peer group exchanges via magazine resources was the everyday interactions between Gill and a friend whom she travelled with on the train to college, with whom she would swap reading material (Southwell College C2). More typical was Gaz's network of fellow R 'n' B fans who were also flatmates: 'There's about seven of us that, kind of like, text each other with perhaps a (record) release date' (University of Salford 3). This locally distributed electronic, mobile information would usually be gathered from the globally distributed electronic medium of the web. Rather than used as an essentially privatised music medium like television, the Internet would seem to have replicated the magazine as a public exchanging resource for these young people who tended to freely access the web at college or university as much as at home. These youth music consumers were often able, therefore, to deploy de Certeau's (1984) tactics through the use of one medium (the Internet) in specific contexts such as gratis college computer rooms to curtail purchasing desires for other (print) media products and thus save financial – without losing cultural – capital. Moreover, the only contact many respondents had with the Internet was in public, peer group contexts of exchange due to its common domestic absence. The everyday public presence of music media for young consumers was a striking trend in various research contexts of which I will now discuss.

The 'publicisation' of media consumption contexts

The preoccupation with television in media studies has perhaps overstated the domestic sphere as the most influential media consumer context in some people's everyday lives. Television is the most privatised of all (music) media and this is perhaps why large-scale demographic survey analyses have shown that the age band from fifteen to twenty-four years – those young people who are most likely to seek public entertainment – consume less television than any other age band (Gauntlett and Hill 1999). The following accounts of the pervasive presence of music media in respondents' everyday education, work and other public – particularly leisure – contexts will argue for a revised approach to media studies which accounts for the interactive dynamics between privatised and 'publicised' consumption practices. It seems that a fundamental property of music media are their capability to be received aurally or visually, and consumers are often empowered with their choice of music reception in everyday practices such as working out in the gym or drinking socially in bars when they are simultaneously consuming many other products that compete for their undivided attention. However, this undivided consumer attention to a given product or combination of products in co-present interactions with other products and consumers, whilst seemingly plausible based on evidence about the publicised realm of non-purchasing intensive use presented earlier, is constantly sought at the phase of production but rarely granted at the phase of reception.

School and college[7]

The significance of school or college breaks as weekly contexts for consuming music was relatively high according to the findings in Table 6.1, particularly when it is assumed that all other public contexts were not as regimented and regulated. At least four out of the eight further education (FE) institutions used to locate respondents had televisions in canteens tuned into one of the non-terrestrial music-orientated channels through each weekday. It seems safe to presume that music television in schools and colleges was a facility driven by the desires of students more than parents, teachers or governors. Survey findings certainly suggested that respondents preferred cable and satellite music television channels to sporadic music-based programmes on the five terrestrial channels: 257 out of 324 replies (79 per cent) on preferred music television channels/programmes referred to satellite or cable transmissions, with only the remaining 67 replies (21 per cent) referring to terrestrial transmissions. However, for many respondents without access to non-terrestrial channels at home, their presence at friends' homes but more likely every day at school and college generated important social contexts for music media consumption. These contexts outside the educational agendas of supervised classrooms and within the recreational spaces of common rooms and canteens, according to Richards, 'can be productive of significant cultural innovation and not least through the mixing of perhaps other disparate cultural elements which, confined to the young, are thus brought together into relation with each other' (1998: 149). Particularly recurrent within the interactive peer group dynamics of these sites of 'cultural innovation' were respondents' different views about the freedom of choices that they perceived in consuming mediated music. I will consider these views and the inconspicuous consumption techniques deployed when choices are limited after interpreting the presentation of music cultures experienced within research contexts.

Field notes taken on experiences while visiting educational institutions to conduct interviews consistently recorded the presence of music media, often owned by students and brought with them on a daily basis. I also noted their frequent use while preparing groups for interviews or actually in the process of interviewing. Apart from the obvious if deliberately understated encouragement given to them by a researcher into how music interacted with these young people's lives, my impression from observations of common rooms and canteens in several schools and colleges was that music from CDs, the radio or television would be wholly conspicuous by its absence. If music was not audible it would probably be present in the ears of numerous students via headphones attached to personal stereos. Indeed, Chris and Craig were so keen to present their music for research that on separate occasions they played it through the microphone attached to the cassette recorder from which I was recording interview discussions:

> Craig proceeds to play his CD collection into the mic through an ear phone – 2Pac, 'Till the End of Time', a dance track [. . .] accompanied by idle chat about TV and rock stars [. . .] (Scarcroft College B1)

Chris plays 'Hotel California' by The Eagles into my tape recorder's mic – he is listening to what is his dad's CD on a Walkman that he has taken to college. At the end of the interview he says, 'rock the world' direct into the mic. Chris: Sorry, just had to say that. {Laughs}   (ibid. 3)

Craig would have played to me most of his mobile record collection on a CD player owned by the college had a lesson not been in progress. He used this CD player to present his collection to peers 'every now and again until Dave [his teacher] comes and tells us to turn it off' (ibid.). At Wilson High School a CD player was carried by one of my respondents to the room in which we conducted a group interview where he promptly played a 2Pac CD as a background soundtrack for completing questionnaires (A1). In the sixth form hut at Pickles High School I noted

Two CD players, one of which is playing hip hop or rap tracks. One lad shows me a D-12 album which is later given an airing while I am interviewing the girls.   (B1)

These were just a few examples of how some respondents consumed music media at school and college for presentation to others and not only, it seemed, to myself as a researcher. Such presentations of music tastes and cultures would become attractive to some peers but repelled by and perhaps deliberately avoided by others.

This tension between different music tastes and cultures presented by and to students of often diverse ethnic and cultural backgrounds involved both conspicuous and inconspicuous techniques in music consumption to serve those more or less willing to participate in contexts of 'cultural innovation'. Some less willing respondents considered music television channels at college to be dull compared to the inconspicuous use of personal stereos to avoid censure from teachers and prevent boredom:

Tom: [. . .] (Music television), that's always, like, all this pop and you just get sick after a while.
Sohel: In this particular class we listen to, er=
Tom: Walkmans.
Sohel: Walkmans, not when he's (the teacher's) speaking but when we're [on with your own work.
Mo'aaz: [[. . .] own work.
DL: I see, right.
Tom: We listen to some music.
?: And the teachers don't want it.
DL: Yeh, yeh.
Mo'aaz: They seriously think that we borrow pencils off each other.

DL: Right.
Tom: Cause as a class we all get on, right, and we just share and swop and we just do whatever but some teachers just have a go at us.
(Northborough College A1)

Dave described the peer group dynamics that operated in the common room at his school which had become a battleground between different groups for presenting their innovative music tastes to others:

Dave: The amount of people who buy different things. It can get annoying and it can get stressful cause, like, people just wanna put their thing on and/people wanna listen to dance music all the time, people just wanna listen to the radio or people just wanna listen – I don't know, there's three of us who just wanna put, like, indie on so we're always, like, just struggling to get someut on so/ - but I always bring my CD player so I've got that in my bag so just – if I'm bored I just listen to that at break. (Richmond High School 3)

When freedom of choice to consume music in these contexts became restricted, Dave resorted to his personal stereo to avoid the music tastes of other students that he disliked in the same way that Tom and his classmates used personal stereos to react against rules imposed by teachers.

So who were the students that engaged in *conspicuous* music media consumption at school and college? At both Richmond and Pickles High Schools male groups were perceived by both male and female others to dictate what was played on CD players at break and lunch times. At Natton College, however, female respondent and part-time DJ Sam claimed that she was the main presenter of music innovation:

DL: But isn't, like, someone playing their own music, you want to play yours.
Sam: Well, I tend to take control, don't I? {Laughter}
DL: Oh right.
Sam: Cause no one else really brings in music and I'm probably – like me, I probably bring in the most [. . .] (D2).

Despite male dominance with regard to which CDs were played at Pickles High School, an older group of performing arts students appeared to operate a reasonably democratic usage of the karaoke machine, which provided a dual purpose: first, as a means of break-time entertainment; and second, as a training tool for the singing lessons that comprised part of their course (A1). Here was an instance of how a music medium used perhaps more for home or pub entertainment provided young people in everyday co-present interactions with an innovative resource for displaying and exchanging their skills and tastes through (leisurely and educational) performances.

Work

Work time for these young people tended to mean paid part-time rather than education-related work, which is why I deal separately with this characteristic of their everyday lives. Many respondents took part-time jobs outside their full-time education to pay for leisure activities among other things. Perhaps not surprisingly given the routine, temporary, junior positions that they generally filled, these young people could not always depend on having facilities for consuming music and were less likely to have a choice in the music that they consumed in work contexts where facilities existed. Nonetheless, typical types of workplace – pubs, restaurants, shops and supermarkets – would often use music media to some degree, even if these smacked of the muzak variety such as the commercial radio station operated by a supermarket chain where Emma worked (Southwell College B2). Where some freedom to use music media was permitted to employees, however, such permission seemed to be gratefully received. Rachel and colleagues who worked at a shoe shop in Bolton would 'take a load of CDs in, play what we want' (ibid.). Similar freedom was granted to a respondent who worked in a small clothes store in Manchester:

> *Jolene: I can bring my own music in there and then other people that work there can bring their music in and we just, like, listen to, like, hip hop and things all day, and you know, like, most shops won't allow that cause you can't play that music but this shop that I'm working at – it's like, it fits in with that new sort of [. . .]*
> (Natton College 3)

Jolene never quite finished her point here but the gist of it was that the place where she worked was considered to 'fit in' with a new attitude to young, temporary employees as important figureheads for a teenage customer base. DeNora's and Belcher's observations of clothing retail stores found that 'customers immediately encounter assistants who may be read both as fashion "models" and model customers – "ambassador users" of the brand' (2000: 87). The shop where Jolene worked was located in a part of Manchester's city centre known for alternative fashions geared towards the youth market. This employer no doubt practised a liberal policy with regard to employees' rights to wear their own choice of clothes and play their own choice of music at busy weekend hours. As well as being seen as a model worker, Jolene would also be targeted as a 'model customer' along with actual shop customers at club nights which would be advertised on flyers and distributed in-store 'cause they know, like, people'll see 'em' (ibid.). A complex, empowering relationship between Jolene's music media use at work and the commercial marketing activities of clubs, which sell nights based on music offerings, shows how closely the publicisation of media consumption in this work context intersected with non-mediated, public music leisure contexts.

Other public contexts

Media consumption occurred in many more public contexts attended with regularity by young people outside school and work. A list of 'Other public places' in which respondents stated that they consumed music included 'town', ice hockey games, football matches, cars, buses, singing lessons, music rehearsals, gym and the cinema.[8] With the possible exception of 'buses', all these other public places typically feature music media presence. Notes from simple observation of a rugby league match at Old Trafford, a football stadium in Greater Manchester, recorded the overt function that mediated music served as stimulus to a buoyant crowd atmosphere:

> The attendance is 61,000 – a record for the Final. And music is a key ingredient of this carnival, overtly entertaining occasion. 'YMCA' by The Village People blasts out from speakers as a spot-kick is converted. Similar tunes are played after a try is confirmed on the big screen. If a spot-kick is missed, music is conspicuously absent. People dance on their seats and participate in this friendly, family, party atmosphere – a very different experience to the hostile behaviour more often observed at football matches.
> (Rugby Super League Final: 19 October 2002)

Mediated music use at sporting events is certainly not a recent phenomenon but it seems to have become more pervasive at certain events such as rugby league and football matches, possibly due its success at ice hockey games (Crawford 2000) and boxing contests where use of music media to influence crowd behaviour is long-established.

Going out to 'town' to pubs, bars and clubs is also likely to involve quite high levels of mediated music experiences, whether or not these are consumed casually and even unconsciously. Recorded music played by DJs or jukeboxes, karaoke equipment, music television channels and increasingly the Internet are examples of media commonly found in pubs. Music media loaded with global associations even served a localised function to transmit and display the real-time actions of customers to others in one bar:

> Television screens show 'real-time' dancers (i.e. tonight's customers) on the raised platform to the rear of the bar. These screens are placed in the main bar area so that the dancing area is represented in the areas more likely to be non-dancing areas as a means of encouragement to non-dancers [. . .] Our group of postgraduate conference attendees are dancing near to the front

entrance, in an area that would not ordinarily be used for dancing but provides plenty of space compared to the more conventional dancing spaces
nearer the rear where the cameras roll.
(Walkabout, Manchester city centre: 11 p.m. 9 May 2002)

Like at the rugby league match, this media use appeared to be a device to
promote crowd involvement in creating a desirable atmosphere where customers would be encouraged to dance and project a sense of fun and
friendliness to the more casual, non-dancing clientele. Where mediated
music use at 'town' leisure venues was absent, an alternative seemed to be
offered in relation to the populist norm by attracting customers that preferred the sound of silence as a background to verbal interaction:

> A Wetherspoon's pub, which means no music and no football (or television at
> all) [. . .] Customers are intent on conversation early on – an alternative not
> afforded by the louder music played at the dance-orientated bars and clubs
> that they might move on to later, when talking would turn to gestures and
> moves.   (Moon on the Water, Manchester city centre: 8 p.m. 10 May 2002)

The strong associations between the Wetherspoon's chain of pubs and
their policy to bring back the traditional British public house *sans* entertainment media is testimony to the widespread ordinariness of mediated
music and other entertainment in the contexts of a 'night out'.

Productive consumer literacies

Media uses by and influences on young people can be understood as
processes of learning how to consume and produce texts in socio-cultural
contexts. What Willis et al. (1990) refers to as a 'DIY culture', in which
technologies made available to lay consumers are utilised and combined to
produce texts laden with 'grounded aesthetics', is indicative of such learning processes. Nonetheless, learning how to use media through interactions with influential others not always requires an end product in the
material sense. Young people in my sample articulated a sophisticated level
of knowledge learnt from consuming as well as producing mediated music.
Further, the common assumption that entertainment media are consumed
and not produced by the vast majority of young people without the technological and institutional means of global entertainment conglomerates
should be challenged. It cannot be denied that global music media products are far more powerful than what is produced in bedrooms or colleges.
What can be denied is the assumption that these music media products are
used in passive, unproductive ways. The phase of media consumption thus

becomes so dislocated from the institutionalised phase of media production that its intricate complexities deserve analysis per se. This necessary turn towards an understanding of consumer behaviour and perceptions is perhaps the definitive point at which the IRP is replaced by the SPP (see Chapter 4). Concepts of spectacle and performance – applicable both to processes of consumption and production – are better able to analyse literacies formed through media consumption but subsequently able to inform everyday producer as well as consumer practices. I will begin by arguing that overtly consumer practices generate literacy skills by illustrating moments of reflexivity indicative of music media texts as educational resources for young people. I will then consider how practices that include elements of consumption and production generate literacies not only for educational but also innovative ends. A brief case study of karaoke use will conclude this section.

During a group interview discussion about music television channels, a debate arose about the extent to which certain channels aired mainstream or alternative music. Claire argued that MTV Base played 'alternative music' but Ian disagreed and instead felt that such channels showed how 'the music industry is just dictated by record companies saying, "Here, play this"' (Richmond High School D2). A particular target of Ian's critically reflexive line was 'mainstream rock' in that 'They [MTV] say it's meant to be alternative.' He then considered 'ten-year-olds going around wearing hoodies' to be influenced by such music played on these channels. Claire then asked: 'Does it matter that ten year-olds are going around wearing hoodies [. . .]?' to which Ian replied, 'No, but, I mean, it's a popular thing – it's something that's mainstream. A lot of people like that sort of stuff' (ibid.). This debate was clearly framed by a perceived dichotomy between mainstream and alternative music that was read off mainstream meanings (see earlier discussion for equivalent definitions of populist and alternative tastes). Ian's criticism of people younger than himself whom he perceived to like mostly mainstream music had been honed through learning experiences in which the characteristics of others are judged through their music tastes and practices. In schools and colleges where students are defined by others based on criteria such as their age (i.e. form or cohort), interests and abilities, their music media cultures serve another defining criterion which is significant throughout many of these young people's educational lives. Dave's perception of the differences between two music magazines is also founded on a dichotomy between populist and alternative media which is projected on to reflexively informed prejudices about the tastes of their readers: '*NME* tries to find new bands and, like, just reports what they see and things like that, and *Q* just reports, like, what the record company wants you to hear I think' (ibid. 3). These examples of reflexivity are a direct outcome of literacy processes fine-tuned during the everyday social experiences of school and college contexts that having nothing to do with reading, writing or arithmetic.

As outlined previously in this chapter, respondents not only could learn how to distinguish alternative from populist or mainstream music media but also how to distinguish between various music genres based on evolving sensibilities acquired through intensive use. The level of sophistication required to define music into particular genres should not be underestimated given a present-day proliferation of genres very different to the traditional division between pop and rock. The finding from 430 replies on preferred music genres and/or acts in which 355 replies (83 per cent) referred to genres and only 75 replies (17 per cent) to acts further indicates a tendency among respondents to favour talking about their favourite genres or types of music rather than a favourite band or performer. Table 5.4 shows the wide distribution of tastes for genres across the sample.

A total of 34 different music genres were referred to as preferences by respondents. Although it could be argued that the most popular types – R 'n' B, pop and rock – suggested the populist tastes of a majority of respondents, this fragmented array of genres more significantly points to

Table 5.4 Preferred music genres/acts

	N	%
R 'n' B	49	11
Pop/chart	40	9
Rock	36	8
Garage	34	8
Dance	30	7
Rap	26	6
Hip hop	20	5
Metals	17	4
Indie	15	3
Any/most	13	3
Punk	9	2
Soul	8	2
Alternative	7	2
Trance	6	1
Bhangra/Indian	6	1
Others	114	27
TOTAL	430	(99)

a lack of cohesion between these young people and any particular music cultural – never mind subcultural – style. It may also be evidence of 'an apparent transfer of authority to consumers' (Abercrombie 1994: 56) as the popular music industry struggles to avoid fragmentation. Making sense of each of these types of music often requires complex knowledge about specific textual facets such as the rate of beats per minute or the relationship between the lyrics and the melody. For instance, Sam intricately and instantly distinguished rap from hip hop: 'Most people think they're the same but they're not. Hip hop's more dance music, rap's just all about the lyrics and dead slow. You, sort of, get rap without the music' (Natton College D1). Similarly, Louise learnt to tell the difference between dance and garage music by reading the faster, heavier beats in the latter genre (Richmond High School A1).

Consumer literacies manifested themselves in mediated music uses of more productive kinds than merely listening to, viewing and talking about music media. So far in this chapter the Internet has been characterised by its intensive music media use, particularly as a means of discovering, downloading, copying and exchanging music within peer groups. Thornton's (1995) categorisation of the web as a micro-medium akin to fanzines and listings that represent the most credible forms of clubbers' media seems to be apt with regard to its use by some young people in this study. However, the Internet is used in particularly productive ways as a consumer-led site for developing networks of online users who desire to learn the latest about the specific 'music world' that they most appreciate and who use peer-to-peer software such as Gnutella to transmit a 'search request from user to user until the file is found' (Jones and Lenhart 2004: 187). Leng (Manchester Metropolitan University 3) exchanged music with likeminded others who simultaneously logged on to a website database at icq.com. She also found out about music events through this online chat room. Similarly, several respondents had registered their details on the databases of MP3 file-swapping sites such as audiogalaxy.com, where users would download music directly from the hard-drive files of other online users rather than on a central server such as the now defunct napster.com service. The blurred distinction between consumption and production practices is certainly at the foreground of this arguably illegal use of web technology. Nonetheless, such productive consumer practices are not only learnt via electronic interactions. Two respondents in separate interviews confessed to purchasing a CD from a retail shop, copying it on to a blank CD at the cost of a few pence, and then returning the original version to the shop with receipt and a tale about how they had bought the wrong CD (Kevin, Richmond High School C2; Chris, Scarcroft College 3).

Like the Internet, the karaoke machine was a music medium used for ends that are neither clearly producer or consumer in character. The afore-mentioned performing arts students at Pickles High School participated in karaoke both for fun and vocal training. Another group of performing arts students at Scarcroft College spent most Thursday evenings together at a local pub karaoke night. Jen described how she would often meet her friends at the pub directly from college, so that for her this public enter-tainment venue functioned as an extended site of performative practices following those enacted in an educational venue (3). She had sung a Belinda Carlisle hit on one occasion because she knew the words but this sat uneasily with her tastes for heavy rock. However, she felt that her singing style was unsuitable for the rock songs that she preferred to listen to. Chris was perhaps the most committed karaoke goer and it was he that I met in the pub during observation research seven months after I had last inter-viewed the group. Perhaps pleasure in singing explained his immediate career plans, which I noted following our conversation:

> Chris is applying for a job in Pontins next year and would like to work at the Blackpool site. He knows the place 'inside out' because this was the venue for many annual family holidays when he was younger. He loves Pontins so much that he wants to work there before returning to study. Needless to say, entertainment is the kind of work that he is seeking out.
> (The Brook Tavern, Worsley, Salford: 9.30 p.m. 17 October 2002)

Whilst Chris's performing arts interests were by no means typical of respondents' interests as a whole, his use of a music medium to hone pro-ductive consumer literacy skills that might be drawn on in future occupa-tional contexts could be applied to Internet file-swappers, CD pirates, DJs, performance dancers, singers and – of course – musicians who together represented a significant proportion of the sample. Musician Steven's rec-ollection that, 'I think I started listening to rock when I were ten, when I started to learn guitar' (Richmond High School C1) is a further example of how media literacies can be formed and informed by consumer and pro-ducer practices. In the final section of this chapter I will focus on another framework for understanding young people's media uses and influences that overlaps with the notion of literacies as temporal processes exemplified here by what Steven recalls of his younger years.

Everyday life narratives

Hermes's (1995) deployment of repertoire analysis which focused on interview responses that recurred on different occasions rather than isolated, extraordinary responses provided a sympathetic method for selecting biographical excerpts from one-to-one discussions. Although the majority of my respondents were interviewed in groups, the definition of 'repertoires' applied by Hermes to her individual interviewees' life histories equally can be applied to my discussions with respondents who mostly shared friendship ties: 'repertoires are available knowledge that readers will refer to in everyday talk' (1995: 26). The 'knowledge' that I sought from respondents had not been intentionally framed by a life-narrative agenda but much of it was drawn from past experiences, some of which recalled early childhood memories. Clearly the impact of family influences on these young people's music media histories explains the abundant availability of knowledge from biographical sources as opposed to contemporary sources such as topical events, the latest fashionable trends or popular products. Nevertheless, talk in the past tense or of an impersonal bent referred to experiences that were given an almost timeless familiarity within hypothetical everyday life contexts. Therefore, whilst life narratives are often assumed to contain past memories that are independent from present-day contexts, what I term 'everyday life narratives' are meant to capture progressive processes by which past experiences inform present-day ones, the latter of which depend on the former for guidance. Everyday life narratives thus endorse the methodological spirit of radical contextualism (Ang 1996) as previously applied to the notion of self-presentations (see Chapter 4), and to an interactionist approach centred in the local and intergenerational (see Chapter 3). Here I will distinguish radically contextual narratives about how music media are used to convey temporal moods 'here and now' with deeper embedded personal histories in which music media use structures definitive life passages.

The large extent to which mediated music choices depended on respondents' moods in reaction to specific events and interactions is evident from several interchanges. For example, Vicky responded to my request for any further comments towards the end of a first-stage interview with the question: 'have you ever wondered why when you're depressed you listen to, like, depressing music, don't ya?' (Richmond High School C1). She listened to 'slower' music if depressed but 'if I'm just in a bad mood I like rock'. She continued:

Vicky: I know when I feel, like, a bit – which is weird that you would do this – but when I feel, like – like crying or, like, just really tired or that, I just play dead sad kind of music, you know, like, a love song or something. {Laughs}
{Some laughter}

Dave: Every – everybody does that sort of thing but, like, other day I was – I was, er, organising some paintball thing for this weekend – I was just so stressed when I got it all organised.
DL: Yeh.
Dave: I just banged on all my favourite tunes and just come to bed – went to bed and I was sound.
DL: Right.
Kevin: Ah that – I was trying to think of it then. Er, have you heard of Basement Jaxx, / 'Where's Your Head At'.
Dave: ['Where's Your Head At', yeh.
Vicky: Oh, I [...]=
Kevin: It's a – it just makes [you want to get up and dance, that song – it just makes you happy, dunnit? I hate dancing, like, [. . .] you just wanna go out, like.
(ibid.)

Little input from myself as interviewer consolidates the view that Vicky's comments about music as a conveyor of moods resonated strongly with at least two others in the peer group. Kevin's change in emotional state while listening to a Basement Jaxx track included the urge to dance even though he hated dancing. Other instances of the intimate, immediate function of music in young people's everyday life narratives were Lucy's account of how she listened to music radio when alone but 'when I'm with others it's usually CDs [. . .]' (Southwell College 3) and Beate's contrary account of listening to the radio while making new friends at her hall of residence (University of Salford 3). Radically contextualist responses borne out of the self-presentations of respondents and gatekeepers involved in fieldwork also drew on life-narrative perspectives. At the end of an interview with Kevin, he acted as a gatekeeper by telling me that he would choose his friend Dave as my next interviewee because 'He's a music man' (Richmond High School 3). The dynamic interactions between senior staff and junior students at FE institutions also led to attempts to deconstruct stereotypical views about adults' – old life narrators – ignorance of young people's music tastes. Observation notes on one of my gatekeepers, the Head of Sixth Form at Pickles High School, recorded how she seemed 'to try and impress the nearly all-male class with her knowledge of artists' names and the names of music genres' (9.30 a.m. 17 September 2001).

As well as mediated music use in specific everyday contexts flagged by temporal moods and self-presentational performances, music could dig deeper into young people's personal histories.[9] The influence of elder family members on respondents' tastes was recalled on various occasions. Gaz's mother influenced his music choices: 'I remember, when I was little it probably influenced me because my mam was very into Jackson Five, a lot of Motown, Diana Ross' (University of Salford 3). However, she also liked Cliff Richard and Rick Astley, which Gaz did not. Moreover, her influence was perceived by her son to have extended through to his current tastes in the 'new soul movement' that he felt borrowed sounds from the older soul that his mother had first introduced to him. Jolene's taste for new soul artists was similarly inspired by her parents, who played soul music at home which steadily 'rubbed off' on her (Natton College 3). On two separate occasions the influence of elders on respondents' music tastes was denied in an immediate context and instead displaced to a time 'when you're young' (Justin and Sophie, Scarcroft College A1) or 'when you're very young' (Tom, Northborough College A1). Although Chris felt that parents had also influenced his music media use at a younger age, he responded to taunts from others in the peer group about his mother's adoration for Elvis Presley with 'There's nothing wrong with Elvis, there's nothing wrong with him' (Scarcroft College B1). Like Gaz's personal history, it would appear that the influence of his mother on Chris's music choices persisted from early to present everyday life contexts. Table 5.5 highlights some important distinctions between influences that tend to be revealed in the two types of everyday life narratives delineated above.

Although these distinctions appear to be qualitatively valid, I return to a fundamental point about everyday life narratives made earlier in this section. These types of narratives capture progressive processes by which the past informs and also guides present-day experiences. So whilst a distinction between radically contextual and embedded narratives holds firm, either type frames and guides the other. As such, both narrative types are sympathetic with Mannheim's (1952) standpoint on the need to detail the individual voices of each generation as it evolves through a history which it makes through its own idiosyncrasies. The youth generation's radically contextual accounts of peer group music exchanges, for example, are guided by more embedded experiences influenced by familial – and therefore

Table 5.5 Everyday life narratives on music influences

Types of narrative	Main influences
Radically contextual/immediate	Personal
	Peers
	Younger on elder family members (rare)
Embedded/historic	Personal
	Elder on younger family members (common)

necessarily intergenerational – interactions in which borrowing and acquiring practices first emerge. So everyday life narratives of mediated music practices communicate young people's intergenerational as much as their intra-generational self-identities and self-presentations.

Young people's everyday life narratives are perhaps more self-reflexive than those of older life narrators, given that they tend to typify learning histories. Learning to experience love and eroticism, for instance, tends to occur and find articulation at a young age (Giddens 1992). More emphasis is placed by young people – along with society as whole – on learning by experience than is placed on and by those who have already learnt by relatively considerable experience (i.e. older people). As discussed in the previous section, what older people such as teachers and parents tend to consider as 'literacy skills' are quite different from the productive consumer literacies that young people prefer to become competent in, such as reading populist commercial agendas in music television channels (Ian, Richmond High School). If young people's everyday life histories are synonymous with their everyday learning histories, it becomes clear that their competencies in articulating affiliation to particular mediated music cultures through everyday life narratives will depend upon their level of learning about them. Levels of learning are therefore inextricably linked with levels of involvement or experience. For example, those intensive media users of heavy rock music over several years will have acquired widespread knowledge through learning about populist, alternative and alternative-cum-populist acts. Their everyday life narratives about this youth music culture will have become more embedded than the merely radically contextual narratives of upstart rockers. The contextually bound and disposable nature of much mediated music demands that genuinely intensive users (i.e. fans) of a given genre are capable of keeping up with the ebbs and flows of the latest news and releases about that genre. Those who lacked a sufficient learning history with regard to a given youth music culture such as Gary (a casual consumer of heavy rock) also lacked the narrative capacities to associate themselves with the embedded narratives of competent and experienced learners such as Rick and Conor (intensive rock users). Not being competent at narrating learning histories with regard to certain youth music cultures, however, did not mean that casual media consumers lacked productive literacies per se. As evident from the selective aural reception of music television channels while doing homework (Claire, Richmond High School), casual consumers tended to learn different types of – in this case, multi-task – competence expressed through radically contextual narratives.

Summary

The central issue that has threaded through this chapter is that of involvement in mediated music consumer and producer practices. Different levels of involvement have been framed along a continuum from intensive use to casual consumption of music media. Models of consumption cycles or spirals as well as consumer/producer dichotomies have been problematised by the everyday productive tactics (de Certeau 1984) that young people deploy to bypass phases in the feeding back of use values to producers. Tactics such as copying others' recorded music collections or accessing news through websites in gratis college contexts are certainly facilitated by the omnipresence of music media across both the private and public realms of young people's everyday lives. Rather than being considered as a realm in which young people tend not to enact music practices unless within the confines of bedrooms, the private, domestic, familial realms of everyday life have been shown to exert key influences on respondents' music consumption and production. Casual media consumers in particular attach very privatised, personal meanings to music products such as hi-fi systems situated in the living rooms where they had grown up. Intensive media consumers, on the other hand, tended to retain very publicised meanings to music products that were very often not even purchased directly from producers (e.g. CD recordings exchanged in peer groups) but could still be previewed and appreciated through attentive use without ever becoming appropriated into the privatised sphere of ownership. Previewing mediated music with more or less attention by differentially involved youth music practitioners was everywhere and to everyone afforded by their daily public contexts. Access to music on the Internet, on non-terrestrial television channels or on CD players at schools and colleges, or access to music media at work as well as in various public leisure contexts was – to varying extents – inclusive of all.

Heterogeneous mediated music involvement led to differences in the types of productive consumer literacies and everyday narratives that young people articulated. Those intensive media users who tended to present alternative tastes to the exclusion of other, populist consumers expressed literacy skills in finely distinguishing between the textual properties of different music genres or deconstructing the commercial ploys of global media conglomerates. More casual consumers with mainly populist, inclusive tastes, on the other hand, demonstrated productive literacies by combining music with multiple related practices such as chatting online or training for educational ends. Different types of everyday life narratives tended to inform these literacies in reference to immediate and embedded learning histories. Intensive mediated music users developed specialist knowledge about specific youth music cultures over significant learning histories whilst casual consumers tended to draw on more immediate histories of critically detached, selective media reception through radically contextual narratives. It would be a mistake, though, to interpret greater levels of literacy skills among intensive compared to casual music media consumers. There are different types – but not necessarily different levels – of literacies.

Degrees of involvement, then, have been applied to the uses, influences, productive literacies and everyday narratives of young people's mediated music cultures. The following chapter will attempt to draw associations between the involvement continuum shown in Figure 5.1 and an accessibility continuum of co-present music practices. The argument presented in this thesis with regard to the distinct but interrelated facets of mediated and co-present music practices will be operationalised by showing how the combination of these two sets of everyday practices impinges on young people's identities and performances. Given that my research has aimed to situate mediated and co-present music leisure practices in young people's everyday lives, it seems valid to argue that the findings here might apply to all forms of leisure that involve comparable mediated and co-present practices.

Notes

1. See previous discussion on the fallacy of 'exotic data' in some ethnographic accounts, particularly in relation to subcultures (e.g. Willis 1978) and fans (e.g. Shank 1994).
2. Expenditure on music merchandise was relatively much lower: 131 respondents (56 per cent) spent less than £10 whilst just 22 respondents (9 per cent) spent £50 or more on T-shirts, fanzines, posters and other merchandise in the past year.
3. Appreciating mediated music brings exposure to the media marketing tool known as 'the genre', which will be discussed later in this section
4. Despite Thornton's (1995: 114) claim about the inadequacy of 'mainstream' as a sociological concept, her account of the meaning of mainstream public entertainment is, ironically, perceptive enough to resonate with my own concerted exploration of casual (and often at the same time mainstream and populist) music practices.
5. Bashment sound seems to have Caribbean roots in dance-hall traditions. This sound is named after a New York DJ called Steelie Bashment and 'in its present form has been going for about three years although Steelie Bashment has been in the business himself for the past 15' (http://www.bbc.co.uk/1xtra/dj_biogs/dj_steelie_bashment.shtml, accessed May 2005).

6. There were 36 out of 114 (32 per cent) males compared to 12 out of 118 (10 per cent) females who consumed one or more hours of Internet music each week on average.

7. To clarify, school best describes the educational context of respondents in further education institutions which also included provision of compulsory secondary education. College describes the contexts for respondents both in exclusively further and higher education institutions.

8. Kassabian's (2002) concept of 'ubiquitous listening' seems appropriate to the omnipresence of mediated music in public contexts, nor are such contexts specific to young people. Music in most public places, though, is only likely to be listened to in a subconscious or background manner – hence my preference for the term 'consumption' rather than 'listening', which implies a greater level of focused music interaction than is usually the case.

9. Indeed, music digs deep into older people's personal histories as revealed by DeNora (2000) and Dolfsma's (2004) oral-history interviews with respondents who experienced youth during the rise of pop music in 1950s and 1960s Holland. I would partly agree with Dolfsma (2004: 436) that 'Analysis of the narratives of consumers bring out a more complex picture than is usually presented in everyday discussion of pop music' but at the same stress the importance of analysing mundane, everyday consumer narratives in relation to more historical ones: 'It is the everyday and normal which frames and helps define the special' (Sloboda and O'Neill 2001: 415).

CHAPTER 6

Public Music Practices

Qualitatively distinct from young people's music media uses and influences, this chapter will interpret empirical findings into youth music cultures in public contexts where co-present consumer and producer practices provide the foreground for social interactions. Like the pervasive presence of music media in public contexts as shown in Chapter 5, the following findings will nevertheless reveal how public music consumers and producers often project media influences on to everyday performances. My use of the term 'practice' (as outlined in Chapter 4) is central to the intentions of this book to situate music within the routine and often mundane contexts of young people's everyday lives. The term 'use' is deployed more frequently in the previous chapter because mediated music was more usually consumed – albeit often for productive ends – than produced by respondents. However, it seems better suited to refer to young people's *practices* in public music contexts where the relationship between consumption and production tends to be ambiguous. Bakhtin's (1984) concept of the carnivalesque as a feature of everyday public life can be applied to the notion of public music practices. Carnivalesque practices as outlined earlier were defined as regular acts of human (or animal) agency, such as the speaking of a particular argot or 'cris'. The sixteenth-century carnivalesque marketplace according to Bakhtin's interpretation of Rabelais's novels was where 'Sound, the proclaimed word, played an immense role in everyday life as well as the cultural field. It was even greater than in our days, in the time of the radio' (1984: 182). Indeed, the cultural field and everyday life were 'all drawn into the same dance' (1984: 160) so that theatrical conventions were drawn into the art of hawking and poetic renditions served as oral advertisements for all to participate in without clear division between producers and consumers. Bakhtin's metaphor of a dance captures the sense of disorder in an informal economy where it is never clear who leads (performs) and follows (spectates). Public music practices discussed here are broadly defined on a similar basis as those everyday consumer and producer interactions that were regularly accessible to respondents in carnivalesque contexts, where perceptions of social classifications tended to be dynamic rather than static.

Access to the contexts of public music practices, however, was more problematic for some young people than others in my sample. Attempts to avoid inspection or escape such contexts altogether were frequently described in interviews. Inspection contexts typically included such sites as clubs and bars, which have been cited by some theorists following Maffesoli (1995) as examples of eclectic consumer spaces that attract neo-tribal, emotional communities (Bennett 1999; 2000; Malbon 1999). The first part of this chapter will assess to what extent public music practices provided access to the eclectic consumer and producer sensibilities of respondents. The notion of eclecticism will be understood in relation to perceptions of exclusiveness and inclusiveness when accessing various public contexts. The second section will show analyses of questionnaire findings, and will evaluate the relationship between young people's accessibility to public music practices and their involvement with these practices as well as those music media uses analysed in the previous chapter. The third section will develop concepts of presentation and identification to understand how young people manage others' impressions of themselves and judge others' impressions through interactive music practices. The significance of global music media influences on how young people form these identifications and presentations will then be evaluated. Fifth, these global influences will be compared to local influences by exploring how space and place relate to public music experiences in terms of scenes and localities, before both sets of influences are incorporated into a much more detailed analysis of promenade performances than has been attempted thus far. In particular, similarities in the contextual facets of carnival and promenade performances will be empirically informed.

Consumption and production

When young people consume or produce music in public contexts, they also simultaneously consume or sometimes produce other experiences. Many public music venues are licensed for the consumption of alcoholic beverages. Added to the cost of these and other refreshments are ticketed admissions and means of transport to venues, together with prerequisites such as suitable clothes and cosmetics to facilitate accessibility to certain music practices. The club cultures studied by Thornton (1995) and

Malbon (1999) served as contexts in which music was central to consumer and producer experiences. Thornton's clubbers invested highly in subcultural capital to draw distinction between their 'hip' selves and mainstream music practitioners. Malbon's clubbers, on the other hand, 'often define themselves in terms of their preferred music(s) and the associated crowds thereof' (1999: 80) through which they created a sense of belonging wherein important memories and emotional experiences could be collectively consumed and produced. In the following discussion of fieldwork findings into a range of public music practices, I will argue that clubbing as a music practice was perhaps perceived with the most vivid sense of exclusiveness by respondents, some of whom drew distinction between their own and others' tastes akin to displays of cultural or even subcultural capital. However, club contexts were also perceived as eclectic spaces in which consumers with different music tastes could unite together. Nonetheless, a sense that club contexts could create belongings and inclusiveness was rarely articulated, although other inclusive music practices were evidently perceived. Discussion of young people's general public music consumer and producer practices, then, is understood here along an *accessibility continuum* from exclusion to inclusion, in which eclectic practices lie somewhere in-between.

Exclusiveness

The term 'exclusiveness' is broadly applied here to public music practices in which certain consumers and producers were distinguished or distinguished themselves as more favourable practitioners than others. Cultural capital becomes a more valuable currency as access to practices becomes more exclusive. Knowledge and material resources represented forms of cultural and financial capital whose significance recurred in several interview responses. Exclusive age and dress codes in certain public contexts were regularly talked about by respondents and observed during fieldwork. Practices in which a specific type or genre of music was perceived to be consumed or produced were more likely to create distinctions that excluded other taste groups. Niche production practices encouraged by those fragmented music tastes that characterised the sample (see Table 5.4) would target specific taste cultures that excluded a huge proportion of consumers who either disliked, or lacked the eclectic sensibility to try and like, the end products. One respondent spoke about how his friends had formed a band and produced music to be accessible on the Internet for consumers – including Artiste and Repertoire (A and R) staff at record companies – with tastes for their type of music (Pickles High School B1). Another respondent, Sam, was in the process of seeking full-time work as a DJ but her experiences at Buzz FM, a local radio station in Manchester, had developed consumer as well as producer sensibilities to build a larger collection of recorded music that was 'a bit more jumpy than I've got, you know, so I won't ever run out of anything like that' (Natton College D2). Partly influenced by 'the person who's in charge of Buzz,' Sam's decision to develop a material resource through knowledge of a particular music genre – in this case, hip hop – suggests that exclusive co-present consumer and producer sensibilities are harboured by mutual accessibility to niche-mediated practices.

Exclusive access to non-mediated music practices was particularly evident in club and certain bar contexts. Perhaps a group of black Caribbean female respondents were the closest resemblance to clubbers high in subcultural capital. Jolene, Sam and Tanya relayed widespread knowledge and experience of special club nights at venues throughout northern England. A regular fixture for Jolene and Sam – and sometimes Jolene's mother – was a soul night on the first Wednesday of each month at a club in Warrington. Jolene had travelled considerable distances without her own means of transport (she was too young to drive, aged sixteen) to club venues in Liverpool, Sheffield and Leeds: 'I'd like to go other places but, like, you need transport and everything, so if you can't get transport then just go town' (ibid. 3). Jolene herself, then, was excluded from exclusive club practices due to the age-related circumstances of her restricted mobility without reliable transport resources. Despite the growth in sociological literature about transport (particularly cars) as a facilitator of mobility (e.g. Miller 2001), there seems to be a dearth of research into how means of transport impact upon those who have them or do not – an issue that resonates especially strongly with young people. One of the few studies to address this issue explains in similar terms the wider significance of the sense of frustration felt by Jolene as the result of inequalities in 'the ability to participate in car culture [. . .] Absence of the car can clearly lead to feelings of social exclusion' (Carrabine and Longhurst 2002: 192–3).

Other exclusive music practices such as clubbing holidays were also subject to necessary financial as well as cultural capital:

Jolene: We're supposed to be going, erm, Aya Napa in August but that's if we save up enough but I don't know if we will yet. And that's, like, we're going there because of the music as well cause it's, like, garage – it's a garage, erm – it's, like, a garage holiday cause loads of garage people go out there – MCs and things, and R 'n' B as well. They'll, like – they'll be loads of things. They have beach parties and everything and loads of MCs over there so/ that's why people usually go Aya

Napa. And, like, Pay as You Go who we went to see last week – they're usually in Aya Napa, like, Spain and everything.   (ibid.)

As well as attending clubs with her daughter and daughter's friends, Jolene's mother also appeared to be the main organising and driving force behind this prospective clubbing holiday. The intergenerational relationship between Jolene's mother and her younger club goers was made more intimate by the fact that, at thirty-three years of age, she was a relatively young mother of a sixteen-year-old daughter. This type of exclusive family holiday can therefore be distinguished from the more inclusive kind that tends to proceed when parents are older and children are younger. Tanya had planned to go holidaying with Jolene and Sam but clearly felt excluded after her expenditure became bound to a family holiday in Canada of the more inclusive kind.

Other than clubs and clubbing holidays, even more typically mainstream public entertainment contexts could create perceptions of exclusiveness to young people. Laura's tastes for pop music and knowledge of going out at night in Bolton town centre explained her preference for bars such as Revolution and Yates that played this type of music:

Laura: [. . .] when you first start going out you find out which places were [. . .] sort of playing what. And if you don't like the music you won't go in. I've found that. Some places I won't go in on a certain night because they have a certain theme night – all dance and all eighties or all [. . .] sixties stuff.
DL: Right.
Laura: Or, like, all brand-new pop, so it also depends what night you go out.
DL: I see. So you tend to go to the kind of variety [[. . .] where I suppose =
Laura: Yeh, more – sort of more pop than all just dance [. . .]   (Richmond High School B1)

Interviewed at the same school, Claire and her friends also preferred these 'big franchised' town-centre bars rather than pubs because they provided better facilities for dancing (ibid. 3). Claire, like Laura, preferred pop music and expressed populist tastes but nevertheless perceived an exclusive practice in seeking out this type of music in public venues rife with rock, dance, hip hop, R 'n' B and garage affiliations. Another example of exclusiveness in accessing Bolton's public music venues was the decision by Alex and his friends to only attend a mainstream club called Atlantis on Fridays when 'It's normally dance music' and no longer on Thursdays when 'they play pop and you have to go upstairs (for dance music)' (ibid.). In this instance, the exclusiveness of a practice geared towards consumption of a specific type of music had been accentuated by experiences of eclectic public music (i.e. club) contexts.

As well as exclusiveness created by differences in tastes, young people's age and dress differences distinguished certain individuals from others in specific music practices. Beate avoided student club nights in Manchester because at twenty-five years of age she felt uneasy about looking old to others (University of Salford 3). Many public music venues in towns and cities with significant student populations target young student consumers by offering discounted admission fees with ID, often strictly in the form of a National Union of Students (NUS) card. In some venues on certain nights an NUS card is not only a benefit but essentially a passport for admittance. Many young people, of course, found themselves excluded from these venues for appearing to be – and frequently being – too young to consume alcohol in public by law. Dress as well as age restrictions were strictly enforced in certain clubs and bars:

> Dave: That's why I don't like going clubbing. Cause, like, you have to wear a certain thing. You have to, like, wear your shirt and you have to wear your black pants and you have to have, like, your posh shoes and stuff like that. I don't like dressing up like that [. . .] I just prefer to dress the way I wanna and go to, like, a club that plays the music I like but there aren't one in Bolton [. . .]
> (Richmond High School 3)

Dave clearly perceived a correlation between club policies on dress codes and the types of music that they played. He imagined his indie rock preferences to be practised in clubs with lenient admission policies. Gaz also associated strict dress codes with exclusive public music practices which he felt were pretentious and undesirable: 'R 'n' B clubs and hip hop clubs have got a bit of a bad reputation' (University of Salford 3). In such clubs dress codes are sometimes placed on particular brands of clothes and shoes that are associated with criminal groups, particularly of young black men. Exclusive age and dress codes partly triggered impression management practices to be discussed later in this chapter.

Inclusiveness

My definition of 'inclusiveness' in relation to public music practices applies to contexts where consumers and producers did not perceive distinctions between themselves and other young people but rather accessed such practices to instil a sense of belonging. Those deemed inclusive practices to some youth groups were thus still exclusive to others. A sense of inclusiveness differed from that of exclusiveness, though, because it remained unaware of its exclusionary consequences given its low requirements of cultural as well as financial capital. Many of the eclectic club practices outlined in the next section were more exclusive than inclusive because they tended to be accessed only by groups with narrow music tastes who followed prerequisite age and dress codes. Vicky's point that, 'You meet people' hints at how clubs might function as sites for what Maffesoli (1995) theorises as 'sociality' and Malbon (1999) partly endorses through participant observations of clubbing. Nevertheless, both Maffesoli and Malbon consider sociality to signal a decline in individualism but interview responses here express the individualist processes involved in such sociality. Louise's personal experiences of social interactions at a particular club (see Figure 6.1) further point to how inclusiveness is perceived in individualist contexts:

> Louise: [. . .] going to Atlantis has made me – made me start to know other people.
> Laura: Yeh, it does =
> Louise: Of what they're like and, erm, / you start to know the people.
> (Richmond High School AB2)

Perhaps the only other means through which club contexts provided inclusive access to young people was by relaxing age restrictions. A group of white and Indian males at Northborough College attended a once monthly night at Atlantis for people aged under eighteen years (A1). The same club permitted those aged over eighteen years for weekly student nights but restricted access only to those aged over nineteen years for the busier public nights at weekends. Claire and her peer group had mutually decided to attend student club nights where access was likely to include them all on the basis of their age, and where cheaper admission fees and drinks encouraged group members who lacked monetary resources. On weekend nights Claire's group would attend local bars to reduce transport costs incurred by a five-mile journey to and from Bolton town centre:

> Claire: Instead of going into Bolton, you know, cause we won't spend as much money cause obviously it's, like, ten pound into Bolton and ten pound back, and then it's getting in a club and then your drinks, so sometimes we'll just go down to Middlebrook cause it's easy and then we'll – we'll, say, / go for something to eat and then stay in there all night. (ibid. 3)

Inclusiveness was practised in this instance through collective peer group decisions to place convenience and economy above music tastes on a list of entertainment criteria.

Other inclusive music practices generally placed less emphasis on

Figure 6.1 Group collectivist and individualist sociality on the Atlantis
dance floor. (Photograph: D. Laughey)

specific or eclectic music tastes as motivations. More important for these
music practices were the friendship or family-group contexts in which
they occurred. Some bars and pubs as well as concert venues, cafés,
churches and schools provided sites for perceived practices of inclusion.
Gaz's network of friends that had partly formed through shared music
tastes favoured a bar called Revolution near Manchester's universities to
some extent out of 'musical choice' but also because its location amid a

Figure 6.2 Inclusive, open–plan DJ-ing practices at Revolution.
(Photograph: D. Laughey)

large student population created 'a really good atmosphere, decent people, decent prices' (University of Salford 3). The inclusiveness of consumption and production practices at Revolution was manifested by what Gaz considered to be 'good DJs' who took requests from customers to play certain tracks (see Figure 6.2).

Some respondents accompanied elder family members to bars and pubs to facilitate age inclusion:

> *Jamie: [. . .] there's, like, loads of violence going on in the pub [. . .] they had to have security on and this guy goes 'have you got any ID?' and I said 'no' and he goes 'well, I can't let you in,' my mum goes 'WHAT,' and he goes 'he's got no ID,' and my mam goes 'I'm his ID, I'm his mam [. . .],' so puts her head down and just walked in laughing.* (Wilson High School A1)

Concert venues also provided inclusive familial practices. Parents sometimes attended concerts with respondents (Dave with his father, Richmond High School C1; Gill with her mother and sister, Southwell College C2), whilst James and his uncle had performed together in a jazz band at gig venues that they also regularly attended (Southwell College B1).[1] Small 'gig' venues such as Manchester's Night and Day generated a sense of inclusiveness between bands and audiences, where the latter were invited to access knowledge about the former in their inevitable quest towards commercial success (see Figure 6.3):

> I include my email details for the band's mailing list. This form is situated on the vending desk – a petty version of the more sophisticated retail and merchandising operations at larger gigs. A young woman sells T-shirts and CDs – products of the bands playing tonight (three in all). (Night and Day, Oldham Street, Manchester city centre: 8 p.m. October 2002)

Hilary frequented the same café in Bolton town centre where music was played, both with her father and on other occasions with friends (Southwell College 3). Stacian's tastes in gospel music were influenced by her Christian beliefs and inclusive church attendance practices alongside her grandparents (Natton College 3). Finally, schools provided peer group music practices of inclusion based on populist tastes. Tom felt that in these everyday contexts 'what everybody else likes you, kind of, follow [. . .] It's not all independent – it's a group thing' (Northborough College A1) and Chris stated that, 'At first it's just, like, you don't want to be different from everyone else, you listen to their sort of music, and after a while you just get used to it' (Scarcroft College B1). The pervasive influence of familial and educational contexts on young people's music practices is often neglected in the concern for more visible and spectacular contexts. Familial influences are assumed to occur during phases of private, domestic, mediated consumption (see previous discussion of Silverstone (1994)). On the contrary, co-present as well as mediated music practices were frequently enacted by family members or classmates beyond those original contexts of identity formations.

Eclecticism

I have chosen to contrast eclectic with inclusive music practices because the neo-tribalism that treats these two phenomena as synonymous proved inadequate when applied to analysis of these empirical findings. Eclecticism in its neo-tribalist usage defines a variety of personal consumer experiences that collectively construct – rather than are constructed by – a sense of communal identity. Bennett's (2000) case study of urban dance culture conveyed its collective and inclusive response to mainstream nightlife practices. However, the incongruity between eclecticism and inclusiveness was emphasised in my research by the finding that the former remained mostly limited to clubbing practices whilst the latter was rarely articulated through such practices. Although many clubs provided eclectic spaces where customers could choose to consume their

Figure 6.3 Inclusive support networks at Night and Day.
(Photograph: D. Laughey)

preferred type of music or try out different types, this finding insufficiently indicated widespread eclectic sensibilities without producing data on how many clubbers regularly moved between these different musical experiences.[2] Observations at Bolton's Club Ikon noted the stark difference between the club spaces and clubbers on the two floor levels:

> The upper floor serves out chart music under the slogan Pop Ikon, a pastiche of the logo for *Pop Idol*, the recent hugely popular television talent show. Here there are two projection screens that occasionally show videos of the track that plays concurrently. This floor in particular hints of the sexual motives behind club-going. The parameters of the dance floor are male-dominated while the dance floor itself is mostly the terrain of females. Key 103 promotes Pop Ikon and in turn the radio station is advertised on banners around the upper floor. The 'happy house' floor seems less explicitly about sexual relations, more about heavy bass, frantic dancing and arm-waving, and building a shared sense of musical appreciation [. . .] The DJ booth is quite small and tucked into a corner of the dance floor. By contrast, the dance floor upstairs is more hierarchical (perhaps more like Mecca dance floors) in that the DJ is positioned above the dancers in a relatively large, clearly visible booth.   (17 October 2002)

On this Thursday night it appeared that offers on alcoholic beverages were at least as important to Club Ikon's marketing as their eclectic music offerings. There was no strict dress code, so that many customers in casual dress appeared to have come directly from pubs. Perhaps predictably, these customers were attracted more by the late drinking hours than the diversity of music and tended to congregate on the upper floor, where they appeared to remain for most of the night. The following conversation between interviewees consolidates a sense in which this club effectively offered exclusive rather than eclectic music experiences:

> Kevin: Say, Ikon in Bolton, that does my head in.
> DL: What sort of music do they play there?
> Kevin: It's just dance =
> Vicky: Dance [. . .]
> Kevin: But everything sounds the same – every new song sounds the same.
> DL: Right, yeh.
> Vicky: I only like a bit of dance music [. . .] but sometimes I wish they'd play more, like, R 'n' B and hip hop stuff.   (Richmond High School C1)

Eclectic club spaces would only make a genuine impression on clubbers' practices, then, if they proved sufficiently different to actualise alternative music experiences.

With eclectic music accessibility doubtful on a significant scale, a few instances in which such practices were perceived are nonetheless noteworthy. I described previously how Alex and his friends avoided the eclectic music spaces offered on Thursdays at Atlantis in favour of exclusively dance music consumption on Fridays. By contrast, Claire and her friends preferred the music on Thursdays at this club: 'you see, they have two levels. They have R 'n' B on the top and they have pop, dancey stuff on the bottom, so it's, like, a good range of different music [. . .]' (ibid. 3). Nicky and Gavin attended club nights with South Asian friends where their group might temporarily split up to consume different types of music in a club's different rooms:

> *Gavin: A lot of Asians do like R 'n' B and hip hop, so they play it in one room and play bhangra in another.*
> *DL: (to Nicky) So what happens if all your friends want to go and listen to bhangra?*
> *Nicky: They do, and stay in that room.*
> *DL: Oh, you're on your own in that room.*
> *Nicky: You meet people [. . .] dance.*   (Natton College A1)

In this example Nicky's eclectic consumer practices conveyed a sense of inclusiveness, albeit through individualist actions. Similarly, Beate preferred to go alone to dance in clubs rather than sit down with her student friends in pubs 'because then I don't need to care for anyone else [. . .] I can go where I want and when I want' (University of Salford 3). Eclecticism also applied to bars where accessibility in terms of selecting and moving between such contexts was less exclusive compared to clubs. Jolene and her clubbing friends could tolerate eclectic music consumption in different bars that could be easily and cheaply entered and exited but 'we don't go in a club for three or four hours if it's not the music that we want or not the people or something' (Natton College D2). Indeed, many town-centre bars at the time of research provided music on different floors akin to clubbing provisions, such as Manchester's Old Monk, where 'If you like garage you can go downstairs, if you like R 'n' B you can stay upstairs' (Sam, ibid.). These bars as well as more traditional pub and various other contexts enabled a greater degree of inclusive accessibility than clubs that could only rarely be perceived as neither more exclusive nor more eclectic.

Figure 6.4 summarises the main characteristics of an accessibility continuum applicable to young people's practices in any specific public music culture as gleaned from interview discussions and observations. The variety of choice sensed by respondents in their eclectic public music consumer and

Exclusiveness	Inclusiveness
Specific tastes	Broad tastes
Niche sensibilities	Mainstream sensibilities
High cultural capital	Moderate cultural capital
High financial capital	Moderate financial capital
Group collectivist	Individualist
Club and bar contexts	Various public contexts

Figure 6.4 An accessibility continuum for public music practices.

producer practices would dictate where they might be positioned along this accessibility continuum. Those respondents who attended clubs where more than one musical space was made available but who nonetheless displayed group preference for accessing a niche space would collectively practise exclusive eclecticism. By contrast, individualist consumers who preferred to access public music experiences alone were able to practise relatively genuine eclecticism inclusive of mainstream and niche spaces. The concept of accessibility will now be developed in relation to that of involvement as explored in the previous chapter.

Accessibility and involvement

Analyses of questionnaire replies revealed no correlation between levels of accessibility in public and involvement in mediated music practices. Therefore, it would be invalid to suggest that the accessibility continuum above could be mapped on to the involvement continuum (see Figure 5.1). It is not the case that, for example, respondents who tended to be intensive music media users also generally tended to be exclusive public music practitioners. This section will instead explore more complex relationships between types of consumption and production, and their accessibility and involvement by the sample. Whilst music media were more or less accessible to all respondents – even if not always in domestic contexts – public music practices provided different experiences based on accessibility *and* involvement. First, I will interpret questionnaire findings on differences in involvement across various public music practices and apply these findings to those on accessibility outlined in the previous section. These interpretations will then inform a second set of analyses which will explore the complex relationship between different youth groups' mediated and public music practices. Understanding this complex relationship is crucial to the objectives of researching music in young people's everyday life contexts, wherein media frequently enjoy public presence and public practices nearly always are mediated to some degree.

First, Table 6.1 shows the temporal involvement of the sample in various everyday sites of public music practices. Exclusive practices in club and certain bar contexts clearly comprised relatively high degrees of consumer involvement in terms of time. However, typical contexts for inclusive practices like concert venues and schools were also sites where quite high degrees of involvement in music consumption could occur.[3] Interview responses revealed that sites both for potentially inclusive and exclusive access to music practices were visited on a typical night out. These responses more acutely revealed that increasingly intense involvement in music practices during a typical night out sometimes corresponded with increasingly exclusive accessibility to such practices. The dancing activities engaged in by Claire

Table 6.1 Public music consumption on average each week (hours)

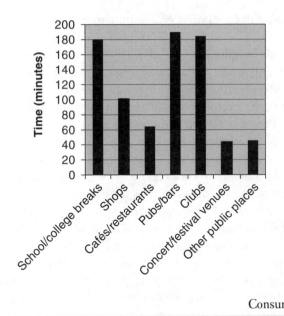

	Consumption time
Pubs/bars	3 hours 10 minutes
Clubs	3 hours 4 minutes
School/college breaks	3 hours
Shops	1 hour 42 minutes
Cafés/restaurants	1 hour 4 minutes
Other public places	45 minutes
Concert/festival venues	44 minutes

and her friends would begin in pubs and bars before often culminating in clubs: 'We normally start, like, furthest away from the club and then have a drink in each and then go to the club' (Richmond High School 3). Similarly, the exclusive clubbing practices accessed by the black Caribbean female group at Natton College would usually follow less exclusive bar practices where involvement in drinking rather than music and dancing would be more intense (D2). Melissa expressed how alcohol consumption was central to her preferred bar contexts but other consumer priorities – music of which was one – formed the criteria for more exclusive club contexts:

> *Melissa: No, I'm not bothered about the music. When I go to bars it's not about the music, it's about drink.*
> . . .
> *Right, when I go out clubbing it I've gotta pick a good club cause I'll be there all night but in a bar [. . .]*   (Natton College B1)

Music as a criterion for public entertainment, then, was prioritised in the case of clubs because increasingly exclusive accessibility posed the threat of self-imposed boredom.

Bi-variate and multi-variate analyses of questionnaire replies partly contradict interpretations from interview discussions and observations with regard to the exclusiveness of certain contexts. Music consumption in pubs and bars was significantly co-related to both ethnicity and social class. In terms of ethnicity, 22 out of 27 (81 per cent) respondents from ethnic minorities compared to 54 out of 135 (40 per cent) white respondents consumed less than three hours of music on average each week in pubs and bars. In terms of social class, 33 out of 57 (58 per cent) respondents with a parent or parents who had at best an 'intermediate, routine and manual occupation' compared to 22 out of 71 (31 per cent) with a parent or parents who had a 'managerial and professional occupation' consumed less than three hours of music on average each week in these same contexts. Findings suggest, then, that those least likely to consume music in pubs and bars were young people from ethnic minorities and those from the lower social classes. However, a possible sense of exclusion felt by young people of certain ethnic and class backgrounds in particular public places was perhaps confined to pubs and bars. Music consumption in clubs was experienced by a far more even distribution of young people across ethnic and social class differences, and by implication provided less exclusive accessibility than music consumed in pubs and bars.

Gender differences in exclusive and inclusive public music practices are illustrated in Table 6.2. The exclusiveness of club contexts is apparently

Table 6.2 Gender and public music consumption

Distribution	
Even	**Skewed**
Pubs and bars	Cafés and restaurants
Clubs	Shops
School and college breaks	Concert and festival venues

neither manifested in terms of gender nor ethnic and social class differences. The even involvement of young consumers across different social variables in clubbing practices suggests that perhaps only age was a significant factor in accessing these contexts. The inclusiveness of music consumption in school and college contexts is reflected by an even distribution of involvement across gender – as well as ethnic and social class – lines. However, various other public music contexts hinted at exclusiveness in terms of gender differences in their involvement: 27 out of 62 (44 per cent) females against 12 out of 76 (16 per cent) males replied that they consumed two or more hours of music in cafés and restaurants each week on average. As there is no apparent alternative public music site for mostly male young people (pubs, bars and clubs were frequented by males and females in numbers that differ little either way), it can be assumed that they were likely to allocate more time and space to private music consumption. Twice as many female than male respondents (26 out of 81 replies against 13 out of 84 replies) spent three or more hours on average each week consuming music in shops. Furthermore, 50 out of 91 (55 per cent) females against 32 out of 83 (39 per cent) males replied that they had spent £30 or more on concert and festival tickets in the past year.

The overall finding that those public contexts with skewed distributions attracted a greater proportion of female than male music consumers points to a simple conclusion that female respondents were more likely to be visible than male respondents in a variety of public music consumption sites. Contrary to previous assumptions (McRobbie 1990; Frith 1983), it would appear not that young females in this sample represented a largely invisible group of music consumers in private contexts such as bedrooms, but that they consumed music in everyday public contexts such as cafés, restaurants and shops that tend to be neglected by ethnographers in pursuit of subcultural or club cultural 'spaces'. An exception to this neglect is DeNora's and Belcher's in-store observations of female responses to music in clothing retail contexts, in which they found that 'younger women are more likely to view shopping as a leisure time pursuit, more likely to visit a shop with no specific objective in mind and to shop in friendship groups' (2000: 92). Contrary to exclusive subcultural gender categories, though, the intensive involvement of young women in leisurely shopping, café and restaurant going seems to attach a sense of inclusiveness to these public music sites more than any sense that they might *intentionally* exclude young men.

In regard to production practices, involvement was not marked along any social variable. It can be assumed, therefore, that the niche sensibilities of exclusive music production or the mainstream sensibilities of inclusive music production were not partaken in by certain demographically delineated youth groups more than others. Expenditure on music instruments for production such as mixing desks, guitars and computer software averaged only £39 in the past year.[4] This low expenditure reflects the statistic that 74 out of 232 respondents (32 per cent) participated in music production. Whilst this proportion of music producers – approximately one to every three young people – represented a minority, it can nevertheless be probably regarded as quite considerable in relation to the proportion of music producers in the wider population. The largest producer group (33 out of 74 or 45 per cent) comprised conventional musicians who generally practised inclusive production through mainstream sensibilities.[5] Nonetheless, more exclusive, niche production such as performance dancing and DJ-ing represented another large producer group (30 out of 74 or 41 per cent). More mainstream, inclusive music practices appeared to have declined in involvement as several respondents grew older and left regimented school to enter informal college contexts. Hilary 'used to play the keyboard' and had lessons at school but no longer expressed interest in improving her keyboard skills, whilst Lucy used to play the flute: 'I don't think I'll go anywhere with it. It was when I was at school. I used to be in the orchestra and have lessons but now I just/ don't really do anything with it' (Southwell College 3). Active production practices of exclusiveness as well as inclusiveness ultimately required intensive levels of involvement.

Findings from questions about involvement in public music practices, then, partly reflected but also contradicted findings from interview discussions and observations about the accessibility of these practices. In trying to compare young people's accessibility to public music with their involvement in music media practices in the second part of this section, then, it seems more useful to understand such complex relationships by way of a dual configuration of continua rather than a continuum or table of binary oppositions, which only proved sufficient for contrasting the features of either set of practices. The four groupings in the model shown in Figure 6.5 do not represent a typology and are not intended to describe personality types or

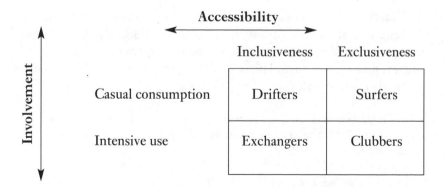

Figure 6.5 An involvement and accessibility model for youth music
practitioners.

fixed categories of youth music practitioners. Many respondents' radically
contextual consumption and production of music in different everyday contexts meant that they frequently appeared to move around these groupings,
with the qualification that it was highly unlikely that they could move from
one extreme to another (i.e. from drifter to clubber). It was previously found
that music practices sometimes increased in exclusiveness and intensity
during a night out. In this case, practitioners might well start the night in
one grouping and finish it in another. Definitions of these four groupings
are clearly required here to detail the complex relationships between everyday mediated and co-present experiences.

Drifters among the sample were characterised by casual consumption
of music media and inclusive access to public music entertainment.
Respondents tended to be drifters when music was perceived only as a
background soundtrack to other activities such as homework or drinking.
This drifter figure would seem to parallel the life strategy of Bauman's
(1996) stroller, who in turn shared features of the *flâneur*, although the
former would stroll around multimediascapes by 'zapping' remote controls
rather than around shopping malls and city streets in the latter's case.
However, the term 'drifter' is preferred here to convey the manner in
which some young people had little awareness of their music consumer and
producer practices even though their everyday life contexts regularly fea-
tured music within earshot. Music often played a minor role in these young
people's everyday lives. Although music would be infrequently purchased
or experienced in public contexts where high amounts of financial capital
were necessary, its pervasive presence through casual media such as radio
perhaps explains drifters' populist tastes and mainstream sensibilities. The
all-female group at Southwell College were mostly drifters. 'Anything

that's on the radio' (C1) was Hilary's response to a question about the kind of music that she liked. At sixteen years of age these respondents were perhaps only taking a few early steps towards experiencing public music contexts on a regular basis. Hilary's brief experience of 'moshing'[6] moved her briefly into the realm of surfing practices which she ultimately disliked:

> *Hilary: [I went with one of my friends the other week in (?Dawson) which is a bit further – but have you ever been moshing dancing?*
> *Gill: Oh, God.*
> *DL: You mean, like, [heavy.*
> *Hilary: [Moshing. Just everybody like, 'Woo'.*
> *Gill: Yeh.*
> *Hilary: [. . .] I just, kind of, went into't corner and hid. {Laughs}*
> *DL: Right. Is this in a pub or club?*
> *Hilary: A pub.*   (Southwell College C2)

As Figure 6.6 illustrates, moshing is an intensive public music practice that would require a drifter to move beyond a casual consumer role just to experience such a practice. Recruitment from one grouping to another would therefore usually involve an at least transitory experience of surfing or exchanging practices.

Figure 6.6 Moshing at The Star and Garter (Manchester city centre) gig venue. (Photograph: D. Laughey)

Surfers were characterised by casual media consumption but exclusive access to public practices. Those surfers among the sample, then, tended to invest more significance – in terms of time and money – in co-present rather than mediated music experiences. Both these experiences, however, would involve surfing, either across multimediascapes or nightscapes. The tourist figure (Bauman 1996) that sought novel experiences outside mundane everyday life contexts closely resembles this surfer figure. Like drifting practices, surfers would generally perceive music to play a functional role as a background to other activities such as seeking sexual relations or intoxication. However, if specific types of music *texts* were immaterial to the pleasures of surfers, specific practices associated with exclusive music *contexts* were of paramount importance to these young people. If surfers' mediated music tastes tended to be populist, their sensibilities were more often than not towards what they perceived to be niche co-present music practices. Claire and her friends engaged in surfing by seeking out broadly chart-based music consumption in what she considered to be niche public contexts that were distinguished from those where exclusively rock, dance, hip hop and other music genres prevailed. Similarly, Rizwaan's casual media consumption of bhangra music bore little relation to his decision to place friendship ahead of music preference at exclusive bhangra nights, where he would effectively become a surfer among many clubbers: 'I don't like it, like, I don't buy it, but I go with my friend' (Natton College E1).

Exchangers were those respondents who typically engaged in inclusive public music practices but intensively consumed music media. Exchangers tended to invest more significance in mediated than co-present practices. Music texts and technologies would be more important to the everyday lives of exchangers than exclusive music contexts. Whilst exchangers' tastes would often be alternative and specific to particular music genres, their sensibilities leaned towards mainstream public practices of inclusion. For example, Ian and Lindsay (Richmond High School) went out within a friendship group formed through shared tastes in alternative rock to inclusive concert venues rather than to town-centre rock clubs or bars, where they might have drawn more immediate distinction between themselves and other music taste groups. Very intensive music media users who rarely if ever engaged in public music contexts would still effectively perform exchanging practices in the peer group contexts of schools and colleges where such practices most frequently occurred (as discussed earlier in this chapter). For example, Gemma's average mediated consumption exceeded nine hours each week across recorded music, music television and Internet music but she never consumed co-present pub or club music. Interestingly, regular exchanging practices in which Gemma would burn MP3 files on to blank CDs for her friend Rachel (Southwell College) were met with what, at certain times of the week, would have been different uses by the receiver. Rather than remain a static exchanger, Rachel consumed music for five hours on an average week in both bars and clubs. Rachel would therefore move between exchanging and surfing or even – if the music that she consumed in bars and clubs related specifically to her mediated preferences – clubbing practices. Use of Internet music to enable cultural exchange adds an important present-day dimension to the exchanger figure. Whereas the now almost obsolete practice of home-taping was subject to the possession of friendship ties with peers (i.e. a certain degree of social capital), MP3 file-swapping is a more inclusive and accessible means of exchanging music than has ever been available before.

Finally, *clubbers* engaged in intensive media use and exclusive public practices. Being a clubber refers more to a sense of membership in a specific music taste group than to the particular context of clubbing. However, the term is also apt because clubs were mainly perceived as sites for exclusive music consumption and production. Music tended to play a central role in these young people's everyday lives. Relatively high levels of cultural and financial capital characterised clubbing practices. The learning processes required of clubbers included gaining media literacy skills for distinguishing dance music genres by numbers of beats per minute:

> Jolene: We just move a certain way with whatever music it is. Like, garage you, kind of, move a bit different than R 'n' B, you know. It's a bit faster, garage, so you would move a bit different, and like, hip hop, you'd dance different as well with that.
> DL: Yeh. So you just – do you do it, like, trial and error? You, kind of, get on the dance floor and then, sort of, work out the pace, or do you actually prepare beforehand, sort of?
> Jolene: It's, like, you've done it so many times so that you don't really need to prepare anything. It just comes and you just do it.   (Natton College 3)

Clubbers developed a sense of alternative self-identities that were clearly distinct from the mainstream sensibilities of surfers. Unlike exchangers, these clubbers tended to exchange and display knowledge or resources only within clubbing practices which excluded those without the eclecticism to try out such practices. Black Caribbean female respondents Jolene, Sam and Tanya typified clubbers by practising levels of cultural capital akin to the subcultural kind associated with the concept of club cultures. This group would travel considerable distances to niche club nights where specific DJs and MCs performed.

These groupings of music practitioners into four distinct figurations should be understood as more fluid than fixed. Young people in individual or group contexts could switch between these figurations in the duration of a single night out. The case of Gemma and Rachel also points to how those who participate together in one grouping might use such social interactions to complement different music practices in other groupings associated with separate contexts (in this case, school and club/bar contexts). Rachel effectively performed the role of an intergroup communicator (Fine and Kleinman 1979) of the latest music products, far from solely drawing her music influences within a single, exclusive grouping along the lines of a subculture. The following section will build on these findings into accessibility and involvement that inform drifter, surfer, exchanger and clubber figurations by applying them to issues of presentation and identification in public music practices. These figurations essentially represented young people's self-identities and self-presentations in interactive everyday contexts.

Presentation and identification

The discussion of performances in Chapter 4 focused on concepts of self-identities and self-presentations. Goffman's ideas about 'teams' and their 'disclosive communication' rituals in interaction with others will be applied to empirical findings into youth group interactions in public music contexts. Goffman (1969a) considered that

> if a performance is to be effective it will be likely that the extent and character of the cooperation that makes this possible will be concealed and kept secret. A team, then, has something of the character of a secret society. (1969a: 108)

The clubbers and surfers outlined in the previous section could certainly be understood as teams in search of effective performances through exclusive, secretive practices. Even inclusive exchangers such as inconspicuous personal stereo users needed to perform like secret societies to escape inspection in dynamic authority contexts (Abercrombie 1994) such as classrooms (e.g. Northborough College A1). The formation of teams in young people's everyday lives is particularly acute in perceptions of selves and others within the social contexts of school and college. It is within these contexts that many friendship groups form teams in competition with other teams. The performances of these teams are progressively removed from their original contexts towards other public music contexts such as pubs and clubs as members grow older together. Butler's (1990; 1999) theories on gender playing in which such processes of identification are conceived to be performative rather than predetermined will be applied to the age-playing practices of youth teams after I have shown that practices in impression management and judgement are fundamental for public music practitioners.

Impression management

The arts of impression management for Goffman's team collectives included measures to maintain loyalty and solidarity among members who might stray out of line in interactions with outsiders and 'disclose to them the consequences for them of the impression they are being given' (1969a: 208). An example of such a disclosure would be an individual among a group of friends whose physical appearance communicated to bouncers outside a club that the group as a whole were underage. At Atlantis in Bolton during a student night when relatively relaxed age restrictions (eighteen years or over) compared to weekend nights perhaps encouraged underage youth groups to attempt age-playing performances while queuing to enter the club, certain individuals had seemingly disclosed too much:

> I notice behind me a pair of young males who have been refused admittance passed the trio of doormen, probably for looking suspiciously underage. Another group of girls observed outside the club had also been turned away and stood aimlessly outside, wondering what to do and where to go next. The doormen wear smart suits and ties. One of them asks my partner to leave her coat in the cloakroom and pay the £1 admission charge. I assume that coats are not permitted because they provide a means for concealing alcohol and other substances going in and out of the club.   (11.15 p.m. 11 July 2002)

Another apparently unfavourable team disclosure to club security staff, then, was a member who wore a coat. At Club Havana in Manchester – where security was tighter than anywhere else during my field observations – it appeared that the thick black coat that I was required to depart with, added to my lone presence, had disclosed unfavourable impressions to two bouncers who followed me into the toilet shortly after I had entered the club, 'suspicious of me, I am sure, but pretending to look for someone else (they search two cubicles)' (11.30 p.m. 31 October 2002). My impression was that these bouncers suspected me of being a drug dealer.

Impression management techniques were mostly deployed by clubbers and surfers, by those young people who participated in exclusive public music practices. Claire and her friends 'dressed up' for clubs 'because you don't get in the clubs if you're wearing jeans [. . .] if you're just wearing normal, everyday clothes you don't get in' (Richmond High School 3). Alex and his friends dressed like each other on the basis of 'what people usually wear to go out' (ibid.). Similarly, Gavin and Nicky deliberately managed impressions of themselves by means of dressing to 'fit in' to different club contexts:

> Gavin: I think club fashion's, sort of, what you wear, innit? Cause I don't think, people don't really, some people do want to really, really stand out or not really be bothered what they wear but most people just wanna mingle, don't they, and just fit in. They want to fit in and be nice but they don't really wanna – no one really wants to stand out so if they – like, I'm really boring, black man, black shoes and a black top, and if it's summer I might wear a white top [. . .] you know what I mean.
> Nicky: It depends where I go. If I go to, like, a special night then I'll dress up, but if I'm just in Manchester or around then I'll wear a fancy pair of jeans [. . .]
> . . .
> Gavin: Yeh, if I went to, like, Club Havana, quite rough, quite ghetto-y, I'd probably wear something that you find people wearing. I wouldn't wear the same clothes in one place as I would in another.   (Natton College A1)

Gavin felt that his fashions were influenced by those of others in the different clubs that he had experienced because his choice of clothes in these contexts helped to manage impressions of himself as a regular member of the clientele. The impression management techniques required to mingle in with a particular club crowd could only be acquired by Gavin through meticulous observations of others. Therefore, this clubber's attempts to guide the impressions of others with regard to his music self-identity or 'front' would initially require him to engage in surfing practices. Eventually Gavin would acquire familiarity with likeminded clubbers and no longer need to manage his 'back': 'When an individual or performer plays the same part to the same audience on different occasions, a social relationship is likely to arise' (Goffman 1969a: 27).[7] Despite the prevalence of impression management in club and certain bar contexts, even those young people who avoided exclusive public music practices would occasionally feel obliged to manage impressions of their music identities and tastes to others outside their friendship groups (i.e. teams) in everyday school and college contexts. These contexts also provided the breeding ground for the arts of impression judgement.

Impression judgement

Impression judgement is not a Goffmanian concept. Included in his discussion of impression management were 'the protective measures used by audiences and outsiders to assist the performers in saving the performers' show' (1969a: 207) but Goffman's dramaturgical model of performer (team) and audience (outsider) relations accounted little for judgemental or hostile reactions. Given that 'Performers can stop giving expressions but cannot stop giving them off' (1969a: 111) it seems unlikely that impression management techniques could enable self-presentations which *managed* the perceptions of others to all intents and purposes. Impression–judgement techniques generally served to distinguish the music tastes and performances of one team of young people from another. However, team members were not necessarily peers but possibly traversed generations within family groupings. An example of impression judgement practices in which members from different generations were perceived to belong together in teams opposed to other intergenerational teams occurred during a debate between a group of fifteen-year-old males and their middle-aged teacher. These boys expressed disgust at a recent school disco where no garage music had been played, but their teacher argued that parents would not have danced to such music. This claim was strongly rejected by several boys who declared that garage was the preferred music choice of their elders (Pickles High School: 9.30 a.m. 17 September 2001). This teacher later expressed to me her judgement that most of the students at Pickles – these garage fans included – held very conservative music tastes except a group of gothic rock fans whom she described in positive terms as 'bohemian' like the students of art colleges in central Manchester.

It seemed in this example that two teams of music practitioners with different tastes and values included members that cut across generations. The 'bohemian' students and their teacher formed one team, which stressed creative, artisan-like values with regard to music as well as fashion and other generally spectacular lifestyle choices. An entirely different intergenerational team formed by the male students and their parents placed less emphasis on displays of individual creativity and more emphasis on shared tastes for a choice of music (i.e. garage) that infiltrated into their various everyday life contexts such as the car and the school disco. These two distinct teams are not dissimilar to the two oppositional groups of mixed generational demographics that were observed by Paul Corrigan (1979) during a school concert (as discussed in Chapter 3). Along with Corrigan's interpretation of a group of working-class schoolboys, I would argue that for the team comprising the male garage fans 'there is involvement and creation of their own kind of action' (1979: 113) in everyday practices of impression judgement outside those conventionally practised by the spectacular team of bohemian students. It is identification with unconventional – even perhaps deviant – values that enabled these young garage fans and their parents to 'cut across the simplistic generational boundary drawn by the concept of "teenage culture" ' (1979: 113) so as to judge others and be judged as part of an intergenerational team.

The example above included parents and teachers in young people's presentations of their music cultures within educational contexts. These contexts seemed to be where stereotypes and prejudices about others' music cultures abounded:

Shahid: Do you not see them walking around college – all dog collars and that?
(Northborough College B1)

Claire: [. . .] at our school you can definitely tell in the sixth form (who likes what music).
(Richmond High School D1)

Chris: I mean, you look at people who listen to, like, heavy metal and that lot, they're all wearing, like, dark clothes, black and all that lot=
Kathryn: Not necessarily.
Chris: And you look at people, they listen to pop and they're all wearing dead light clothes.
Craig: Right, if you see – if you see someone in town, right, and on one side of you is dressed, like, dog collar, big leather coat [. . .] and all that.
Jen: Basically me. {Laughs}
{Laughter}
Craig: And you see this other, like, lovely little thing with, like=
Chris: Pink colour skirts and everything.
Craig: Yeh, pink right, you do – you've got some idea, you know what I mean. You wouldn't say, 'Yeah, she's into Slipknot'/ but you've got some idea.
(Scarcroft College B1)

The general consensus in interview discussions was that certain physical appearances indicated affiliations for certain music cultures. There were exceptions to the rule such as Steven. He shared the alternative music tastes of Ian and Lindsay but differed from them by wearing conventional clothes and hairstyles. Nevertheless, he considered judgements based on stereotypes to be more or less accurate as 'on the whole you don't tend to get people who dress in the hood jacket or whatever and don't listen to that kind of music [. . .] It, kind of, works one way but not the other' (Richmond High School D1). Lindsay's alternative music tastes were reflected in her dyed red hair and nose-ring. She was clearly conscious of how others judged her tastes in music and other cultural items through her physical appearance. The impression judgements of others, though, merely reinforced her sense of being different from normal young people on a deeper, personal level: 'It's not, "Oh, I listen to this music, therefore I dress this way," it's just that I just feel different and probably because I like different music as well" (ibid.). Lindsay's sense of distinction from populist music practitioners at the same time reinforced her sense of belonging to an inter-generational team of alternative performers that included peers like Ian and elders like her mother: 'I get me mum to paint a witch on to my back when I'm going out' (ibid. D2). Impression judgement techniques were inclusive to the sample and their familial relations, and from time to time would be deployed by clubbers, surfers, exchangers and drifters alike to consolidate team loyalty and solidarity.

Age play

Butler's thesis on gender trouble, which argued that gender or any other 'identity is performatively constituted by the very "expressions" that are said to be its results' (1999: 33), can be applied to the age trouble that some young people performed in their everyday public music practices.[8] Rather than passively accepting predetermined age identities, some respondents constructed identifications with particular age categories other than their biological ones. Identifications might be defined differently from identities in that the former are transitional processes whilst the latter are constant entities at any given moment (Malbon 1999). These age identifications were akin to those of middle-aged groups who were observed performing public music practices such as clubbing so as to ostensibly reconstitute their age identities, also known as 'feeling eighteen again'. Age-playing techniques deployed by those respondents under the permitted age to perform certain music practices clearly were intended to make them appear older to facilitate inclusion into exclusive contexts where they would effectively become surfers at first. Justin's point that 'you dress to be older' (Scarcroft College A1) is worthy of contemplation. His use of the verb 'be' instead of 'look' perhaps emphasised the necessity of a complete perfor-mance in enacting age-playing techniques. This technique as well as those of growing stubble (Chris, ibid. 3), wearing a cap (Matthew, ibid. 1) and accompanying older friends and siblings on nights out (Kevin, Richmond High School 3) were hardly novel or subversive but nevertheless consoli-dated effective team performances.

The use of fake identity (ID) cards was a widespread technique of age play that represented more subversive identifications. Whilst this tech-nique was by no means novel either, the sophisticated means by which some young people invested in credible pieces of plastic – that were much more credible than the amateurish ID cards of which most public music gatekeepers had become wise – revealed the considerable lengths that would be taken to perform effectively age identifications. Several respondents with favourable experiences of using fake ID cards spoke about a 'buzz' or emotional 'high' in successfully performing such identifications. Many respondents who had been unsuccessful in previous attempts spoke about new ID cards that they already owned or intended to own which created anticipations about effective future performances in accessing exclusive music practices. Chris, who had used the same fake ID card to access a number of pub contexts for several years despite still being only seventeen years old, now no longer felt that he required it: 'some places, it's like, they do ask you for ID so I'll go "I've not been asked for ID for ages, so I don't carry it with me no more"' (Scarcroft College 3). Justin talked about one sophisticated type of ID card that he had considered purchasing:

> *Justin: There's a thing on the Internet, this fake ID [. . .] you know, with your photo on and its supposed to – it's got a hologram on, and on the back, if they still don't believe it, it's got a number and it actually – if you ring the number it actually says you are 18 [. . .]* (ibid.)

Rizwaan similarly knew how to obtain a student ID card from his college on which he could state that his age was eighteen rather than seventeen to enable him to access clubbing practices (Natton College E1).[9] This age-playing technique was widespread albeit not foolproof. Knowledge of fake ID cards was often gleaned through advertisements on the Internet or in magazines targeted at young (mostly male) readers such as *FHM*. I will now turn to many other ways in which media seemed to influence respondents' presentation of and identification with public music practices. The influences of associative mediated music items such as clothing fashion accessories in particular impacted upon these young people's co-present impression management and judgement perceptions.

Media influences

The pervasiveness of media consumption in public music contexts (see Chapter 5) was matched by the pervasiveness of media influences on public music practices. Mediated influences on co-present music consumers and producers emerged from globally and locally disseminated texts. However, global media influences were evident among different figurations of youth music practitioners whilst local media mostly influenced the clubber figure. The omnipresence of global media practices across all four groupings suggests that McCracken's notion of 'grooming rituals' as instruments for transferring meanings from products to consumers potentially applied to all youth music practitioners:

> The 'going out' rituals with which one prepares for 'an evening out' are good examples here because they illustrate the time, patience and anxiety with which an individual will prepare him or her self for the special public scrutiny of a gala evening or special dinner party. (1990: 86)

However, these grooming rituals tended to be played down by respondents or displaced on to others to different degrees according to their positions within the involvement and accessibility model. Disavowing any transfer of personal meanings from music products enabled certain practitioners to detach and distance themselves from the banalities of passionate consumption. Before detailing young people's responses across these four groupings to media influences on the presentation of their selves in everyday music practices, an overall analysis of how these influences were frequently articulated through radically contextual everyday life narratives indicates their significance in understanding global as well as local cultural phenomena.

Although Jen presented herself as a female goth metal fan by typically wearing baggy combat trousers, a dark hooded top and bandanna to college, she tried to manage others' perceptions of her music cultural identity by not focusing all her energies into an exclusive domain of mediated music influences:

> DL: {to Jen} You don't like to be considered a goth?
> Jen: Well, I'm a mixture.
> . . .
> Jen: I don't like to be classed as just one thing.
> DL: No, no.
> Jen: I'm lots of things.
> DL: Yeh, right.
> Jen: A bit of a rocker, mosher and sometimes a – it depends on what mood I'm in.
> (Scarcroft College B1)

Jen's intensive use of mediated goth metal coupled with her sense of performing fluid identifications within a range of music practices indicated her closest resemblance to the exchanger figure. Another exchanger appeared to be her friend Sophie, who also managed fluid impressions of her music affiliations through radically contextualist performances. In college Sophie would express allegiance to goth music culture by wearing a Korn T-shirt and Doc Martin shoes, but 'I tone it down when I go to the concerts and stuff and have my make-up all down my face [. . .] and I usually end up wiping it off [. . .] The only time I can put my make-up on probably is when I'm, you know, just going out shopping' (ibid. A1). Radically contextual narratives about clubbing and surfing experiences were also articulated in interview discussions. Shahid recalled surfing experiences of clubber practices:

Shahid: [. . .] you know when people take drugs – to get on the level they listen to music – and then they take ecstacy tablets to get on the level – usually you see it in clubs. Over 18 clubs, they take ecstacy tablets and they drink with it and then they put it on the level with the music. (Northborough College B1)

Shahid's perception of the links between clubbing and drug consumption – perhaps partly created by news media reports – articulated a radically contextualist narrative about how certain co-present as well as mediated music practices enabled mood changes. Perceptions of media influences on the clothing fashions of other youth practitioners also articulated a sense of radical contextualism. Sohel remembered 'when Craig David started wearing that denim jacket and denim jeans, and that was the trend and I think it still is' (ibid. A1) and Amy remembered the reaction to Geri Halliwell's public appearance dressed in a butterfly top: 'every shop started selling it then, and then they all bought it because she was wearing it' (Richmond High School A1). Radically contextual narratives on music media influences only occasionally included personal declarations of being influenced by global cultural practices. Nonetheless, the following responses suggest that distinct groups of youth music practitioners absorbed such globalised and sometimes localised influences to different extents.

Clubbers like Jolene perceived local more than global media influences on her public music practices. As opposed to 'moshers and gothic people [. . .] (that) wear dark make-up and dark clothes', her impression management techniques for attending an R 'n' B club were felt to be based on personal decisions: 'there's no specific way to dress, I mean – you just dress the way you wanna really, just as long as it's dressed up' (Natton College 3). Jolene acknowledged that she might derive ideas about physical appearance from music videos featuring her favourite artists such as the rapper Snoop Dogg. However, localised media such as flyers more directly influenced the public music practices of Jolene and her fellow clubbers. This group would use flyers and magazine listings to organise short-term nightlife schedules:

Jolene: [. . .] if you're going somewhere else and the people that give out the flyers know which events to go to, to get what kind of people that are into that music –

so if they have garage nights on or an R 'n' B night they'll go and they'll give the flyers to all the people that have been there cause they'll know that they'll wanna go to this.   (ibid.)

These localised media – synonymous with micro-media (Thornton 1995) – influenced clubbers' practices to an immediate, quite sublime extent. Their attendance at a particular club night brought Jolene and her friends into contact with these media-marketing devices to encourage club consumer loyalty. Indeed, Jolene referred to flyers as important resources for building knowledge about clubbing practices. Many flyers that offered discounted admission fees provided exclusive financial as well as cultural capital: '£8 entry – some people have VIP tickets that get them a £4 entry fee' (The Nightspot club, Wigan Pier: 11 p.m. 19 October 2002). Conspicuous consumption of localised media enabled these clubbers to distinguish themselves from populist music practitioners who appeared more influenced by global media texts. For example, those young people who copied the dance routines of choreographed pop acts like S Club were judged to be inferior to these clubbers, who enacted their 'own moves' when dancing to bashment or hip hop music (Tanya, Natton College D2).

Surfers and exchangers, on the other hand, tended to be indistinguishable in regard to media influences from which globally disseminated texts held sway over those disseminated locally. Even flyers that advertised exclusive guest appearances by popular media stars at franchised bars such as Life in Bolton had non-local motives in promoting celebrities such as a Big Brother contestant across a national circuit of appearances at different branches of the same bar (10.30 p.m. 17 October 2002). Similarly, local media such as CDs and merchandise in the surfing practices of small concert venues tended to have national and global intentions for the rising bands of tomorrow's *Top of the Pops*. Goldrush, the headliners at Night and Day on the night when I visited the venue, had already signed to a label and released a single which had entered the Top 60 in the national charts (8 October 2002). Even those surfers who engaged in exclusive music practices nonetheless casually consumed the chart-based mediated music available on radio and television, which to some extent influenced their co-present music experiences. On the other hand, exchangers' intensive media uses might have effectively created niche or alternative music tastes but their inclusive practices catered for broad tastes which predominantly meant global pop music consumption. Several respondents in these two groups borrowed ideas about physical appearance from globally mediated music texts. Jawaria considered

Jennifer Lopez to be a role model (Northborough College B1) and Colleen admitted that she 'really did try and dress like The Spice Girls when they first came out' (Scarcroft College B1). Similarly, Dave had bought 'shoes that Noel Gallagher wears' but stressed that 'I wouldn't dress exactly like him' (Richmond High School C1), whilst Neal's tastes for nu-metal bands like Blink 182 had persuaded him to change an aspect of his physical appearance sported by global metal stars: 'I'll start spiking my hair up and everything' (Wilson High School C1). Unlike clubbers, surfers and particularly exchangers generally avoided impression judgements of specific music cultures. Instead these young people expressed hostilities towards much broader youth cultural groupings: 'I think in America the people are more influenced by the actions they see' (Mo'aaz, Northborough College A1).

Finally, drifters distinguished themselves from other youth music practitioners by perceiving limited global or local music media influences, or at least remaining inconspicuous about their levels of music involvement. Hilary and Gill, for instance, borrowed fashion ideas not from pretentious music media products such as celebrities but from non-music media such as teen magazines:

> *Hilary: [. . .] I think it's mainly, erm, teenage magazines that we get things like (fashion ideas) from – you know, like* More *[. . .].*
> *DL: Yeh. So you still, sort of, get those kind of magazines?*
> *Gill: Yeh, I think they're more down to earth, kind of.* (Southwell College C2)

Gill perceived these general interest magazines to present more realistic fashion and physical appearance images than those presented by music-based media. Gill also consumed music magazines, which she exchanged with her friend on the train to and from college, so her drifting practices were not ignorant of potential media influences in contexts where she could quite easily slip into exchanging practices. Rather, the casual consumption of both music and non-music media enabled distinctions to be drawn between drifters and other youth music practitioners. If Gill occasionally became an exchanger, Hilary – as already discussed – occasionally engaged in surfing practices but only to reinforce her identification as a predominant drifter:

> *Hilary: Well, like – I go out with my friends that, like, dress as Slipknot hoodies and things.*
> *DL: Oh right.*
> *Hilary: And the music's the influence.* (ibid.)

Hilary's judgement that the global music band Slipknot influenced her friends' but not particularly her own fashions was a frequently deployed displacement technique among drifters. Undesirable surfing experiences with these friends, including that of moshing, enabled Hilary to draw a distinction between herself and others based on different extents of music media influence. Drifting judgements were not the same as clubbing judgements, though, because drifters distinguished themselves by judging all other youth music groupings whereas clubbers distinguished themselves by judging *particular* groupings. Although local music media only significantly influenced clubbers' public music practices, localised influences in the shape of public music contexts penetrated deeply into the majority of these young people's everyday lives and will now be analysed in relation to the mostly global media influences in evidence here.

Space and place

The notion of 'cultural space' was used by Straw (1991) to understand how various music practices could interact with each other in local scenes where the influences of globalisation facilitated differentiations in these practices. However, it has already been argued that only clubbers sought differentiation and distinction from other public music practitioners. Clubbers like Sam and Jolene were two of only a small proportion of respondents who differentiated between their practices in hip hop, garage, rap and bashment music, and those of others around the Manchester scene:

> Sam: [. . .] Manchester's not really that good.
> Asifa: No, it's [. . .]
> . . .
> DL: [. . .] And so what sort of music tends to get played in Manchester that you don't really like? Pop music or=
> Sam: No, I don't like that.
> Jolene: Pop and dance, [that's the stuff I don't really like.
> Sam: [Just all – all the other stuff that I don't like – it's not rap, anything else.
> DL: So you like the stuff that's not pop – that's like=
> Jolene: Definitely, I don't like pop at all. Dance, indie, rock – none of them.
> (Natton College D1)

Sam and Jolene consequently looked further afield to engage in clubbing practices within a scene that geographically encompassed at least a sixty-mile radius around Manchester. Similarly but this time on a national scale, Gavin and Nicky perceived differences between the 'multicultural' music

scene in their inner-city Manchester locale and the narrow, populist music
scene in a less diverse community:

> *Gavin: [. . .] we're multicultural cause we're in Manchester and in inner-cities*
> *you got a lot of/ different people, haven't ya, and different influences, yeh.*
> *DL: Yeh, so how do you like R 'n' B? Who got you into garage or house or what-*
> *ever?*
> *Nicky: It, kind of, came on the scene.*
> *. . .*
> *DL: But how do you get to the, sort of, unusual sounds that no one hears?*
> *Gavin: You have to go – yeh, but inner-city record shops will sell multicultural*
> *[. . .]*
> *Nicky: Like, if you go in HMV you've got an R 'n' B section, reggae section,*
> *rock section, pop, do you know what I mean, and all the chart stuff.*
> *Gavin: Yeh, but if you live in Manchester city centre, the HMV's gunna be*
> *different than if you live in, let me think of it, Carlisle.*
> *Nicky: Yeh, it probably would be.*
> *Gavin: If you live in Carlisle I don't think their HMV will be the same as*
> *Manchester.*
> *Nicky: They'd see what the market was [. . .]*
> *Gavin: Their manager would say, 'Well, when they come and say no, well we won't*
> *sell many of that and we won't sell many of that, cause there's no point in us taking*
> *two thousand,' then what they'll say, 'Yeh, but we'll sell popular music, yeh, we'll*
> *have five thousand of them and three thousand of them.*   (ibid. A1)

This differentiation between everyday music practices in large, diverse and
small, mostly white urban populations could be interpreted in relation to
Straw's concepts as examples of the difference between music scenes –
exemplified by Manchester – and communities, like in Carlisle. In contrast
to the uniformly populist practices of communities, scenes are spaces such
as record shops that represent the eclectic practices of a range of distinct
youth music practitioners. Although Carlisle might still be conceived to
have a music scene, it is a homogeneous and static scene compared to the
fluid, transient scene or scenes that interact and vie for supremacy in
Manchester.

However, music scenes full of multicultural spaces were rarely perceived
by non-clubber groups. Instead the music practices accessible to young
people within Manchester, Bolton and the outlying areas would be compared to those practices accessible in other areas on national or even international scales to generate an inclusive sense of a cultural locality
consisting predominantly of recognisable places rather than indefinite,
variable spaces. For instance, a weekly gig night for unsigned bands at
Manchester's Band on the Wall was advertised as 'Showcase Well North of

London' to convey the view that the capital was not the only place to be 'spotted' in performance by record-industry figures. For surfers such as Laura who had experienced nights out in several English cities, her memories of those experiences were couched in terms of the places rather than the spaces where she had been: 'Down in Reading that was all pop [. . .] and jazz – all the pubs had jazz on. Then I went down to Hull where [. . .] sixties, eighties stuff' (Richmond High School B1). Reading as a music locality was perceived differently to Hull rather than specific music spaces in Reading, such as clubs being differentiated from clubs in Hull. A much wider association between music and place characterised Laura's surfer/tourist recollections. For exchangers such as Beate the most striking difference between Manchester and experiences of public music practices in her native country was licence restrictions that were ultimately determined by differences in place (i.e. national laws) more so than spaces within places: 'all the clubs are closing at, I don't know, two thirty, three o'clock./ It's different from Germany so I have to hurry up to go out early [. . .]' (University of Salford 3).

The sense in which a majority of respondents framed public music contexts as places more than spaces was further evident from how particular contexts became associated with their regular clienteles, the majority of whom were local people. Typical age and ethnic demographics of these clienteles equated to knowledge with a very localised but nonetheless valuable currency. In terms of age demographics, respondents at three different locations referred to 'grab a granny' club nights which were avoided because of the perception that significantly older women and men would be in search of sexual encounters with younger others such as themselves (Louise, Richmond High School A1; Sara and Helen, Natton College: ibid.; Ian, Wilson High School: ibid.). Anicca avoided three local pubs in the Hulme area of Manchester because they were frequented by an old, rough clientele (Natton College C1). At the other end of the age spectrum, Michelle referred to a local club as a 'kindergarten': 'I tell you what, there's too many kids going in Atomic's now [. . .] About 13-year-old go in there. It's bad' (Wilson High School A1).[10] In terms of ethnic demographics, particular club and bar contexts sometimes represented the cultural diversity within localities around Manchester and Bolton. For Louise, who lived in a mainly white community in suburban Bolton, an early surfing experience at a town-centre club provided a swift introduction to a diverse cultural locality other than her familiar one:

Louise: I've only really been once – I was with my sister and it was, like, I walked in and it knocked me [. . .] total black people, right, it was an R 'n' B night [. . .]

{DL laughs}
Louise: It was scary. Everybody was black apart from us. (Richmond High School A1)

Alex similarly defined a Bolton town-centre bar in relation to what he perceived to be its regular clientele – 'Harvey's is black' – and Vicky expressed preference for this bar and others frequented by black people in Manchester because of the 'chilled-out', relaxing music played in them (ibid. C2). Despite the multicultural diversity of music practices that co-existed in the fieldwork region, these different practices were rarely contextualised solely within the cultural spaces of scenes but nearly always within the geographical places of localities that were defined by the communities that peopled them. The preponderance of globally distributed media influences (as outlined in the previous section) and locally perceived public music practices (as detailed in this section) surrounding young people's everyday lives provided the resources for their promenade performances.

Promenade performances

Given that the term 'promenade' can refer to a type of concert in which spectators and performers co-participate to create a musical atmosphere, it might be regarded as unsurprising that findings into respondents' concert and gig practices revealed promenade performances. Perhaps more surprising was the pervasiveness of promenade performances throughout these young people's public music practices. These performances indicated interactive practices where performers and spectators, producers and consumers would be intimately and collusively related to each other. These youth music 'performers' – like those recorded by Mass-Observation in 1930s and 1940s Britain – emphasised demonstration and display in their everyday leisure activities. To summarise findings from early youth music cultures and media (see Chapter 3), globally mediated music influences penetrated into highly localised music practices through two phases. First, the reception phase provided knowledge about the latest tunes, dances and fashions to come on to the scene. This phase therefore demonstrated mediated promenade performances. Second, the exhibition phase involved selection of this knowledge to demonstrate co-present promenade performances. However, the extent to which different youth groups experienced such performances varied considerably. Clubbers tended to engage in both reception and exhibition phases but only unintentionally demonstrated their complete promenade performances to non-clubbers. Surfers were the most likely group to witness and imitate clubbers' demonstrations at the phase of exhibition, but they bypassed mediated promenade performances. On the contrary, exchangers intensively engaged in such performances at the phase of reception but less often exhibited them or had them exhibited in co-present promenade contexts. Finally, drifters were the only group who rarely engaged in music-based promenade performances during either phase, although such performances were likely to be encountered in non-musical leisure contexts. Observations and interview responses will now fill in more details about how promenade performances were enacted in different contexts by different youth music practitioners.

As regards clubbers and surfers, the architecture of certain clubbing places catered for spectators and performers to foster collective involvement. For example, one club venue with a sense of exclusiveness enabled observation from

> the balcony of this church-like dance arena where dancers on the dance floor below can be viewed from all four sides. The dance floor includes a platform near its centre and another at one side for those who wish to exhibit their pleasure in motion. Motion is the name of the game here. At times as I stand in relatively passive observation I feel awkward and out of place as all around me – even in spaces considerably removed from the dance floor – show flight of foot and arm, including several shows of stamina and athleticism.
> (The Nightspot club, Wigan Pier: 19 October 2002)

Self-consciousness of giving off expressions to clubbers and surfers about my drifter role encouraged me to 'wait in the wings' of these exhibition contexts, where I still encountered promenade performances incongruous with my own, insipid one. The spectacle of clubbing practices on dance floors encouraged promenade performances by both demonstrators and imitators:

> One white male dancer shows off his athletic dancing skills and tries to encourage his black friend to show off his dancing skills in turn, which he fleetingly obliges to do. Two female dancers are a captive audience for this keen dancer. Mirrors play a part here – especially one by the stairs through which people glance at their reflection (narcissism encouraged).   (Bar Juice, Bolton town centre: 1 November 2002)

The use of mirrors in Bar Juice (see Figure 6.7) not only created a false impression of its spaciousness but enabled surfers in particular to witness how closely their own dancing styles imitated those more accomplished

Figure 6.7 Exclusive promenade performances in dance and talk at Bar Juice.
(Photograph: D. Laughey)

exhibitions from clubbers. Mirrors have always played an integral part in dance studios and perhaps it is no coincidence that the upper floors of the building that housed Bar Juice 'once were used by the Bolton Dance and Leisure Club, a now defunct dancing school that perhaps catered for older customers in its latter days' (Bar Juice, Bolton Town Centre; 19 July 2002).[11]

Promenade performances also abounded in more inclusive public music contexts. While sitting in a Manchester bar early one Friday evening, my partner and I were politely requested by a member of staff to relinquish our seats 'to make way for what becomes this late-opening bar's central dance floor for the rest of the night' (Springbok bar, Manchester city centre: 8.15 p.m. 19 April 2002). Exhibitory phases of performance were thus fostered by the policies of dance entertainment venues to remove chairs and tables so as to facilitate fluid interactions by means of walking, shuffling and dancing. Territorialisations of dancing spaces (Berk 1977; Malbon 1999) in mainstream club contexts where surfers and exchangers were perhaps most likely to interact further facilitated demonstrations and displays: 'The raised platform that forms the upper level of the dance floor is for the more committed dancers (this is crowded all night); the lower level is less crowded and for more casual dancers' ('Pop Ikon' on the upper floor of Club Ikon, Bolton town centre: 17 October 2002). Those exchangers or even drifters on the lower level could imitate the more exclusive clubbing practitioners that congregated above. Similarly at the Ritz,

> Many customers are dressed in seventies clothes and hairstyles, some more extravagantly than others. The keen ones are also likely to want to join the Love Train crew on the Ritz's stage – once the platform for dance bands when the Ritz was a Mecca ballroom. The close interactions between performers and dancing customers/spectators here is a striking example of how participatory and exhibitionist the whole 'night out' experience becomes. One male customer dressed like John Travolta, for instance, took the invitation to dance with a female member of *Love Train* and the two danced like the romantic couple in the film *Grease*. (Ritz, Manchester city centre: 9 October 2002)

The male customer who danced like John Travolta was a promenade performer who had vividly engaged in both mediated and co-present phases where he had first gained knowledge through presumably viewing the video of *Saturday Night Fever* and then selected this knowledge for exhibition purposes. Here was a rare instance of a clubber who – along with another clubber who was also a producer – intentionally demonstrated his niche sensibilities to non-clubbers within inclusive music practices. To become a clubber, of course, this young man would have needed to engage in exchanger practices so as to become familiar enough with the dance routines to be able to competently demonstrate and display them (see Figure 6.8).

Exchangers were most likely to experience promenade performances while audience members at concert and gig venues. Although these youth music practices were co-present, their mediated influences were starker than those which penetrated into most other co-present practices. These influences were at their starkest when global media stars made local concert appearances. For Gaz and his network of exchangers, a Beth Orton concert at the intimate Academy venue was preferred to that at the more formal, corporate Bridgewater Hall: 'There was more of an atmosphere (at the Academy) – I think people were more willing to, kind of, cheer her on and communicate with her' (University of Salford 3). Gaz considered the quality of communication from both directions to provide a measure for the success or failure of a given concert. At the Academy 'Beth' communicated more with the crowd in response to positive feedback from receptive exchangers such as Gaz's group: 'We'd all cheer and obviously make her chuffed' (ibid.). At smaller gig venues in particular, this inclusive sense of

Figure 6.8 Inclusive promenade performances as demonstrated at the Ritz.
(Photograph: D. Laughey)

collusion between consumers and producers typified the reception phase of promenade performances that might ultimately lead to an exhibition phase if exchangers moved into surfer roles. At different venues I struggled to distinguish performers from spectators. At O'Shea's (an Irish pub in Manchester city centre), a band was observed for well in excess of one hour tuning instruments alongside expectant spectators who occasionally conversed with them (2 November 2001). As regards Night and Day and Band on the Wall,

> A key similarity between the two venues is the way that performers and spectators are closely related both spatially and socially. Bands at both venues set up while talking to friends and family, who eventually distance themselves from their counterparts as the performance emerges (it hardly ignites at a moment's notice). Guitars are tuned, instruments and technical equipment are brought in and taken away through a melêé of spectators.
> (8 October 2002)

A slight difference between these two venues, however, was that the more established bands at Night and Day distanced themselves further from spectators than the unsigned acts at Band on the Wall. Becker's (1951) account of how professional jazz musicians strove for critical distance from 'square' audiences perhaps is supported by these comparative observations. By implication, promenade performances for exchangers tended to increase in intensity and exclusiveness when greater intimacy between producers and consumers ensued.

Finally, although drifters generally avoided promenade performances of the musical type in their everyday lives, their engagement in a whole variety of other public leisure activities would potentially bring them towards contexts of demonstration and display. Microcosms of leisure resorts can these days be found in leisure complexes such as Bolton's The Valley Centertainment Park, where a cinema is juxtaposed with the Atlantis club venue. Young cinema goers with little interest in public music practices would ultimately be obliged to present their drifting promenade performances in loosely co-present interactions with non-drifters outside different leisure venues. Similarly, drifters who found themselves relieved of their tables and chairs at dance-orientated town-centre bars would be left to promenade around the quieter territories of such contexts unless they chose to lift off their initial self-presentations and replace them with those acquired through selected knowledge in interactions with more involved youth music practitioners. Promenade performances, therefore, are exclusive to no groupings of youth music practitioners or youth leisure practitioners per se.

Summary

In this chapter I have attempted to explain the different extents to which qualitatively distinct co-present practices are nevertheless informed by and able to inform mediated music practices. Rather than couch public music practices in terms of an involvement continuum which poses more empirical problems than measuring music media involvement, a more significant – albeit correlated – framework for understanding such practices has been suggested by a continuum of accessibility from exclusive to inclusive consumption and production. Exclusiveness is typified by certain club and bar contexts where niche production practices backed by specific music consumer tastes equipped with high levels of cultural and financial capital prevail. At the other end of the accessibility continuum, inclusiveness occurs across various public music contexts wherein broad consumer tastes and mainstream producer sensibilities render moderate levels of cultural and financial capital acceptable. It has been argued through the perceptions of respondents that the notion of eclectic co-present music practices in sympathy with a neo-tribalist theoretical perspective on the decline of individualism (Maffesoli 1995) is much removed from practices of inclusion. Instead, eclecticism sits uneasily between inclusiveness and exclusiveness along the accessibility continuum. Eclectic as well as inclusive production sensibilities like the provision of club spaces for different music consumer tastes, for instance, in practice led to several respondents reinforcing their sense of exclusiveness by remaining within a given musical space rather than sampling a broader range of these spaces.

This accessibility continuum for public music practices in combination with the involvement continuum for music media uses (outlined in the previous chapter) can be construed along two axes wherein four groupings of youth music practitioners emerge. These groupings or figurations are useful categories for not only combining mediated with co-present music practices but also for emphasising how these two sets of practices are intimately juxtaposed in young people's everyday lives across education and work as well as leisure contexts. Such categories are also assumed to be transient in accordance with these young people's radically contextual everyday interactions. Exchangers in education contexts such as Gemma and Rachel (Southwell College), for example, might remain exchangers by night (Gemma) or become surfers and perhaps – later at night – clubbers in leisure contexts (Rachel). However, the transitory nature of these categories of youth music practices should not be regarded as entirely relativistic. These categories should be applied to specific youth music cultures (e.g. hip hop) rather than young people's music practices in general.

As such, it might be clearer to perceive how someone would encounter serious difficulties by attempting to move from a hip hop drifter to a hip hop clubber within a matter of hours or days. On the other hand, it seems reasonable to conceive of the relative ease in which young music practitioners might move from hip hop exchangers to surfers or from hip hop surfers to exchangers on an everyday basis. Perhaps less easy but certainly possible would be a rapid movement from hip hop surfer/exchanger to hip hop clubber or drifter.

The reason why the involvement and accessibility model for youth music practitioners (Figure 6.5) is not entirely free flowing in its fluidity is because its four groupings depend on their categorisation not only through perceptions of the self but also of others *vis-à-vis* the self in everyday, interactive performances. Impression management techniques to perform presentations and identifications (Goffman 1969a) therefore need to be balanced against impression judgement techniques. So in order to impress judgement by other clubbers as to his clubber performance in certain club contexts, Gavin (Natton College) deployed impression management techniques within surfing practices by dressing to 'fit in with' the fashions of other clubbers. Age-playing techniques were likewise akin to life strategies (Bauman 1996) in facilitating movement towards the more exclusive groupings within the involvement and accessibility model. Again, the success or failure of age play like all other youth music performances depended on the judgement of others – in this case, public entertainment gatekeepers such as bouncers – as well as the management of the self. Unlike impression management techniques that were almost exclusively practised by clubbers and surfers, impression judgement techniques applied mostly to surfers, drifters and exchangers. These four groupings also tended to be distinguished by their articulations of the spaces and places in which they consumed and produced music. Whereas clubbers tended to perceive specific music spaces such as independent record shops as indicative of a scene in which the music of different cultures could survive and interact, other youth music practitioners tended to attach musical meanings to familiar places within a close-knit, geographically circumscribed locality.

Adapting theoretical insights on carnivalesque and carnival practices (Bakhtin 1984; V. Turner 1987) to the previously devised notion of promenade performances helps to detail the wider significance of these four youth music practitioner groupings to the interactive relationship between young people's globally mediated and locally co-present cultural influences. Within the ordinary, routine characteristics of respondents' everyday lives, promenade performances represented extraordinary moments of display and demonstration to different extents. Clubbers' intensive involvement in mediated music at the phase of reception and exclusive access to co-present music at the exhibition phase meant that they were engaged in promenade performances which they would – usually unintentionally – both display and demonstrate to others. The surfer figure, by contrast, generally retained casual consumption of music media at the reception phase but attached exclusiveness to their public music practices at the phase of exhibition, so surfers would display but be unequipped to demonstrate promenade performances. The exchanger represented an inversion of the surfer figure. Intensive involvement at the mediated music reception phase but inclusive accessibility at the co-present music exhibition phase meant that exchangers were engaged in demonstrating rather than displaying promenade performances. Finally, drifters' casual music media consumption coupled with their inclusive public music practices characterised passive promenade performances without display or demonstration in music contexts, although they – along with the exchangers – could not avoid moments of display in other everyday mediated and co-present leisure contexts. Amongst other things, the concluding chapter of this book will compare the concept of (promenade) performances informed by sociological understandings of everyday life practices to less helpful conceptual frameworks around homogeneous, intra-generational youth cultural worlds.

Notes

1. Questionnaire replies from James stated that he spent £200 in the past year on concerts or festivals, most of which were at small gig venues around the Manchester area accompanied by his uncle and father.
2. Such data production ultimately fell outside the resources and intentions of this research. Further research is required to improve an understanding of the extent to which clubbers practise eclecticism.
3. The finding that nearly twice as much expenditure over the past year on average had been on bar and club admission fees (£66) compared to concert and festival tickets (£36) supported interview findings which suggested that exclusive music practices demanded higher degrees of consumer involvement in terms of money (i.e. financial capital) than inclusive practices.
4. By contrast, expenditure on music equipment for consumption such as CD players, blank record formats and headphones averaged £111 in the past year. Respondents in general were far more accustomed to consuming than producing music.
5. Although conventional musicians clearly excluded others who did not have the resources or ability to play musical instruments, such exclusion was not a motivation and did not often appear to create a barrier – in the way that it might have for professional musicians (Becker 1951).

6. Moshing meant dancing violently in a crowd to heavy rock music.
7. Gavin's experiences here resemble a previous theoretical standpoint in support of 'front region' and 'back region' performances (Goffman 1969a) in Chapter 4.
8. Sympathetic if not synonymous with the notion of age play and age trouble is that of 'age crime'. Shauleen described herself and was described by her older cousin Ruth as an 'age criminal' for going out to clubs underage (Natton College C1). Despite emphasising at the beginning of discussions that all responses would remain confidential, on several occasions interviewees were reluctant to recount their age-playing experiences for fear either that I might pass over recorded evidence (i.e. the cassette tape used for transcription purposes) of their criminal activities to the police or that I was an undercover police officer. The omnipresent sense of inspection in many respondents' everyday lives inevitably infiltrated research contexts.
9. It was not clear, however, how Rizwaan could obtain an NUS card as advertised on a wall at the college, where proof of age in the form of passport, birth certificate or previous NUS card was required.
10. Aged sixteen years, Michelle might be said to have contributed to the 'bad' (i.e. underage) reputation of this club – particularly when it appears that she speaks from experience.
11. Many clubs today are housed in the same buildings as their dance-hall predecessors (e.g. the Ritz, Manchester, which has offered dance entertainment since its Mecca origins in the 1930s), which points to the endurance of their purpose-built designs in spite of historical changes in dancing styles and music technologies.

CHAPTER 7

Everyday Youth Music Cultures and Media

I will now succinctly tie together previous theoretical propositions and empirical analyses that have attempted to understand how music interacts with young people's everyday lives. These empirically informed theoretical propositions are to be applied throughout to the five aims outlined in the introduction. The three sections of this chapter will address these aims collectively so as to show how the book as a whole has been underpinned by a consistent and sustained research agenda. First, I will propose a situational interactionist model for the study of everyday youth music cultures and media. This model will not only address the initial aim of this study – to analyse the literature on subcultures, club cultures and post-subcultures from an interactionist perspective – but will also be informed by ideas and findings that have attempted to address other aims, such as to respectively situate and contextualise local youth music practices (both mediated and co-present) in relation to other leisure, education and work activities. Similarly, the second and third sections of this chapter draw on distinct ideas and findings but attempt to apply them across each of the five aims. As such, notions of intergenerational narratives as well as localised performances are shown to be consistent with the theoretical model of situational interactionism as earlier advocated.

A situational interactionist model

The model outlined here contains features that will be compared with those that have hindered a structuralist or postmodernist framework for understanding music in young people's everyday lives. The first feature of this situational interactionist model is its central focus on the local, familial and traditional contexts for everyday youth music cultures. A second feature is this model's conceptualisation of youth music practices as the consequences of learning to follow certain rules of enactment (Schatzki 1996) or of honing literacies, the success or failure of which determines the growth or decline in these practices. And third, this model details differences with regard to young people's involvement in and accessibility to certain mediated and co-present music practices. This third feature of the model details different groupings of youth music practitioners – clubbers, surfers, exchangers and drifters – and ultimately stems from thorough consideration of the other two features. I will provide evidence to support each of these three features from findings produced through the interactionist approach to youth music cultures and media as adopted in the preceding chapters. A diagrammatic representation of this situational interactionist model is shown in Figure 7.1.

First, a situational interactionist is better able than an orthodox structuralist model to focus upon the everyday contexts of youth music cultures. These everyday *contexts* of music consumption and production are not always encoded with meanings and values akin to the *texts* that have provided sources for semiotic analyses of youth subcultures. Such local, familial and traditional contexts are more likely to be mundane than sensational, recurrent for a majority than extraordinary for a minority of young people. Furthermore, the texts and contexts studied with regard to subcultures and their contemporary revisions have been assumed to project the national or even global concerns of certain youth groups in opposition to those of nationally or globally dominant cultures. Music texts therefore have been structured within a stylistic framework of subcultural deviance or resistance to oppressive political institutions rather than situated in relation to the local and familial cultures of young people. Rock 'n' roll music, for instance, was contextualised in the constructed subcultural world of motorbike boys (Willis 1972; 1978) as one dimension to a nostalgic vehicle through which a particular group of young people

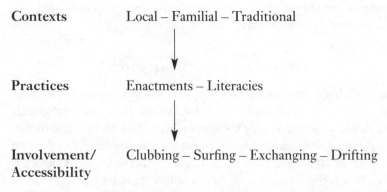

Contexts   Local – Familial – Traditional

Practices   Enactments – Literacies

Involvement/   Clubbing – Surfing – Exchanging – Drifting
Accessibility

Figure 7.1 A situational interactionist model.

expressed their resistance to the commercial function of contemporary music. Singles were preferred to albums because the act of consuming these texts reflected the fast-moving contexts of biking in homologous relation to the speed of the bikes, rapid argot and so on. However, research into this and countless other constructed youth cultural worlds has centred entirely on those – mostly leisure – contexts which have facilitated collective expressions of music consumption and production.

In comparison, a situational interactionist model proposed here includes these leisure contexts but does not exclude all those other everyday contexts in which music plays a significant role for a majority of young people. It is those local, familial and traditional contexts that comprise the micro-cultures in which young people interact on an everyday basis (Wulff 1995) and that have been neglected by structuralist models in which youth music cultures become situated solely inside an intra-generational milieu tied together regardless of localised variations. A focus on the micro-cultures of young people's music consumption and production is beneficial to understanding the range of everyday contexts where this consumption and production can occur, whether it be schools, buses, supermarkets, bedrooms and so on. For example, Claire's preference for albums over singles is explained in practical terms that are very different to those explanations of the motorbike boys' preference for singles over albums:

> Claire: [. . .] I'll buy an album but I don't buy singles.
> DL: Yeh.
> Claire: Cause they just annoy me / cause, like, I suppose when you put them on the CD and then they're over in, like, three songs and then, but with an album you can put it on and then just leave it and do your work while it's on, whereas singles you have to just put 'em back, change 'em.
> (Richmond High School 3)

In everyday educational contexts of homework, then, this young music consumer preferred texts that could conveniently function as non-intrusive background soundtracks to these contexts. Whilst rock 'n' roll singles were structured into an overarching framework for meaningful youth cultural lifestyles in the contexts of the motorbike boys' subculture, the use of albums by Claire is meaningful in far more mundane, localised situations and certainly not in terms of deviance from societal norms or resistance to commercial incorporation. In this example and many others from fieldwork analysis it has been evident that music is far more often situated by young people in relation to various contexts of education, work and leisure than structured within a single, coherent lifestyle context reminiscent of bohemian youth (Young 1971).

The second feature of a situational interactionist model is its greater attention to the everyday, heterogeneous practices of youth music cultures. The signifying practices of youth cultures as detailed in structuralist and post-structuralist models of youth subcultures have tended to be read from second-hand accounts in newspapers and on record sleeves rather than from the first-hand accounts of practitioners. Where first-hand accounts of practices are provided, these accounts are necessarily biased towards those spectacular practices engaged in by committed participants to certain homologous styles. An apt example of such an account is that of the David Bowie lookalikes who were interpreted – perhaps accurately – as embodying very narrow music, dress and other stylistic practices (Hebdige 1979: 60). However, these Bowie lookalikes presumably enacted far more conventional music practices outside concert attendances. As with the problem of contexts, therefore, the problem faced by structuralist theories of youth music cultures has been ignorance of the multitude of everyday practices other than highly committed leisure ones in which music is pervasively present. Moreover, a general lack of ethnographic information about changes in the practices of youth music cultures seems to have arisen from theories of homology and appropriation premised on studying such cultures at given flashpoints in time. These theories, inspired by the subcultural resistance thesis, work around a static model of practices that are assumed to begin and end within the confines of particular youth cultures without being externally received or diffused.

A situational interactionist model, by contrast, is able to examine how the practices of different youth music cultures can interlock and thus is able 'to study the dynamics of transmission of subcultural elements' (Fine and Kleinman 1979: 16). Conceptualising practices as learning processes rather than signifying ends, this book has sought ethnographic depth in analysing how young people's everyday music practices are developed and enacted. The notion of productive consumer literacies (see Chapter 5) in particular enables an understanding of the often close correspondence between young people's music consumer and producer practices. Practices of resistance to wider social and political structures have tended to be interpreted as either solely consumerist (e.g. Hall 1992) or radically productivist (e.g. Fiske 1987; 1989a; 1989b) in reaction to institutionalised, capitalist forms of production. Everyday producer practices according to a situational interactionist model, however, are centred on everyday activities of consumption in the same way that speed readers produce different readings of texts from those that might have been encoded for intended consumption by authors (de Certeau 1984). These everyday practices of productive consumer literacy are therefore not always radically innovative but very often educational in their outcomes. Instances of practices that had clearly developed from learning and depended on continual honing in order to be successfully enacted were the readings through which some respondents distinguished music genres in terms of numbers of beats per minute. These practices at the same time distinguished certain productive youth music consumers from less productive others. As such, young people who copied the dance routines of choreographed pop acts like S Club were judged to be inferior practitioners compared to clubbers who enacted their 'own moves' when dancing to bashment or hip hop music (Tanya, Natton College D2). Likewise, learning how to perform certain types of dance through instruction or demonstration in the contexts of early youth music cultures enabled the acquisition of social equipment to gain approval in the presentation of self and the judgement of others.

Third and perhaps most importantly, a situational interactionist model can explore variable levels of involvement in and accessibility to everyday youth music cultures and media. On the contrary, a structuralist model has effectively constructed exclusive semiotic spaces that define youth groups homogeneously *against* other groups and ignore the everyday interactions between young people (and others) *within* these different groups. The concept of club cultures (Thornton 1995), whilst a useful rejoinder to the semiotic bias of subcultural accounts, remains trapped in a structuralist model by lacking detailed sociological examination of young people's everyday involvement in and access to such cultures. Too much emphasis has been placed on emotionally committed youth music consumers and producers – a flaw in studies of fandom (e.g. Schwichtenberg 1993) as well as subcultures, club cultures and post-subcultures – to the disregard of a majority who might be thought to experience uneven levels of involvement and accessibility. Applied to Goffman's (1963) concepts of main and side involvements, music as well as every other artefact comprising the homologous styles of youth subcultures is deemed to be a main involvement around which subcultural members' lives are structured. An interactionist model improves upon this structuralist tendency to favour 'exotic data' (Naroll and Naroll 1963) by accounting for both main and side involvements as well as variations in accessibility which impinge upon young people's opportunities to become involved in certain contexts of consumer and producer practices. Goffman's example of how American adolescents' use of portable radios 'has guaranteed a source of absorbing side involvement that can be carried into a multitude of different situations' (1963: 49) illustrated the significance of music as an omnipresent sound-filler for young people in a variety of public contexts through an interactionist perspective. Issues around uneven accessibility to youth music together with other cultural practices were well illustrated by reflexive accounts of my own fieldwork experiences, which pointed to the sense of intrusive inspection that infiltrated many respondents' everyday lives.

The situational interactionist model proposed here acknowledges variations in the extent to which young people become involved in and choose to access everyday youth music cultures and media by outlining four distinct, yet fluid, groupings or figurations of practitioners. Clubbers are the grouping that most closely resembles the typical research participants in orthodox structuralist and postmodernist accounts of youth music cultures. These young music consumers and producers are intensively involved in mediated and access exclusive co-present music practices. Sam and Jolene (Natton College) were involved in mediated clubbing practices such as – in Sam's case – building a record collection of hip hop music for DJ-ing purposes, and they accessed co-present clubbing practices by sometimes travelling considerable distances to attend specialist club nights. Professional dance instructors who were regular readers of *Danceland* and practised the latest step routines contained therein would be pre-war examples of clubbers. Surfers, by contrast, share access to exclusive public music practices such as dance clubs but differ from clubbers by being only casually involved in music media practices. Rizwaan's (ibid.) involvement in bhangra club nights depended upon the appeal of the co-present experience itself and was certainly influenced by the friend with whom he accessed these surfing contexts more so than the music, his casual consumption of which was evident from mediated contexts. Similarly, those early youth dancers who attended dance halls with the intention of striking up social and sexual relations rather than perfecting their knowledge of music and dance routines (also observed by Mungham (1976) several decades later) would essentially perform surfing practices.

Exchangers are the inverse of surfers in that they access inclusive co-present practices but are intensively involved in mediated music practices. Gemma (Southwell College) was a typical exchanger in that her productive consumer practice of downloading music files from the Internet and copying them on to blank CDs for the benefit of others bore no relation to her reticence about engaging in co-present music practices outside the inclusiveness of a local pub. Given the public contexts of Mass-Observation's ethnographic research, examples of exchangers are inevitably more elusive. It might be suggested, though, that those young factory workers in 1930s and 1940s Britain who were perhaps too young or too poor to afford access to dance halls and other public music venues nevertheless performed exchanger roles by collectively teaching themselves the lyrics to songs heard on the wireless or gramophone, or printed in magazines. Early enthusiasts who built gramophones and wirelesses to loan, give or sell to others would clearly cut the figure of exchangers. Drifters, on the other hand, are the inverse of clubbers in that they are casually involved in music media and access inclusive public music practices. Perhaps due to their young age and appearance, Hilary, Lucy, Sarah and Gill (Southwell College) had hardly experienced exclusive co-present music contexts but – for the moment at least – appeared not to seek such contexts given their casual involvement in mediated music practices such as listening to the radio. Early youth music drifters, like exchangers, would have largely escaped the eye of Mass-Observers. Even during this period, though, the omnipresence of mass music media in everyday life generated distaste as well as taste. Two female assistants at a male directive respondent's workplace were belittled for singing 'snatches of jazz tunes' (DR 1194: January 1939). This male respondent fits into the role of drifter by performing a detachment from the lowbrow culture of jazz but being unable to distance himself from associated cultural and media practices.

The previous example of drifting practices within youth music cultures suggests the fluidity of these four groupings as practitioners grow older, acquire new tastes, reside in different locations and so on. Allowing such fluidity is essential to understanding the dynamic relationship between mediated and co-present youth music practices which this situational inter-actionist model seeks to achieve. Rather than always highlighting the different ways in which mediated and co-present practices structure youth music cultures, this model attempts to situate the two sets of practices in young people's everyday consumer and producer contexts to reveal ways in which mediated practices might *complement* as well as contradict co-present music practices and vice versa. In the following two sections I will show how a pair of key themes that have emerged from an interactionist approach to researching music in young people's everyday lives are consistent with the situational interactionist model outlined here. Thematic examinations of intergenerational narratives and localised performances will show how such phenomena are centrally situated in young people's everyday music con-sumption and production. What is more, these two themes would be incon-ceivable to studies of subcultures, club cultures and post-subcultures operating – as they have invariably – within a structural Marxist framework.

Intergenerational narratives

In Chapter 5 I suggested two types of everyday life narratives through which respondents articulated their mediated music practices: radically contextual narratives about how music media are used to convey temporal moods 'here and now'; and deeper embedded personal histories in which music media use structures definitive life passages. However, on further consideration it would appear that such narratives are not confined to mediated but extend to co-present practices and therefore to everyday youth music cultural 'repertoires' (Hermes 1995; Richards 1998) or 'maps' (DeNora 1999) in general. Although my methodological approach to interviewing had no intentions of requesting respondents' life narratives, and indeed could not expect to receive them given that most of the interviews were conducted in group-based rather than personal situations, on many brief and on several in depth occasions, I was given autobiographical insights through the recalling of both near and distant memories. These narratives were sometimes about family and other times about peer group events. Regardless of the precise situation for these everyday life narratives, each generated meaning comparative to other possible situations. In particular, a clear distinction between radically contextual narratives about peer group and embedded narratives about familial interactions held firm in young people's vivid perceptions of their personal histories. Therefore, the term 'intergenerational narratives' would seem appropriate to the way in which respondents framed their autobiographies of everyday music consumption and production. I will now develop the definition of such a term by proposing that its associative theme fits neatly into a situational interactionist model of youth music cultural contexts, practices, involvement and accessibility as presented earlier in this chapter.

Intergenerational narratives are situated in the interactive local, familial and traditional contexts of everyday youth music cultures. Such situations persist whether these narratives refer to immediate or embedded everyday life contexts. A starting point for the differences between these two types of narrative is Table 5.5 but the findings contained in this table were based on music media contexts alone. However, I would like to modify these findings to account for narratives about public music contexts too. In the case of immediate or radically contextual narratives about music consumption and production, the local contexts for young people's public music experiences were closely associated with familial and traditional contexts. The familiar surroundings of schools, colleges, shops, revisited holiday destinations, pubs and cafés, for example, were hardly the kinds of public contexts studied by theorists of spectacular, intra-generational youth music cultures operating within a subcultural paradigm. Some respondents accompanied elders to these public music contexts on a daily, weekly or yearly basis. Hilary and her friends (Southwell College 3) regularly accompanied her parents to a café in Bolton town centre where the playing of background music was nevertheless noticeable. The familiar experience of consuming and producing music in the public contexts of schools and colleges, on the other hand, generated radically contextual, intergenerational narratives about the superiority of respondents' and their parents' music tastes against those of teachers (e.g. as observed at Pickles High School). In the case of embedded or historic intergenerational narratives, Lucy (Southwell College 3) still participated in the annual family tradition of holidaying in Blackpool and experiencing a variety of public music contexts therein. Local and familiar mediated music contexts for immediate intergenerational narratives included Dave's (Richmond High School C1) bedroom, where he listened to music as a means of expressing personal moods in reaction to stressful interactions with friends and elders. Similar mediated contexts for embedded intergenerational narratives included Ryan's (Scarcroft College 3) domestic consumption of eighties music originating from his father's record collection and a historical image of his father's youth.

Intergenerational narratives can also be conceived to articulate both mediated and co-present music practices as literacies and enactments consistent with the situational interactionist model. Radically contextual and embedded narratives about youth music practices articulate learning processes (Becker 1953). With regard to radically contextual narratives about co-present music practices, pertinent examples were the various age-playing techniques (see Chapter 6) enacted by young people so as to escape inspection from gatekeepers. The enactment of such techniques as part of the practices of going out to experience night-time music entertainment would be honed by learning from previous mistakes. By the same token, prolonged enactment of age-playing techniques would eventually articulate embedded intergenerational narratives about such public music practices once the arts – or literacies – of impression management were perfected or no longer required to be enacted: 'some places, it's like, they do ask you for ID so I'll go "I've not been asked for ID for ages, so I don't carry it with me no more"' (Chris, Scarcroft College 3). Chris articulated this narrative at seventeen years of age and presumably such a narrative would become much deeper embedded in his intergenerational perceptions once he reached an age where the enactment of age-playing practices would not even be considered. Enactments and literacies with regard to immediate intergenerational narratives about mediated music practices included Beate's (University of Salford 3) practice of listening to music on the radio while learning about the strength of new friendships in relation to more familiar ones in her native Germany. The enactment and learning of mediated music practices articulated through embedded intergenerational narratives was exemplified by Gaz's (University of Salford 3) practice of initially becoming influenced by his mother's tastes in soul music before adapting these tastes to those for the 'new soul movement', which he felt – vis-à-vis his mother's tastes in the older soul sounds – to be distinctly his own.

Intergenerational narratives are further capable of evincing variations in involvement in and accessibility to everyday youth music cultures and media. Immediate and historic narratives about music consumption and production situate young people themselves and in the judgement of others within one of the four fluid groupings of practitioners (clubbers, surfers, exchangers and clubbers). These intergenerational narratives are grounded in a situational interactionist model that can account for the fluid dynamics that generate uneven levels of involvement and accessibility to music contexts and practices over a young – and gradually older – person's life course. Radically contextual and embedded narratives about involvement in and accessibility to music experiences have already combined co-present with mediated music practices (as presented in the previous chapter) so there is no need here to provide separate examples in relation to these two sets of practices. Instead, the two types of narratives are considered here to apply to each of the clubbing, surfing, exchanging and drifting figurations of youth music practitioners in general. Radically contextual intergenerational narratives about clubbing practices were evident, for instance, in Jolene's (Natton College 3) acknowledgement that she might derive ideas about physical appearance from music videos featuring her favourite rap artists, who also gained favour with her mother and other family members. Such intergenerational narratives were also used to articulate surfing practices such as Claire's (Richmond High School 3) seeking out of broadly chart-based music consumption – akin to her mediated music practices as influenced by those of her father – in what she considered to be exclusive public bar and club contexts. Exchanging practices perceived through radically contextual intergenerational narratives included Kevin's copying of up-to-date music releases on to blank CDs from MP3 files for use by familiar others: 'if someone wants an album I just do it for them' (Richmond High School C1). And drifting practices perceived through these types of intergenerational narratives included Hilary's (Southwell College C2) disassociation with the heavy rock music favoured by her friends, which in turn informed an embedded intergenerational narrative about domestic music consumption detailed below.

Embedded intergenerational narratives, likewise, can be applied to the four groupings of youth music practitioners distinguished by their levels of involvement and accessibility. Clubber narratives of this type included Tanya's (Natton College 3) about her preference for dancing to hip hop as opposed to pop music, where the former genre of music was far deeper embedded in her familial interactions than the latter, more disposable genre. Surfer narratives of this type were expressed by several respondents who had once accompanied elder family members to facilitate access to exclusive music contexts and practices, but perhaps now accessed them like veterans. Exchangers' embedded intergenerational narratives were articulated frequently during the fieldwork. An example of such a narrative was that articulated by Ian in his early peer interactions with school friend Steven (Richmond High School D1), who had lent him a cassette of Smashing Pumpkins tracks that ultimately influenced Ian's long-term affections for rock music. And drifters' embedded intergenerational narratives about music consumption and production included Hilary's (Southwell College 3) admission that she 'was brought up with' the pop music liked by her parents, which was 'stuck in my head now' and continued to reflect her tastes more so than the heavy rock that was presently enjoyed by some of her friends. It seems clear, in summarising this section, that the theme of intergenerational narratives – given its empirical outcomes – is consistent with a situational interactionist model of everyday youth music cultures and media. In the following section I will argue that another central theme of this thesis, to be termed 'localised performances', is also consistent with the conceptualisation of contexts, practices, involvement and accessibility within this model.

Localised performances

The notion of promenade performances has been proposed to account for interactive practices where performers and spectators, producers and consumers are collusively related to each other (as explored by Goffman 1969a; see also Malbon 1998; 1999). Promenading youth music 'performers' emphasise demonstration and display in their everyday leisure activities. Globally mediated music influences have been shown to penetrate into highly localised promenade performances through two phases. First, the reception phase provides knowledge about the latest tunes, dances and fashions to come on to the scene. This phase in practice demonstrates mediated promenade performances. Second, the exhibition phase involves selection of this knowledge to demonstrate and display co-present promenade performances. Both these phases of promenade performances are firmly situated in everyday local interactions even though the reception phase in particular is loaded with global media influences. In this sense, the concept of 'hybridisation' as applied by Bakhtin (1984) to the mix of localised and globalised identifications inherent to the carnivalesque marketplace would also seem to apply to promenade performance contexts. The term 'localised performances', then, is argued to capture most accurately the processes through which respondents demonstrated and displayed their everyday music consumption and production. I will now develop the definition of this term by proposing that its associative theme sits well with the previously outlined situational interactionist model of youth music cultural contexts, practices, involvement and accessibility.

Localised performances are situated in the interactive local, familial and traditional contexts of everyday youth music cultures. Such situations persist whether these performances occur during the phase of reception or exhibition in promenade contexts. Mediated promenade performances that would ostensibly be exposed to globalised influences are nevertheless overridden by the local contexts of reception through which they are conceived. For example, a group of Indian interviewees (Northborough College A1) shared experiences of mediated, localised performances in the familial contexts of listening to Indian music on Asian Sound Radio. Despite the global (or at least national) broadcasting of this music medium, the phase of its reception for these young people was perceived to be situated in highly localised performances such as that enacted by Farnaz's mother, who listened to the station in the kitchen. Such localised performances were intertwined with the music cultural traditions of Indian households. Furthermore, these cultural traditions seemed not to be confined to the phase of reception. The same group of respondents projected this phase of reception on to a phase of exhibition such that the Indian music preferred by their familial elders became the resource for co-present promenade performances in localised contexts. As Farnaz said, 'where there's bhangra doing, you find out when it is and then you go out that night' (ibid.). This example is one of several in which the contexts of co-present were influenced by mediated localised performances.

Localised performances are also characterised by practices of enactment and learning during the phases of reception and exhibition. The enactment of effective practices during the phase of reception would develop literacies that could lead to further practices being enacted and then honed during the exhibition phase. An example of this mutually dependent dynamic between practices of demonstration and display in mediated and co-present localised performances was those enacted by a group of quarrelsome interviewees at Richmond High School (B1). Conor and Rick enacted their mediated promenade performances in antithesis to those of Gary by demonstrating literacies at being able to distinguish alternative (Nirvana) from populist (Linkin Park) rock bands. Such practices during the phase of reception were required to be learnt before Gary could be conceivably accepted to share Conor's and Rick's acquired musical tastes. Likewise, Gary would be expected to learn the same practices during the phase of exhibition in order to be accepted by Conor and Rick as a genuine, localised performer of alternative music tastes. For now, though, Gary's traditional Friday night excursion to a local pub rendered his co-present localised performances to be differently enacted from those learnt and enacted – initially at the reception but later at the exhibition phase – by Conor and Rick in their search for goth clubs across a thirty-mile area from Bolton to Manchester.

Localised performances also evince different levels of involvement in and accessibility to everyday youth music cultures. As previously suggested in greater depth in Chapter 6, promenade performances are differentiated by the extent to which youth music practitioners are involved in and able to access the phases of reception and exhibition with regard to a given music culture. Clubbers are intensively involved in the phase of reception and able to access exclusive practices during the phase of exhibition, whilst drifters are only casually involved in the reception phase and only willing to access inclusive practices at the exhibition phase. Exchangers are intensively involved in the reception phase but only opt to access inclusive practices in stark contrast to surfers, who are only casually involved during the phase of reception but able to access exclusive practices at the phase of exhibition. Localised clubbing performances, then, were presumably enacted by the man who was observed at the Ritz (Manchester city centre: 9 October 2002) dressed and dancing like John Travolta. The globally distributed video medium through which he would have received *Saturday Night Fever* nevertheless bore minor relation to the localised meanings that his performance bestowed upon those clubbers who accompanied him and those (non-clubbers) who witnessed him during the phase of exhibition. Localised drifting performances – perhaps less surprisingly – were bereft of any markedly globalised or commercially incorporated situations. Instead, these performances tended to be conservative and introspective, such as Hilary's (Southwell College C2) casual involvement with the reception of heavy rock music liked by her friends and her preference for inclusively accessible practices such as listening to light music in cafés.

Localised exchanging performances, on the other hand, tended to be situated closest to globalised influences, but the impact on such enactments of local, everyday interactions was sensed by respondents to a greater degree. The case of Gemma and Rachel (Southwell College B2) well illustrates the localised situations for the consequences of youth music performances, as well as the fluidity of the four groupings of practitioners necessary for adaptations to different interactive contexts for these performances. Whilst Gemma tended to avoid the phase of exhibition following her intensive involvement in copying CDs to exchange with Rachel at the phase of reception – although even the act of exchanging should be situated in the exhibition phase – it was Rachel who projected her exchanging performance on to familiar others in highly localised contexts of exhibition such as local pubs. And localised surfing performances, by contrast, tended to be situated furthest from globalised influences. Gavin's (Natton College A1) perceived need to manage his appearance and tastes for music so as to fit into certain clubbing crowds would have been partly informed by a reception phase in which his mediated localised performances in enacting the tastes of these crowds would have become effective. Ultimately, though, Gavin sensed that regular participation in these clubbing crowds during the phase of exhibition produced the most effective localised surfing (which might later acquire the status of clubbing) performances. I conclude this section by claiming that empirical outcomes that inform this theme of localised performances are consistent with a situational interactionist model of everyday youth music cultures. I will now present a series of overall conclusions that return to address the five research aims outlined in the opening chapter.

CHAPTER 8

Overall Conclusions

Each concluding point hereafter refers to one of five aims that this book has attempted to address. For each point I will evaluate the extent to which the corresponding aim has been fulfilled, as well as summarising the theoretical outcomes that developed from the attempt to address that aim. Each of the aims has shared a common agenda to understand how music cultures and media interact with young people's everyday lives. Music, it has been argued, is a pervasive cultural resource for young people not only in contexts such as clubs, where it functions as a foreground, but in more routine contexts such as schools, where it often functions as a background activity. This pervasiveness extends to a variety of music practices such that young people identify themselves with heterogeneous tastes and performances through the articulation of honed musical narratives and literacies.

The first aim of this study has been to analyse classic theories of youth music cultures as subcultures – together with contemporary 'revisions' of these classic theories in terms of club cultures and post-subcultures – from an interactionist methodological standpoint. The theoretical formation of youth subcultures has been shown to depend more upon a European academic tradition of critical and cultural theory than upon a North American one of empirical sociological research. British cultural studies and the work of the CCCS in particular can be traced back to a critical tradition upholding values of artistic authenticity and critical scrutiny within a structuralist framework or ideal order of high and low culture. This tradition of cultural studies extended its influence to the method of semiotics, which in turn imposed its influence on key structuralist models for the analysis of subcultural texts – particularly music ones – as coded expressions of resistance (Hebdige 1979; Hall 1992; Hall and Jefferson 1993). The subcultural resistance thesis shared similar flaws to the preceding thesis of subcultural deviance. Both sets of theories interpreted youth as an intragenerational unit and music as a statement of *its* exclusive, structurally distinct ideology. Emphasis was disproportionately placed upon either middle-class, bohemian counter-cultures (e.g. Wilson 1970; Young 1971) seemingly free from economic restraints or – at the other extreme – working-class subcultures whose symbolic rather than material resources were structured into a homologous style (e.g. Clarke and Jefferson 1973). Contemporary revisions of subcultures in the form of club cultures and post-subcultures have mostly continued to structure young people and their music *against* rather than *within* parental cultures. A situational inter-actionist model, by stark contrast, attempts to situate music in young people's everyday contexts of localised and intergenerational – as well as intra-generational – interactions. This model has consistently addressed the overall aim to detail the variable as well as homologous characteristics of young people's involvement in and accessibility to music practices.

Second, I have aimed to apply sociological and cultural theories of every-day life to young people's music consumption and production in general, and their enactment of tastes and performances in particular. Theories of tactics based on everyday time patterns (de Certeau 1984) and the carni-valesque as a site of oral and visual conventions for everyday performances (Bakhtin 1984) have been particularly applicable to understanding how music interacts with the ebbs and flows of daily life. A central problem with many perspectives on club cultures and post-subcultures (e.g. Thornton 1995; Rietveld 1993) has been a structuralist preoccupation with the IRP which necessitates that consumers remain relatively alike so as to be collec-tively differential from producers. This book, however, is keen to evince variations *within* everyday consumer and producer practices, and to unpack the collusive relationship between everyday youth music consumers and producers. In order to address this aim, then, I have argued for a more crit-ical definition of practices than the rather simplistic definition of practices as the decoding of signs, as deployed by theorists operating within the IRP. Young people's practices are defined as processes learnt through social – particularly familial and traditional – interactions. As such, these practices can grow or decline depending upon their intergenerational transmission. In line with the conventions of learning associated with carnivalesque and art worlds (Becker 1982; Finnegan 1989) of everyday consumer and pro-ducer practices, attention is turned towards the dynamics between simple (i.e. localised) and diffused (i.e. globalised) rather than towards mass audiences (Abercrombie and Longhurst 1998). Applying this theoretical perspective on everyday youth music practices to the notion of tastes, there-fore, I have argued that concepts of subcultural capital (Thornton 1995 fol-lowing Bourdieu 1977; 1984) and neo-tribalism (Bennett 1999; 2000 following Maffesoli 1996) tend not to detail ethnographically the temporal processes by which young people learn to become involved in and to access music practices, or indeed learn to abstain from such practices. On the other hand, concepts of omnivorousness (Carrabine and Longhurst 1999) and taste narratives (e.g. Richards 1998) tend to be more in keeping with notions of performative youth music practices that are considered to be typified by the concepts of fluid self-identities (e.g. Bauman 1996) and self-presentations (Goffman 1969a).

Third, archival research has aimed to situate contemporary young people's music cultures within a historical context by exploring an early period of youth music activity in Britain prior to the post-war phenomena of subcultures. Although early youth music practices such as jitterbugging hinted at the types of subversive practices expressed by later subcultures such as Teddy Boys, I have suggested an alternative interpretation of these historic practices as part of a wider set of promenade performances within localised and intergenerational contexts. Such an interpretation is grounded in the methodological concerns of the Mass-Observation researchers – from which the archival material was generated – to penetrate 'every part of local life' (M-O 1970, 'Preface': 8). Akin to informal economies of the carnivalesque marketplace (Bakhtin 1984) and of productivist consumer tactics (de Certeau 1984), everyday promenading in the form of dance demonstrations and displays blurred the distinctions between consumption and production, spectacle and performance, the local and the global. Processes of cultural exchange enabled early youth dancers with more or less levels of involvement and competence to transmit (or have transmitted) music practices within contexts loaded with highly localised, familiar meanings – as also indentified by Madge and Harrisson (1939), and Hoggart (1958) in his discussion of generational transmutation.

The fourth aim has been to contextualise the local sites of everyday interaction wherein young people's music cultures are enacted and influenced, detailing the similarities as well as the differences between their involvement in mediated and accessibility to co-present music experiences. The focus in addressing this aim, then, has been to interpret consumer and producer *contexts* as much as *texts*. Research into the medium of television has made substantial inroads in contextualising its everyday reception (e.g. Morley 1986; Liebes and Katz 1993) but research into the consumption and production of music remains largely text-driven. This focus on contexts as much as texts has also led to a need for rigorous empirical information about the localities of these contexts as much as the national or global implications of texts. The terms by which some respondents referred to their music preferences as a result of their cultural backgrounds has supported the methodology that underpins this aim. These young people defined their music cultures as the outcomes of local, familial contexts and globally mediated texts. Peer group music exchanging, by the same token, was as much about the contexts of building relationships and identifications in localised performance contexts such as schools than about the texts that were pirated in the spirit of de Certeau's (1984) tactics. The way in which different leisure, education and work contexts of music practices closely juxtaposed with each other to effectively banish the notion of hedonistic weekends at leisure or long holidays without work, and instead to shift certain leisure times towards weekday nights, would problematise any suggestion that a significant proportion of these young people could find the time and commitment required for spectacular subcultural or indeed club cultural pursuits. Young people's contextual involvement in mediated music texts ranged from intensive to casual levels of consumption. Although access to mediated music contexts was reasonably even across the sample, there were marked differences between respondents' experiences of accessing co-present music contexts which ranged from senses of exclusiveness to those of inclusiveness. The theoretical outcome of this interactionist empirical information is a relatively – but not entirely – fluid model (see Figure 6.5) consisting of four groupings of youth music practitioners: clubbers, surfers, exchangers and drifters. Evaluation of this outcome might criticise these groupings as being effectively personality types but the four figurations are at least a considerable improvement on singular social variables that characterised static subcultural consumption and production (Fine and Kleinman 1979: 11).

Fifth and finally, I aimed to show the relationship between young people's music media and public music practices, which by necessity demanded a model for portraying the relationship between private and public consumer as well as local and global producer practices. Most studies of youth music cultures either have focused entirely on media or – in the case of subcultures – public music consumption and production without suggesting that one might inform the other. On the contrary, this study has applied the four groupings of youth music practitioners that were evinced in addressing the previous aim to the concepts of everyday life narratives and promenade performances. All groups of young people are argued to articulate narratives about the role of music in their everyday lives. Types of narratives differ depending upon the historical situation of music within them. Radically contextual or immediate narratives are particularly prevalent among more casual media consumers (i.e. drifters and surfers) although they are also used by youth music practitioners in the other two groupings. These narratives tend to refer to everyday public interactions in peer group contexts. Embedded or historic narratives, by contrast, are mostly but not exclusively told by intensive music media users (i.e. clubbers and exchangers). These narratives generally refer to every-day private interactions in domestic/familial contexts. The concept of promenade performances is sympathetic with a radically contextualist (Ang 1996) methodological approach. Promenade performances relate to the local and global influences which shape young people's presentation of their music cultures through display and demonstration. Such perfor-mances occur in two phases: the reception phase, which initially occurs through globally mediated practices, and the exhibition phase, which occurs through locally co-present practices. As such, intensive youth music practitioners (i.e. clubbers and exchangers) can effectively display and demonstrate their promenade performances – learnt during the reception phase – to others during exhibition, who may in turn learn to perform in these ways through changing their music practices. However, the highly localised contexts for promenade performances serve also to project influences at the exhibition phase (particularly projected by surfers) on to other youth music practitioners, dependent upon perceptions about the accessibility of such practices. These concepts of everyday life narratives and promenade performances both evince the complementary as well as the contrasting ways in which young people's everyday music media and public music practices interact.

Appendix: Interview Schedules and Transcript Notation Conventions

Interview Schedules

Interviews were conducted in three stages, beginning with 138 first-stage interviewees drawn from the 232 questionnaire respondents that comprised the research sample. Details of the interview stages are given in the table below.

Fieldwork period	Interview [stage]	Interview type	Number in sample	Number of interviews	Number and type of locations
Sept 2001 – Jan 2002	1	Semi-structured focus group	138	24	8 sixth form colleges/school-based sixth form centres
Nov 2001 – Feb 2002	2	Semi-structured focus group	44	8	4 sixth form colleges/school-based sixth form centres
March 2002 – May 2002	3	Semi-structured individual	20 (16 FE and 4 HE students)	20	4 sixth form colleges/school-based sixth form centres and 2 universities

Second-stage interviewees from eight out of the twenty-four groups that had been interviewed during the first stage were revisited on the basis of their representing a range of different findings from questionnaire replies and first-stage interview transcripts. Twenty third-stage interviews with individuals, sixteen of whom were drawn from groups interviewed in the second stage and four of whom were higher education students, aimed to provide more in-depth accounts about interviewees tastes in, and uses of, music in everyday life. It would then be possible to control findings from individual interviews with those from the same individuals in the group situations of the first and second interview stages to examine whether or not different research contexts produced different types or levels of response. The schedule of questions changed for each interview stage and became more or less unique for each interview in tandem with the grounded theory of process in which themes are generated inductively from existing data (Glaser and Strauss 1968). The ethnographic qualities of this multistage, semi–structured interviewing process are exemplified by the absence of any consistent schedule for second–stage interviews.

The number '1' used in analysis of interview responses (Chapters 5 and 6 in particular) indicates a first-stage group interview context, '2' indicates a second- and '3' a third-stage context. The letters 'A', 'B', 'C' and so on identify particular groups of interviewees located in the same educational institution (e.g. 'Natton College A1' identifies group A's first-stage inter-view at Natton College). All names of respondents and colleges/schools are fictitious. Characteristics of the socio–economic geographical locations of the colleges/schools are distinguished in the table below.

Prosperous	Impoverished
Richmond High School, Bolton	Natton College, Manchester
Northborough College, Bolton	Southwell College, Bolton
Scarcroft College, Salford	Pollington College, Salford
Cathbury High School, Bolton	Pickles High School, Manchester
	Wilson High School, Manchester

Names of the two universities from which respondents were drawn are retained on the discretion that higher education institutions are anony-mous enough not to warrant pseudonyms for the sake of confidentiality.

First-stage interviews
A list of six questions were used to set a consistent agenda across each of the group interviews but were not always asked in a particular order or intended to give a rigid structure to these interviews. They were addressed to groups as a whole rather than to each individual within these groups, so as to better enable free-flowing interactional dynamics.

What kind of music do you like?
Who or what influences your music preferences/choices?
Do you listen to music with friends and/or family?

Do you go out to venues where music is played?
What do you do in these venues?
Does music influence your choice of fashions/clothes/hairstyles/how
you look?

Second-stage interviews

Interview schedules were tailored to each group in order to probe into
specific queries gleaned from analyses of first-stage interviews. In practice
this often meant that some of the questions scheduled in the previous
interviews were asked again to encourage greater depth of responses. The
only question that I repeated to all groups at this stage was: have any of
your music tastes changed since I last spoke to you?

Third-stage interviews

These individual interviews – mostly with respondents who had participated in both group interview stages – were designed partly to continue
probing into themes that had arisen from the first and second stages, and
partly to address new and more structured questions that would be likely
to suggest themes yet brought into consideration. Eighteen questions were
scheduled in the order listed below and in addition a few specific enquiries
were tailored to each individual:

Whereabouts do you often go to where music is played?
What do you do there?
Who do you go there with?
Who or what influences your decision to go there?
How do you dress and make yourself look when you go there?
Who and what influences how you dress and make yourself look when
you go there?
Do you get ideas about music and fashion choices from media (tele-
vision, radio, magazines, newspapers, the Internet, etc.)?
Do you exchange music with others? If so, with whom and how?
Have you started listening to any different or new music since the
previous interviews?
Are there any kinds of music that you would never listen to?
Do you have a boyfriend/girlfriend who you go out with on nights?
What do you do in your leisure time other than music-related activities?
Describe to me your typical weekend.
Have you any plans for holidays or short breaks?
Who might you be going with and what will you be doing there?
Do you listen to any of your parents' music?

Does he/she/they encourage you to listen to their music?
Do your parents listen to your music?

Transcript notation conventions

Some of these conventions are borrowed from and some are amendments
to those used for transcript notation by Buckingham (1993: x).

/	Short pause
Pause	Long pause
=	Interruption
[. . .]	Omission of talk within a single response
. . .	Omission of dialogue (i.e. various responses)
?:	Unknown speaker
(? . . .)	Approximate wording due to distorted recording
(. . .)	Additional information to improve sense
{. . .}	Tone indicator e.g. {Ironically}
{to . . .}	Response directed at a particular individual/individuals within a group e.g. {to Gavin and Nicky}
CAPITALS	Emphatic speech
[followed by	Simultaneous responses
[	

Bibliography

Abercrombie, N. (1994), 'Authority and Consumer Society' in R. Keat, N. Whiteley and N. Abercrombie (eds), *The Authority of the Consumer* (London: Routledge), pp. 43–57.

Abercrombie, N. and Longhurst, B. J. (1998), *Audiences: a sociological theory of performance and imagination* (London: Sage).

Abrams, M. H. (1972), 'Orientation of Critical Theories' [from *The Mirror and the Lamp: romantic theory and the critical tradition*] in D. Lodge (ed.), *20th Century Literary Criticism: a reader* (London: Longman), pp. 1–26.

Adorno, T. W. (1945), 'A Social Critique of Radio Music', *Kenyon Review* 8 (2), pp. 208–17.

— (1991), 'On the Fetish Character in Music and the Regression of Listening' (first published 1938) in J. M. Bernstein (ed.), *The Culture Industry: selected essays on mass culture* (London: Routledge), pp. 26–52.

— (1992), 'On Popular Music' (first published 1941) in A. Easthope and K. McGowan (eds), *A Critical and Cultural Theory Reader* (Buckingham: Open University Press), pp. 211–23.

Adorno, T. W. and Horkheimer, M. (1944), 'The Culture Industry: enlightenment as mass deception', *Dialectic of Enlightenment* (New York: Continuum), pp. 120–67.

Ang, I. (1985), *Watching 'Dallas': soap opera and the melodramatic imagination* (London: Methuen).

— (1990), 'Culture and Communication: towards an ethnographic critique of media consumption in the transnational media system', *European Journal of Communication* 5, pp. 236–60.

— (1991), *Desperately Seeking the Audience* (London: Routledge).

— (1996), *Living Room Wars: rethinking media audiences for a postmodern world* (London: Routledge).

Aries, P. (1962), *Centuries of Childhood: a social history of family life* (London: Cape).

Arnold, D. O. (1970a), 'Subculture Marginality' in D. O. Arnold (ed.), *The Sociology of Subcultures* (Berkeley: The Glendessary Press), pp. 81–9.

Arnold, D. O. (ed.) (1970b), *The Sociology of Subcultures* (Berkeley: The Glendessary Press).

Back, L. (1997), 'Nazism and the Call of the Jitterbug' in H. Thomas (ed.), *Dance in the City* (London: MacMillan), pp. 175–97.

Bakhtin, M. (1984), *Rabelais and his World*, trans. Hélène Iswolsky (Bloomington: Indiana University Press).

Baldwin, E., Longhurst, B. J., McCracken, S., Ogborn, M. and Smith, G. (1999), *Introducing Cultural Studies* (London: Prentice Hall Europe).

Barker, H. (1989), *Arguments for a Theatre* (London: John Calder).

Barthes, R. (1993), *Mythologies* (first published 1957), trans. A. Lavers (London: Vintage).

Baudelaire, C. (1964), *The Painter of Modern Life and Other Essays*, edited by J. Mayne (London: Phaidon Press).

Baudrillard, J. (1983), *Simulations* (New York: Semiotext).

Bauman, Z. (1988), *Freedom* (Milton Keynes: Open University Press).

— (1996), 'From Pilgrim to Tourist – or a Short History of Identity' in S. Hall and P. du Gay (eds), *Questions of Cultural Identity* (London: Sage), pp. 18–36.

Becker, H. S. (1951), 'The Professional Dance Musician and his Audience', *American Journal of Sociology* 57, pp. 136–44.

— (1953), 'Becoming a Marihuana User', *American Journal of Sociology* 59, pp. 235–42.

— (1963), *Outsiders: studies in the sociology of deviance* (New York: Free Press).

— (1982), *Art Worlds* (London: The University of California Press).

— (2004), 'Jazz Places' in A. Bennett and R. A. Peterson (eds), *Music Scenes: local, translocal, and virtual* (Nashville: Vanderbilt University Press), pp. 17–27.

Benjamin, W. (1973), 'The Work of Art in the Age of Mechanical Reproduction' (first published 1936) in *Illuminations*, trans. H. Zohn (London: Fontana Press), pp. 211–44.

Bennett, A. (1999), 'Subcultures or Neo-tribes? Rethinking the Relationship between Youth, Style and Musical Taste', *Sociology* 33 (3), pp. 599–617.

— (2000), *Popular Music and Youth Culture: music, identity and place* (Basingstoke: MacMillan).

— (2001), *Cultures of Popular Music* (Maidenhead: Open University Press).

Bennett, A. and Kahn-Harris, K. (eds) (2004), *After Subculture: critical studies in contemporary youth culture* (Basingstoke: Palgrave).

Bennett, A. and Peterson, R. A. (eds) (2004), *Music Scenes: local, translocal, and virtual* (Nashville: Vanderbilt University Press).

Bennett, T. (1986), 'Hegemony, Ideology, Pleasure: Blackpool' in T. Bennett, C. Mercer and J. Woollacott (eds), *Popular Culture and Social Relations* (Buckingham: Open University Press), pp. 135–54.

Berk, B. (1977), 'Face-Saving at the Singles Dance', *Social Problems* 24 (5), pp. 530–44.

Best, B. (1997), 'Over-the-counter-culture: retheorising resistance in popular culture' in S. Redhead (ed.) with Derek Wynne and Justin O'Connor, *The*

Clubcultures Reader: readings in popular cultural studies (Oxford: Blackwell), pp. 18–35.

Birksted, I. K. (1976), 'School Performance Viewed from the Boys', *Sociological Review* 24, p. 63–77.

Boëthius, U. (1995), 'Controlled Pleasures: youth and literary texts' in J. Fornäs and G. Bolin (eds), *Youth Culture in Late Modernity* (London: Sage), pp. 145–68.

Bourdieu, P. (1977), *Outline of a Theory of Practice*, trans. Richard Nice (Cambridge: Cambridge University Press).

— (1984), *Distinction: a social critique of the judgement of taste*, trans. Richard Nice (London: Routledge).

Bradby, B. (1994), 'Freedom, Feeling and Dancing: Madonna's songs traverse girls' talk' in S. Mills (ed.), *Gendering the Reader* (New York: Harvester Wheatsheaf), pp. 67–95.

Bradley, D. (1992), *Understanding Rock 'n' Roll: popular music in Britain, 1955–1964* (Buckingham: Open University Press).

Brake, M. (1985), *Comparative Youth Culture: the sociology of youth culture and youth subcultures in America, Britain and Canada* (London: Routledge and Kegan Paul).

Brown, A. R. (2003), 'Heavy Metal and Subcultural Theory: a paradigmatic case of neglect?' in D. Muggleton and R. Weinzierl (eds), *The Post-Subcultures Reader* (Oxford: Berg), pp. 209–22.

Brown, J. D. and Schulze, L. (1990), 'The Effects of Race, Gender, and Fandom on Audience Interpretations of Madonna's Music Videos', *Journal of Communication* 40 (2), pp. 88–102.

Buckingham, D. (1993), *Children Talking Television: the making of television literacy* (London: Falmer Press).

Bull, M. (2000), *Sounding Out the City: personal stereos and the management of everyday life* (Oxford: Berg).

Butler, J. (1990), 'Performative Acts and Gender Constitution: an essay in phenomenology and feminist theory' in S. Ellen (ed.), *Performing Feminisms: feminist critical theory and theatre* (Baltimore: The Johns Hopkins Press), pp. 270–82.

— (1999), *Gender Trouble: feminism and the subversion of identity* [10th anniversary edition] (New York: Routledge).

Campbell, C. (1987), *The Romantic Ethic and the Spirit of Modern Consumerism* (Oxford: Basil Blackwell).

Carrabine, E. and Longhurst, B. J. (1999), 'Mosaics of Omnivorousness: suburban youth and popular music', *New Formations* 38, pp. 125–49.

— (2002), 'Consuming the Car: anticipation, use and meaning in contemporary youth culture', *The Sociological Review* 50 (2), pp. 181–96.

Carrington, B. and Wilson, B. (2004), 'Dance Nations: rethinking youth subcultural theory' in A. Bennett and K. Kahn-Harris (eds), *After Subculture: critical studies in contemporary youth culture* (Basingstoke: Palgrave), pp. 65–78.

Cartwright, J. (1986), *Road* (London: Methuen).

Chambers, I. (1985), *Urban Rhythms: pop music and popular culture* (London: MacMillan).

Chaney, D. (1993), *Fictions of Collective Life: public drama in late modern culture* (London: Routledge).

— (1994), *The Cultural Turn: scene-setting essays on contemporary cultural history* (London: Routledge).

— (2004), 'Fragmented Cultures and Subcultures' in A. Bennett and K. Kahn-Harris (eds), *After Subculture: critical studies in contemporary youth culture* (Basingstoke: Palgrave), pp. 36–48.

Chatterton, P. and Hollands, R. (2001), *Changing Our 'Toon': youth, nightlife and urban change in Newcastle* (Newcastle: Department of Sociology and Social Policy, University of Newcastle).

— (2003), *Urban Nightscapes: youth cultures, pleasure spaces and corporate power* (London: Routledge).

Clarke, G. (1990), 'Defending Ski-Jumpers: a critique of theories of youth sub-cultures' (first published 1981) in S. Frith and A. Goodwin (eds), *On Record: rock, pop, and the written word* (London: Routledge), pp. 81–96.

Clarke, J. and Jefferson, T. (1973), 'Working Class Youth Cultures', *CCCS Stencilled Paper No. 18* (Birmingham: University of Birmingham).

Clarke, J., Hall, S., Jefferson, T. and Roberts, B. (1993), 'Subcultures, Cultures and Class' (first published 1975) in S. Hall and T. Jefferson (eds), *Resistance through Rituals: youth subcultures in post-war Britain* (London: Routledge), pp. 9–74.

Cohen, A. (1955), *Delinquent Boys: the culture of the gang* (New York: The Free Press).

Cohen, P. (1992), 'Subcultural Conflict and Working-class Community' (first published 1972) in S. Hall, D. Hobson, A. Lowe and P. Willis (eds), *Culture, Media, Language: working papers in cultural studies, 1972–79* (London: Routledge), pp. 78–87.

Cohen, Sara (1991), *Rock Culture in Liverpool: popular music in the making* (Oxford: Oxford University Press).

— (1993), 'Ethnography and Popular Music Studies', *Popular Music* 12 (2), pp. 123–38.

Cohen, Stanley (1980a), *Folk Devils and Moral Panics: the creation of the mods and rockers* (first published 1972) (Oxford: Blackwell).

— (1980b), 'Symbols of Trouble: introduction to the new edition' in *Folk Devils and Moral Panics: the creation of the mods and rockers* (Oxford: Blackwell).

Corrigan, Paul (1979), *Schooling the Smash Street Kids* (Basingstoke: MacMillan).

Corrigan, Peter (1997), *The Sociology of Consumption: an introduction* (London: Sage).

Crawford, G. (2000), 'Theorising the Contemporary Sports Supporter: an ethnography of the supporter base of the Manchester Storm' (University of Salford, UK: unpublished Ph.D. thesis).

Cressey, D. R. (1970), 'Foreword' in D. O. Arnold (ed.), *The Sociology of Subcultures* (Berkeley: The Glendessary Press).

Cressey, P. G. (1932), *The Taxi-Dance Hall* (New York: Greenwood Press).

Cross, G. (ed.) (1990), *Worktowners at Blackpool: Mass-Observation and popular leisure in the 1930s* (London: Routledge).

— (1997), 'The Suburban Weekend: perspectives on a vanishing twentieth-century dream' in R. Silverstone (ed.), *Visions of Suburbia* (London: Routledge), pp. 108–31.

Cuff, E. C., Sharrock, W. W. and Francis, D. W. (1990), *Perspectives in Sociology*, 3rd edn (London: Routledge).

Cultural Trends (1993), 'The Music Industry' (19), pp. 45–66.

— (1995), 'Music and the Music Industry' (26), pp. 27–43.

Davies, A. (1992), *Leisure, Gender and Poverty: working-class culture in Salford and Manchester, 1900–1939* (Buckingham: Open University Press).

de Certeau, M. (1984), *The Practice of Everyday Life*, trans. Steven Rendall (Berkeley: University of California Press).

de Certeau, M., Giard, L. and Mayol. P. (1998), *The Practice of Everyday Life Volume 2: Living and Cooking*, trans. T. J. Tomasik (Minneapolis: University of Minnesota Press).

Debord, G. (1995), *The Society of the Spectacle*, trans. Donald Nicholson-Smith (New York: Zone Books).

DeNora, T. (1999), 'Music as a Technology of the Self', *Poetics* 27, pp. 31–56.

— (2000), *Music in Everyday Life* (Cambridge: Cambridge University Press).

DeNora, T. and Belcher, S. (2000), ' "When You're Trying Something On You Picture Yourself in a Place Where they are Playing This Kind of Music" – Musically Sponsored Agency in the British Clothing Retail Sector', *The Sociological Review* 48 (1), pp. 80–101.

Dolfsma, W. (2004), 'Consuming Pop Music/Constructing a Life World: the advent of pop music', *International Journal of Cultural Studies* 7 (4), pp. 421–40.

Downes, D. M. (1966), *The Delinquent Solution: a study of subcultural theory* (London: Routledge and Kegan Paul)

Drew, R. (2004), ' "Scenes" Dimensions of Karaoke in the United States' in A. Bennett and R. A. Peterson (eds), *Music Scenes: local, translocal, and virtual* (Nashville: Vanderbilt University Press), pp. 64–79.

Easthope, A. and McGowan, K. (eds) (1992), *A Critical and Cultural Theory Reader* (Buckingham: Open University Press).

Edgell, S., Hetherington, K. and Warde, A. (eds) (1996), *Consumption Matters: the production and experience of consumption* (Oxford: Blackwell).

Eliot, T. S. (1948), *Notes towards the Definition of Culture* (London: Faber and Faber).

Epstein, J. S. (1998a), 'Introduction: Generation X, youth culture, and identity' in J. S. Epstein (ed.), *Youth Culture: identity in a postmodern world* (Oxford: Blackwell), pp. 1–23.

— (ed.) (1998b), *Youth Culture: identity in a postmodern world* (Oxford: Blackwell).

Featherstone, M. (1991), *Consumer Culture and Postmodernism* (London: Sage).

Fenster, M. (1995), 'Two Stories: where exactly is the local?' in W. Straw, S. Johnson, R. Sullivan and P. Friedlander with G. Kennedy (eds), *Popular Music – Style and Identity* (Canada: The Centre for Research on Canadian Cultural Industries and Institutions), pp. 83–87.

Fine, G. A. and Kleinman, S. (1979), 'Rethinking Subculture: an interactionist analysis', *American Journal of Sociology* 85 (1), pp. 1–20.

Finnegan, R. (1989), *The Hidden Musicians: music-making in an English town* (Cambridge: Cambridge University Press).

— (1997a), 'Music, Performance and Enactment' in H. MacKay (ed.) *Consumption and Everyday Life* (London: Sage), pp. 113–46.

— (1997b), ' "Storying the Self": personal narratives and identity' in H. MacKay (ed.), *Consumption and Everyday Life* (London: Sage), pp. 65–104.

Fiske, J. (1987), *Television Culture* (London: Methuen).

— (1989a), *Understanding Popular Culture* (London: Unwin Hyman).

— (1989b), *Reading the Popular* (London: Unwin Hyman).

— (1996), *Media Matters: race and gender in US politics*, rev. edn (Minneapolis: University of Minnesota Press).

Fornäs, J. (1995), 'Youth, Culture and Modernity' in J. Fornäs and G. Bolin (eds), *Youth Culture in Late Modernity* (London: Sage), pp. 1–11.

Fowler, D. (1992), 'Teenage Consumers? Young wage-earners and leisure in Manchester 1919–1939' in A. Davies and S. Fielding (eds), *Workers' Worlds: cultures and communities in Manchester and Salford, 1880–1939* (Manchester: Manchester University Press), pp. 133–55.

— (1995), *The First Teenagers: the lifestyle of young wage-earners in interwar Britain* (London: Routledge).

Frith, S. (1978), *The Sociology of Rock* (London: Constable).

— (1983), *Sound Effects: youth, leisure, and the politics of rock 'n' roll* (London: Constable).

— (1986), *The Sociology of Youth*, 2nd edn (Ormskirk: Causeway).

— (1990), 'Afterthoughts' (first published 1985) in S. Frith and A. Goodwin (eds), *On Record: rock, pop, and the written word* (London: Routledge), pp. 419–24.

— (1996), 'Music and Identity' in S. Hall and P. du Gay (eds), *Questions of Cultural Identity* (London: Sage), pp. 108–27.

— (1997), 'The Suburban Sensibility in British Rock and Pop' in R. Silverstone (ed.), *Visions of Suburbia* (London: Routledge), pp. 269–79.

Frith, S. and Goodwin, A. (eds) (1990), *On Record: rock, pop, and the written word* (London: Routledge).

Frith, S. and Horne, H. (1987), *Art into Pop* (London: Methuen).

Frith, S. and McRobbie, A. (1990), 'Rock and Sexuality' (first published 1978) in S. Frith and A. Goodwin (eds), *On Record: rock, pop, and the written word* (London: Routledge), pp. 371–89.

Furlong, A. and Cartmel, F. (1997), *Young People and Social Change: individualisation and risk in late modernity* (Buckingham: Open University Press).

Gadamer, H. -G. (1979), *Truth and Method* (London: Sheed and Ward).

Gammond, P. (1991), *The Oxford Companion to Popular Music* (Oxford: Oxford University Press).

Gardiner, M. E. (2000), *Critiques of Everyday Life* (London: Routledge).

Garofalo, R. (1992), 'Introduction' in R. Garofalo (ed.), *Rockin' the Boat: mass music and mass movements* (Boston: South End Press), pp. 1–13.

— (ed.) (1992), *Rockin' the Boat: mass music and mass movements* (Boston: South End Press).

Gauntlett, D. (1995), *Moving Experiences: understanding television's influences and effects* (London: John Libbey).

— (1997), *Video Critical: children, the environment and media power* (Luton: John Libbey).

Gauntlett, D. and Hill, A. (1999), *TV Living: television, culture and everyday life* (London: Routledge).

Giddens, A. (1991), *Modernity and Self-identity: self and society in the late modern age* (Cambridge: Polity Press).

— (1992), *The Transformation of Intimacy: sexuality, love and eroticism in modern societies* (Cambridge: Polity Press).

Gilbert, N. (ed.) (1993), *Researching Social Life* (London: Sage).

Glaser, B. G. and Strauss, A. L. (1968), *The Discovery of Grounded Theory: strategies for qualitative research* (London: Weidenfeld and Nicolson).

Goffman, E. (1963), *Behaviour in Public Places: notes on the social organisation of gatherings* (New York: The Free Press).

— (1969a), *The Presentation of Self in Everyday Life* (first published 1959) (Harmondsworth: Penguin).

— (1969b), 'On Face-Work: an analysis of ritual elements in social interaction' in *Where the Action Is* (London: Allen Lane), pp. 3–36.

Gold, R. (1969), 'Roles in Sociological Field Observations' in G. J. McCall and J. L. Simmons (eds), *Issues in Participant Observation: a text and reader* (London: Addison-Wesley), pp. 30–9.

Gordon, M. M. (1970), 'The Concept of the Sub-culture and its Application' (first published 1947) in D. O. Arnold (ed.), *The Sociology of Subcultures* (Berkeley: The Glendessary Press), pp. 31–6.

Gramsci, A. (1985), *Selections from Cultural Writings*, trans. W. Boelhower (London: Lawrence and Wishart).

Greenwood, J. (1986), *Blackpool Entertains the Troops* (Blackpool: Cleveleys).

Grossberg, L. (1984), 'Another Boring Day in Paradise: rock and roll and the empowerment of everyday life', *Popular Music* 4, pp. 225–58.

— (1992), *We Gotta Get Out of This Place: popular conservatism and postmodern culture* (New York: Routledge).

— (1994), 'Is Anybody Listening? Does Anybody Care?: on talking about "The State of Rock"' in A. Ross and T. Rose (eds), *Microphone Fiends: youth music and youth culture* (New York: Routledge), pp. 41–58.

Hall, G. S. (1904), *Adolescence: its psychology and its relation to physiology, anthropology, sociology, sex, crime, religion and education* (New York: Appleton).

Hall, S. (1992), 'Encoding/decoding' (first published 1980) in S. Hall, D. Hobson,
    A. Lowe and P. Willis (eds), *Culture, Media, Language: working papers in cultural
    studies, 1972–79* (London: Routledge), pp. 128–38.
— (1996), 'Introduction: who needs "identity"?' in S. Hall and P. du Gay (eds),
    Questions of Cultural Identity (London: Sage), pp. 1–17.
Hall, S. and du Gay, P. (eds) (1996), *Questions of Cultural Identity* (London:
    Sage).
Hall, S. and Jefferson, T. (eds) (1993), *Resistance through Rituals: youth subcultures
    in post-war Britain* (first published 1975) (London: Routledge).
Hall, S. and Whannel, P. (1990), 'The Young Audience' (first published 1964) in
    S. Frith and A. Goodwin (eds), *On Record: rock, pop, and the written word*
    (London: Routledge), pp. 27–37.
Hall, S., Hobson, D., Lowe, A. and Willis, P. (eds) (1992), *Culture, Media, Language:
    working papers in cultural studies, 1972–79* (first published 1980) (London:
    Routledge), pp. 128–38.
Halnon, K. B. (2005), 'Alienation Incorporated: "F*** the Mainstream Music" in
    the mainstream', *Current Sociology* 53 (3), pp. 441–64.
Hammersley, M. (1990), *Reading Ethnographic Research: a critical guide* (London:
    Longman).
Hammersley, M. and Atkinson, P. (1995), *Ethnography: principles in practice*, 2nd
    edn (London: Routledge).
Harley, J. L. (1937), 'Report of an Enquiry into the Occupations, Further Education
    and Leisure Interests of a Number of Girl Wage-earners from Elementary and
    Central Schools in the Manchester District, with Special Reference to the
    Influence of School Training on their use of Leisure' (University of Manchester,
    UK: unpublished MEd dissertation).
Harrisson, T. (1938a), 'Whistle While You Work', *New Writing* 1, pp. 47–67.
— (1938b), 'The Fifty-Second Week: impressions of Blackpool', *Geographical
    Magazine* 6 [Nov. 1937–Apr. 1938], pp. 387–404.
— (1939a), 'The Birth of a Dance', *Picture Post* [7 January], pp. 45–9.
— (1939b), 'So This is Blackpool', *Picture Post* [1 July], pp. 26–32.
— (1961), *Britain Revisited* (London: Victor Gollancz).
— (1976), *Living through the Blitz* (London: William Collins Sons).
Hebdige, D. (1979), *Subculture: the meaning of style* (London: Routledge).
— (1989), 'Towards a cartography of taste 1935–1962' [abridged] in B. Waites,
    T. Bennett and G. Martin (eds), *Popular Culture: past and present* (London:
    Routledge), pp. 194–218.
Heller, A. (1984), *Everyday Life* (London: Routledge and Kegan Paul).
Hennion, A. (2003), 'Music and Mediation: toward a new sociology of music'
    in M. Clayton, T. Herbert and R. Middleton (eds), *The Cultural Study of Music:
    a critical introduction* (London: Routledge), pp. 80–91.
Hermes, J. (1995), *Reading Women's Magazines: an analysis of everyday media use*
    (Cambridge: Polity Press).
Hesmondhalgh, D. (2002), 'Popular Music Audiences and Everyday Life' in

D. Hesmondhalgh and K. Negus (eds), *Popular Music Studies* (London: Arnold), pp. 117–30.

Hodkinson, P. (2002), *Goth: identity, style and subculture* (Oxford: Berg).

— (2004), 'The Goth Scene and (Sub)Cultural Substance' in A. Bennett and K. Kahn-Harris (eds), *After Subculture: critical studies in contemporary youth culture* (Basingstoke: Palgrave), pp. 135–47.

Hoggart, R. (1958), *The Uses of Literacy: aspects of a working-class life with special reference to publications and entertainments* (London: Pelican).

Hollands, R. G. (1990), *The Long Transition* (Basingstoke: Macmillan).

— (1995), *Friday Night, Saturday Night: youth cultural identification in the post-industrial city* (Newcastle: Department of Social Policy, University of Newcastle).

Jackson, P. (2004), *Inside Clubbing: sensual experiments in the art of being human* (Oxford: Berg).

Jagger, E. (2000), 'Consumer Bodies' in P. Hancock, B. Hughes, E. Jagger, K. Paterson, R. Russell, E. Tulle-Winton and M. Tyler (eds), *The Body, Culture and Society: an introduction* (Buckingham: Open University Press), pp. 45–63.

Jenks, C. (2005), *Subculture: the fragmentation of the social* (London: Sage).

Jeffrey, T. (1999), *Mass-Observation: a short history* [first published University of Birmingham CCCS, SP no. 55, 1978] (University of Sussex, UK: M-O Archive Occasional Paper no. 10).

Jones, S. (1988), *Black Culture, White Youth: the reggae tradition from JA to UK* (Basingstoke: MacMillan).

Jones, S. and Lenhart, A. (2004), 'Music Downloading and Listening: findings from the Pew Internet and American Life Project', *Popular Music and Society* 27 (2), pp. 185–99.

Kahn-Harris, K. (2004), 'Unspectacular Subculture? Transgression and Mundanity in the Global Extreme Metal Scene' in A. Bennett and K. Kahn-Harris (eds), *After Subculture: critical studies in contemporary youth culture* (Basingstoke: Palgrave), pp. 107–18.

Kaplan, E. A. (1993), 'Madonna Politics: perversion, repression, or subversion? Or masks and/as master-y' in C. Schwichtenberg (ed.), *The Madonna Connection: representational politics, subcultural identities, and cultural theory* (Colorado: Westview Press), pp. 149–65.

Kassabian, A. (2002), 'Ubiquitous Listening' in D. Hesmondhalgh and K. Negus (eds), *Popular Music Studies* (London: Arnold), pp. 131–42.

Katz, E., Blumer, J. G. and Gurevitch, M. (1974), 'Utilization of Mass Communication by the Individual' in J. G. Blumer and E. Katz (eds), *The Uses of Mass Communications* (London: Sage), pp. 19–32.

Keat, R., Whiteley, N. and Abercrombie, N. (eds) (1994), *The Authority of the Consumer* (London: Routledge).

Kershaw, B. (1994), 'Framing the Audience for Theatre' in R. Keat, N. Whiteley and N. Abercrombie (eds), *The Authority of the Consumer* (London: Routledge), pp. 166–86.

Kidd, A. (1993), *Manchester* (Staffordshire: Keele University Press).

Laing, D. (1985), *One Chord Wonders: power and meaning in punk rock* (Milton Keynes: Open University Press).

— (1986), 'The Music Industry and the "Cultural Imperialism" Thesis', *Media, Culture and Society* 8, pp. 331–41.

— (1994), '*Scrutiny* to Subcultures: notes on literary criticism and popular music', *Popular Music* 13 (2), pp. 179–90.

Leavis, F. R. and Thompson, D. (1933), *Culture and Environment* (London: Chatto and Windus).

Lee, M. J. (1993), *Consumer Culture Reborn: the cultural politics of consumption* (London: Routledge).

Lefebvre, H. (1984), *Everyday Life in the Modern World*, trans. S. Rabinovitch, (New Brunswick: Transaction Publishers).

Liebes, T. and Katz, E. (1993), *The Export of Meaning: cross-cultural readings of 'Dallas'*, 2nd edn (Cambridge: Polity Press).

Lodge, D. (ed.) (1972), *20th Century Literary Criticism: a reader* (London: Longman).

Longhurst, B. J. (1995), *Popular Music and Society* (Cambridge: Polity Press).

— (2002), 'Introducing and Progressing Cultural Studies: disciplinarity, communication and innovation', *Sociology* 36 (2), pp. 429–35.

Longhurst, B. J. and Savage, M. (1996), 'Social Class, Consumption and the Influence of Bourdieu: some critical issues' in S. Edgell, K. Hetherington and A. Warde (eds), *Consumption Matters: the production and experience of consumption* (Oxford: Blackwell), pp. 274–301.

Lury, C. (1996), *Consumer Culture* (Cambridge: Polity Press).

Lynd, R. S. and Lynd, H. M. (1929), *Middletown: a study in American culture* (Brace and World: Harcourt).

McCracken, G. (1990), *Culture and Consumption: new approaches to the symbolic character of consumer goods and activities* (Bloomington: Indiana University Press).

MacDonald, N. (2001), *The Graffiti Subculture: youth, masculinity and identity in London and New York* (Basingstoke: Palgrave).

MacKay, H. (ed.) (1997), *Consumption and Everyday Life* (London: Sage).

McRobbie, A. (1984), 'Dance and Social Fantasy' in A. McRobbie and M. Nava (eds), *Gender and Generation* (Basingstoke: MacMillan), pp. 130–61.

— (1990), 'Settling Accounts with Subcultures: a feminist critique' (first published 1980) in S. Frith and A. Goodwin (eds), *On Record: rock, pop, and the written word* (London: Routledge), pp. 66–80.

— (1993), 'Shut Up and Dance: youth culture and changing modes of femininity', *Cultural Studies* 7 (3), pp. 406–26.

McRobbie, A. and Garber, J. (1993), 'Girls and Subcultures: an exploration' (first published 1975) in S. Hall and T. Jefferson (eds), *Resistance through Rituals: youth subcultures in post-war Britain* (London: Routledge), pp. 209–22.

Madge, C. and Harrisson, T. (1937), *Mass-Observation* [foreword by J. Huxley] (London: Frederick Miller).

— (1939), *Britain by Mass-Observation* (Penguin: Harmondsworth).

Maffesoli, M. (1996), *The Time of the Tribes: the decline of individualism in mass society*, trans. D. Smith (London: Sage).

Malbon, B. (1998), 'Clubbing: consumption, identity and the spatial practices of every-night life' in T. Skelton and G. Valentine (eds), *Cool Places: geographies of youth cultures* (London: Routledge), pp. 266–86.

— (1999), *Clubbing: dancing, ecstacy and vitality* (London: Routledge).

Mannheim, K. (1952), 'The Problem of Generations' (first published 1927) in P. Kecskemeti (ed.), *Essays on the Sociology of Knowledge* (London: Routledge and Kegan Paul), pp. 276–320.

Marchant, O. (2003), 'Bridging the Micro-Macro Gap: is there such a thing as a post-subcultural politics?' in D. Muggleton and R. Weinzierl (eds), *The Post-Subcultures Reader* (Oxford: Berg), pp. 83–97.

Mass-Observation (1938), *First Year's Work, 1937–38* (London: Lindsay Drummond).

— (1940), *War Begins at Home* (London: Chatto and Windus).

— (1970), *The Pub and the People: a Worktown study*, 2nd edn (first published 1943) (Welwyn Garden City: Seven Dials Press).

May, T. (2001), *Social Research: issues, methods and process*, 3rd edn (Buckingham: Open University Press).

Mays, J. B. (1954), *Growing up in the City: a study of juvenile delinquency in an urban neighbourhood* [preface by R. Titmuss] (Liverpool: Liverpool University Press).

Miles, S. (2000), *Youth Lifestyles in a Changing World* (Buckingham: Open University Press).

Miller, D. (ed.) (2001), *Car Cultures* (Oxford: Berg).

Morley, D. (1980), *The 'Nationwide' Audience* (London: British Film Institute).

— (1986), *Family Television: cultural power and domestic leisure* (London: Comedia).

Morris, G. (2001), 'Bourdieu, the Body, and Graham's Post-War Dance', *Dance Research* 19 (2), pp. 52–82.

Morrison, D. E. (1978), 'Kultur and Culture: the case of Theodor W. Adorno and Paul F. Lazarsfeld', *Social Research* 45 (2), pp. 331–55.

Moy, R. (2005 forthcoming), 'Sonic Architecture: home hi-fi and stereo "types"' in J. Croft and G. Smyth (eds), *Our House: the representation of domestic space in contemporary culture* (Amsterdam: Rodopi Press).

Muggleton, D. (1997), 'The Post-Subculturalist' in S. Redhead, D. Wynne and J. O'Connor (eds), *The Clubcultures Reader: readings in popular cultural studies* (Oxford: Blackwell), pp. 185–203.

— (2000), *Inside Subculture: the postmodern meaning of style* (Oxford: Berg).

Muggleton, D. and Weinzierl, R. (eds) (2003a), *The Post-Subcultures Reader* (Oxford: Berg).

— (2003b), 'What is "Post-subcultural Studies" Anyway?' in D. Muggleton and R. Weinzierl (eds), *The Post-Subcultures Reader* (Oxford: Berg), pp. 3–23.

Muncie, J. and Hughes, G. (2002), 'Modes of Youth Governance: political rationalities, criminalisation and resistance' in J. Muncie, G. Hughes and E. McLaughlin (eds), *Youth Justice: critical readings* (London: Sage), pp. 1–18.

Mungham, G. (1976), 'Youth in Pursuit of Itself' in G. Mungham and G. Pearson (eds), *Working Class Youth Culture* (London: Routledge and Kegan Paul), pp. 82–104.

Mungham, G. and Pearson, G. (eds) (1976), *Working Class Youth Culture* (London: Routledge and Kegan Paul).

Murdock, G. and McCron, R. (1976), 'Youth and Class: the career of a confusion' in G. Mungham and G. Pearson (eds), *Working Class Youth Culture* (London: Routledge and Kegan Paul), pp. 10–26.

Naroll, R. and Naroll, F. (1963), 'On Bias of Exotic Data', *Man* 25, pp. 24–26.

Negus, K. (1996), *Popular Music in Theory: an introduction* (Cambridge: Polity Press).

Nott, J. J. (2002), *Music for the People: popular music and dance in Interwar Britain* (Oxford: Oxford University Press).

Oliver, L. (1995), 'From the Ballroom to Hell: a social history of public dancing in Bolton from c. 1840–1911', *Women's History Notebooks* 2 (2).

Olson, M. J. V. (1998), ' "Everybody Loves Our Town": scenes, spatiality, migrancy' in T. Swiss, J. Sloop and A. Herman (eds), *Mapping the Beat: popular music and contemporary theory* (Oxford: Blackwell), pp. 269–89.

Orwell, G. (1989), *The Road to Wigan Pier* (first published 1937) (London: Penguin).

Osgerby, B. (1998), *Youth in Britain since 1945* (Oxford: Blackwell).

Parsons, T. (1942), 'Age and Sex in the Social Structure of the United States', *American Sociological Review* 7, pp. 604–16.

Pearson, G. (1983), *Hooligan: a history of respectable fears* (Basingstoke: MacMillan).

Pegg, C. (1984), 'Factors Affecting the Musical Choices of Audiences in East Suffolk, England', *Popular Music* 4, pp. 51–73.

Peterson, R. A. (1990), 'Why 1955? Explaining the advent of rock music', *Popular Music* 9 (1), pp. 97–116.

Peterson, R. A. and Kern, R. M. (1996), 'Changing Highbrow Tastes: from snob to omnivore', *American Sociological Review* 61, pp. 900–7.

Pini, M. (1997), 'Women and the Early British Rave Scene' in A. McRobbie (ed.), *Back to Reality?: social experience and cultural studies* (Manchester: Manchester University Press), pp. 152–69.

Poe, E. A. (1967), 'The Man of the Crowd' in David Galloway (ed. and intro.), *Selected Writings of Edgar Allan Poe: poems, tales, essays and reviews* (Harmondsworth: Penguin), pp. 179–88.

Polsky, N. (1971), *Hustlers, Beats and Others* (first published 1967) (Harmondsworth: Penguin).

Power, J. (1980), 'Aspects of Working Class Leisure during the Depression Years: Bolton in the 1930s' (University of Warwick, UK: unpublished MA dissertation).

Priestley, J. B. (1934), *English Journey: being a rambling but truthful account of what one man saw and heard and felt and thought during a journey through England during the autumn of the year 1933* (Harmondsworth: Penguin).

Redhead, S. (1990), *The End-of-century Party: youth and pop towards 2000* (Manchester: Manchester University Press).

— (ed.) (1993), *Rave Off: politics and deviance in contemporary youth culture* (Aldershot: Avebury).

— (1997), *Subculture to Clubcultures: an introduction to popular cultural studies* (Oxford: Blackwell).

Redhead, S. with Wynne, D. and O'Connor, J. (eds) (1997), *The Clubcultures Reader: readings in popular cultural studies* (Oxford: Blackwell).

Richard, B. (1998), 'Ravers' Paradise? German youth cultures in the 1990s' in T. Skelton and G. Valentine (eds), *Cool Places: geographies of youth cultures* (London: Routledge), pp. 161–74.

Richard, B. and Kruger, H. H. (1998), 'Ravers' Paradise? German youth cultures in the 1990s' in T. Skelton and G. Valentine (eds), *Cool Places: geographies of youth cultures* (London: Routledge), pp. 161–74.

Richards, C. (1998), *Teen Spirits: music and identity in media education* (London: UCL Press).

Richards, J. and Sheridan, D. (eds) (1987), *Mass-Observation at the Movies* (London: Routledge and Kegan Paul).

Rietveld, H. (1993), 'Living the Dream' in S. Redhead (ed.), *Rave Off: politics and deviance in contemporary youth culture* (Aldershot: Avebury), pp. 41–78.

Roberts, K., Campbell, R. and Furlong, A. (1990), 'Class and Gender Divisions among Young Adults at Leisure' in C. Wallace and M. Cross (eds), *Youth in Transition: the sociology of youth and youth policy* (Basingstoke: Falmer Press), pp. 129–45.

Roberts, K. and Parsell, G. (1994), 'Youth Cultures in Britain: the middle class take-over', *Leisure Studies* 13 (1), pp. 33–48.

Roberts, R. (1971), *The Classic Slum: Salford life in the first quarter of the century* (Manchester: Manchester University Press).

Robins, D. and Cohen, P. (1978), *Knuckle Sandwich: growing up in the working-class city* (Harmondsworth: Penguin).

Robison, S. M. (1936), *Can Delinquency be Measured?* (New York: Columbia University Press).

Ross, A. and Rose, T. (eds) (1994), *Microphone Fiends: youth music and youth culture* (New York: Routledge).

Rust, F. (1969), *Dance in Society: an analysis of the relationship between the social dance and society in England from the Middle Ages to the Present Day* (London: Routledge and Kegan Paul).

Sardiello, R. (1998), 'Identity and Status Stratification in Deadhead Subculture' in J. S. Epstein (ed.), *Youth Culture: identity in a postmodern world* (Oxford: Blackwell), pp. 118–47.

Schatzki, T. R. (1996), *Social Practices: a Wittgensteinian approach to human activity and the social* (Cambridge: Cambridge University Press).

Schatzki, T. R., Cetina, K. K. and von Savigny, E. (eds) (2001), *The Practice Turn in Contemporary Theory* (London: Routledge).

Schulze, L., White, A. B. and Brown, J. D. (1993), ' "A Sacred Monster in her Prime": audience construction of Madonna as low-other' in C. Schwichtenberg (ed.), *The Madonna Connection: representational politics, subcultural identities, and cultural theory* (Colorada: Westview Press), pp. 15–37.

Schutz, A. (1972), *The Phenomenology of the Social World*, trans. George Walsh and Frederick Lehnert (London: Heinemann).

Schwichtenberg, C. (ed.) (1993), *The Madonna Connection: representational politics, subcultural identities, and cultural theory* (Colorado: Westview Press).

Shank, B. (1994), *Dissonant Identities: the rock 'n' roll scene in Austin, Texas* (Hanover: Wesleyan University Press).

Shields, R. (1996), 'Foreword: Masses or Tribes?' in M. Maffesoli, *The Times of the Tribes: the decline of individualism in mass society*, trans. D. Smith (London: Sage), pp. ix–xii.

Shuker, R. (1998), *Key Concepts in Popular Music* (London: Routledge).

Silverman, D. (ed.) (1997), *Qualitative Research: theory, method and practice* (London: Sage).

Silverstone, R. (1989), 'Let Us Return to the Murmuring of Everyday Practices: a note on Michel de Certeau, television and everyday life', *Theory, Culture and Society* 6 (1), pp. 77–94.

— (1994), *Television and Everyday Life* (London: Routledge).

— (ed.) (1997), *Visions of Suburbia* (London: Routledge).

Simmel, G. (1971a), 'The Metropolis and Mental Life' (first published 1903) in D. N. Levine (ed. and intro.), *Georg Simmel on Individuality and Social Forms* (Chicago: The University of Chicago Press), pp. 324–39.

— (1971b), 'The Stranger' (first published 1908) in D. N. Levine (ed. and intro.), *Georg Simmel on Individuality and Social Forms* (Chicago: The University of Chicago Press), pp. 143–49.

Skeggs, B. (1993), 'A Good Time for Women Only' in F. Lloyd (ed.), *Deconstructing Madonna* (London: Batsford), pp. 60–73.

Skelton, T. and Valentine, G. (eds) (1998), *Cool Places: geographies of youth cultures* (London: Routledge).

Sloboda, J. A. and O'Neill, S. A. (2001), 'Emotions in Everyday Listening to Music' in P. N. Juslin and J. A. Sloboda (eds), *Music and Emotion: theory and research* (Oxford: Oxford University Press), pp. 415–29.

Somers, M. (1994), 'The Narrative Construction of Identity: a relational and network approach', *Theory and Society* 23 (5), pp. 605–50.

Spender, H. (1977), *Worktown: photographs of Bolton and Blackpool taken for Mass-Observation, 1937–38* (Gardner Centre Gallery, University of Sussex: Brighton).

— (1982), *Worktown People: photographs from northern England, 1937–38* [edited by Jeremy Mulford] (Falling Wall Press: Bristol).

Springhall, J. (1998), *Youth, Popular Culture and Moral Panics: penny gaffs to gangsta-rap, 1830–1996* (Basingstoke: MacMillan).

Stewart, F. (1992), 'The Adolescent as Consumer' in J. C. Coleman and C. Warren-Anderson (eds), *Youth and Policy in the 1990s: the way forward* (London: Routledge), pp. 203–26.

Storey, J. (1999), *Cultural Consumption and Everyday Life* (London: Arnold).

Straw, W. (1991), 'Systems of Articulation, Logics of Change: communities and scenes in popular music', *Cultural Studies* 5 (3), pp. 368–88.

Straw, W., Johnson, S., Sullivan, R. and Friedlander, P. with Kennedy, G. (eds) (1995), *Popular Music: Style and Identity* (Canada: The Centre for Research on Canadian Cultural Industries and Institutions).

Street, J. (1986), *Rebel Rock: the politics of popular music* (Oxford: Basil Blackwell).

Swiss, J., Sloop, J. and Herman, A. (eds) (1998), *Mapping the Beat: popular music and contemporary theory* (Oxford: Blackwell).

Thomas, H. (ed.) (1997), *Dance in the City* (Basingstoke: MacMillan).

Thomson, R. A. (1989), 'Dance Bands and Dance Halls in Greenock, 1945–55', *Popular Music* 8 (2), pp. 143–55.

Thornton, S. (1995), *Club Cultures: music, media and subcultural capital* (Cambridge: Polity Press).

Turner, G. (1992), *British Cultural Studies: an introduction* (London: Routledge).

Turner, S. (2001), 'Throwing out the Tacit Rule Book: learning and practices' in T. R. Schatzki, K. K. Cetina and E. von Savigny (eds), *The Practice Turn in Contemporary Theory* (London: Routledge), pp. 120–30.

Turner, V. (1987), *The Anthropology of Performance* (New York: PAJ Publications).

Urry, J. (1990), *The Tourist Gaze: leisure and travel in contemporary societies* (London: Sage).

Verhagen, S., Van Wel, F., Ter Bogt, T. and Hibbel, B. (2000), 'Fast on 200 Beats per Minute: the youth culture of gabbers in the Netherlands', *Youth and Society* 32, pp. 147–64.

Wallace, C. and Cross, M. (eds) (1990), *Youth in Transition: the sociology of youth and youth policy* (Basingstoke: Falmer Press).

Wallace, C. and Kovatcheva, S. (1998), *Youth in Society: the construction and deconstruction of youth in East and West Europe* (Basingstoke: Palgrave).

Walton, J. K. (1998), *Blackpool* (Edinburgh: Edinburgh University Press).

— (2000), *The British Seaside: holidays and resorts in the twentieth century* (Manchester: Manchester University Press).

Ward, A. (1997), 'Dancing around Meaning (and the Meaning around Dance)' in H. Thomas (ed.), *Dance in the City* (Basingstoke: MacMillan), pp. 3–20.

Warde, A. (1994), 'Consumers, Identity and Belonging: reflections on some theses of Zygmunt Bauman' in R. Keat, N. Whiteley and N. Abercrombie (eds), *The Authority of the Consumer* (London: Routledge), pp. 58–74.

Webb, E. J., Campbell, D. T., Schwartz, R. D. and Sechrest, L. (1966), *Unobtrusive Measures: nonreactive research in the social sciences* (Chicago: Rand McNally).

Whiteley, S. (2004), 'Introduction' in S. Whiteley, A. Bennett and S. Hawkins (eds), *Music, Space and Place: popular music and cultural identity* (Aldershot: Ashgate).

Whyte, W. F. (1993), *Street Corner Society: the social structure of an Italian slum*, 4th edn (first published 1943) (Chicago: University of Chicago Press).

Wicke, P. (1992), 'The Times They Are A-Changin': rock music and political change in East Germany' in R. Garofalo (ed.), *Rockin' the Boat: mass music and mass movements* (Boston: South End Press), pp. 81–92.

Widdicombe, S. and Wooffitt, R. (1995), *The Language of Youth Subcultures: social identity in action* (Hemel Hempstead: Harvester Wheatsheaf).

Wild, P. (1979), 'Recreation in Rochdale, 1900–1940' in J. Clarke, C. Critcher and R. Johnson (eds), *Working Class Culture* (London: Hutchinson), pp. 140–60.

Williams, C. (2001), 'Does it Really Matter? Young People and Popular Music', *Popular Music* 20 (2), pp. 223–42.

Williams, R. (1966), *Culture and Society, 1780–1950* (first published 1958) (London: Penguin).

Willis, P. E. (1972), 'Symbolism and Practice: the social meaning of pop music', *CCCS Stencilled Paper No. 13* (Birmingham: University of Birmingham).

—— (1978), *Profane Culture* (London: Routledge and Kegan Paul).

Willis, P. E. with S. Jones, J. Canaan and G. Hurd (1990), *Common Culture: symbolic work at play in the everyday cultures of the young* (Milton Keynes: Open University Press).

Wilson, B. (1970), *The Youth Cultures and the Universities* (London: Faber and Faber).

Wise, S. (1990), 'Sexing Elvis' (first published 1984) in S. Frith and A. Goodwin (eds), *On Record: rock, pop, and the written word* (London: Routledge), pp. 390–8.

Wulff, H. (1995), 'Inter-racial Friendship: consuming youth styles, ethnicity and teenage femininity in South London' in V. Amit-Talai and H. Wulff (eds), *Youth Cultures: a cross-cultural perspective* (London: Routledge), pp. 63–80.

Wyn, J. and White, R. (1997), *Rethinking Youth* (Australia: Allen and Unwin).

Young, J. (1971), *The Drugtakers: the social meaning of drug use* (London: Paladin).

Zerubavel, E. (1981), *Hidden Rhythms: schedules and calendars in social life* (Chicago: University of Chicago Press).

—— (1991), *The Fine Line: making distinctions in everyday life* (Chicago: University of Chicago Press).

Archival sources

Mass-Observation Archive, University of Sussex
Worktown Collection, 1937–40 (WC): 3a; 3c; 27e; 27f; 48c; 48d; 48e; 50b; 52a; 52d; 52j; 52k; 55d; 56b; 57a; 57d; 57f; 60d
Directive Replies (DR): August 1938; December 1938; January 1939 (Jazz and Dancing); July 1939 (Jazz Survey); 1941 month unknown; February 1942; April 1942; 1949 month unknown
File Reports 1940–9 (FR): 11A; 49; 197; 295; 499; 538; 592; 1249; 1637; 3162

Index